CITADELS
OF
PRIDE

CITADELS
OF
PRIDE

Sexual Assault,
Accountability, and
Reconciliation

MARTHA C. NUSSBAUM

W. W. NORTON & COMPANY
Independent Publishers Since 1923

For information about permission to reproduce selections from this book, write to
Permissions, W. W. Norton & Company, Inc., 500 Fifth Avenue, New York, NY 10110

For information about special discounts for bulk purchases, please contact
W. W. Norton Special Sales at specialsales@wwnorton.com or 800-233-4830

Manufacturing by Lake Book Manufacturing
Book design by Chris Welch
Production manager: Lauren Abbate

Library of Congress Cataloging-in-Publication Data

Names: Nussbaum, Martha C. (Martha Craven), 1947– author.
Title: Citadels of pride : sexual assault, accountability, and reconciliation / Martha C. Nussbaum.
Description: First edition. | New York, NY : W. W. Norton & Company, [2021] |
Includes bibliographical references and index.
Identifiers: LCCN 2020058441 | ISBN 9781324004110 (hardcover) | ISBN 9781324004127 (epub)
Subjects: LCSH: Sexual harassment. | Sex crimes. | Male domination (Social structure) |
Power (Social sciences) | Courts—Moral and ethical aspects. | Arts—Moral and ethical
aspects. | Sports—Moral and ethical aspects.
Classification: LCC HQ1237 .N87 2021 | DDC 305.42—dc23
LC record available at https://lccn.loc.gov/2020058441

W. W. Norton & Company, Inc., 500 Fifth Avenue, New York, N.Y. 10110
www.wwnorton.com

W. W. Norton & Company Ltd., 15 Carlisle Street, London W1D 3BS

1 2 3 4 5 6 7 8 9 0

CONTENTS

PREFACE

These are revolutionary times for American women and men. A recent flood of testimony has shown that for generations our society has harbored a culture of sexual violence and sexual harassment. Many, many women have been treated as mere objects for male pleasure and use—their dignity disrespected, their inner experiences ignored. This very old problem has entered the foreground of public awareness in a new way, challenging all Americans to heed, belatedly, women's long-ignored demand for justice and equal respect. The decency and basic justice of our society hang in the balance.

The information brought out by the #MeToo movement that began in 2017 is not really new. For more than fifty years American women have been telling their stories of sexual violence and workplace harassment in pursuit of justice for all women, and many creative and determined lawyers and policy makers have been working hard to reshape both criminal and civil law to deal more adequately with both sexual assault (a criminal offense) and sexual harassment (defined in our country as a civil offense of sex discrimination under Title VII of the Civil Rights Act of 1964). One objective of this book is to tell that frequently ignored set of stories, so that we understand that America's march to justice has been long and is the work of many unheralded contributors, not just recent celebrities, valuable though the contributions of the latter have been.

America's unfinished revolution in sexual equality has made progress over the years, and the #MeToo movement has made yet more progress. There remain, however, significant barriers to full accountability. A second major objective of this book is to pinpoint those areas of recalcitrance and to analyze the reasons why they have resisted reform. I'll be arguing that greed is a major impediment: men who seem irreplaceable and who make a lot of money for other people, especially in sports and in the arts and media, are still likely to be insulated from full accountability, their misdeeds covered up. The federal judiciary is another area in which powerful figures, who often seem indispensable to those whose interests they serve, are similarly insulated—at least until very recently, with reforms as yet far from adequate. Defects in accountability stemming from greed require institutional and structural solutions, and I shall propose some for each area.

Above all, I will argue that the vice of pride is at work in the still all-too-common tendency to treat women as mere objects, denying them equal respect and full autonomy. Pride, as I'll define it, is the vice that consists of thinking that you are above others and that other people are not fully real. This vice can be found at the source of several of the deepest problems in our national life, including racial superiority and privilege, and indifference and disdain on the basis of class. One place where pride surely has ruled is in relations between men and women. Dominant men, refusing women recognition as full and equal people, have resisted the creation of laws that empower women to defend their bodily integrity and assert their agency. And even when, nonetheless, these laws manage to be created, many men resist their sway, creating outposts, citadels of pride, where they avoid accountability.

Like any major social-political revolution, ours is "the best of times," meaning a time of budding hopes for full justice. But it is also "the worst of times," a time of pain and turbulence, when established patterns have been challenged but people are very unsure about how to go forward, and are often filled with resentments on both sides responding to the injustices of the past and the magnitude of the changes. When Charles Dickens used those two descriptions to characterize the French Revolution, one thing he had in mind was that a push for justice can lead to an outbreak of retributive emotion that does not serve justice well and that actually retards human progress. Our time contains similar dangers, where women and men are concerned. Ours is a time when women speak clearly and proudly, demanding justice and respect. It is also a time when some men react in fear and anger, resenting lost privileges and demonizing feminism as the cause of their discontent. And, sadly, it is also a time when some women not only ask for equal respect but seem to take pleasure in retribution. Instead of a prophetic vision of justice and reconciliation, these women prefer an apocalyptic vision in which the former oppressor is brought low, and this vision parades as justice.

No. Justice is something very different, requiring nuances, distinctions, and forward-looking strategies to bring the warring parties to the table of peace. I'll argue that on this issue as with so many others, retributive emotion is no help. We all need to go forward somehow into a shared future, women and men, and we need to start building that future now, rather than focusing on the infliction of retrospective pain. That's not to say that part of the institutional solution does not involve punishment of offenders. Punishment is useful, and often necessary, to deter the offender, to deter others from offending, to express society's most important norms, and to educate society as a whole about the importance of good behavior. But punishment accomplishes its legitimate goals only if it is law-based, fair and nuanced, calibrated to the severity of the offense. Our #MeToo moment has seen its share of cases in which punishment has not been nuanced or calibrated, in which mass shaming takes the place of procedural justice. It has also spawned narratives in which reconciliation is dismissed in favor of retributive triumphalism.

Following the lead of both Elizabeth Cady Stanton and Martin Luther King Jr., I shall call for a revolution that fully recognizes the equal human dignity of all people and that moves forward to create a new world, a world in which, as King put it, "men and women may live together"—but let's say "women and men," since it is time for Americans to change the customary order of our thinking. In short, this is a book about justice, but a justice that seeks reconciliation and a shared future.

This justice has a central role for law. Law, and the "rule of law,"

embody a vision of equal dignity and fair due process. And though law is
finite and its processes flawed, American women have been able to turn
to the law, and to legal change, in a way that has not always been possible
for women in nations where the law is more deeply flawed and corrupted
at its very core.[1] But law does its job well only when people understand
it, and in America today people interested in justice for women do not
always understand the relevant laws and their background. A large part
of my purpose in this book is to describe the relevant areas of law, and
their history, clearly, so that any reader who wants to use the law, or to
study it further, will be pretty well placed to do so. This will mean that
my discussion may at times seem technical, because the impartiality of
the law means that it is, in fact, technical, avoiding colorful particulars
and personal narratives. Narratives play a role in the evolution of the
law, since ours is a "common law" system in which law develops incrementally through cases, and I shall be telling the stories of some crucial
cases. But I want my readers to embrace the larger goal of creating a
system that stands for all and is fair to all, standing above any narrative
and (or so it should be) immune to bias and favor. So when you think the
text is abstract, please try to see that this embodies a noble moral ideal!
We have worked hard to win our way past this or that particular story
toward a vision of unbiased justice for all; we should not let the natural
desire for narrative color betray that struggle. Law in that way embodies a vision of reconciliation: each tells her story, but not just for herself,
seeking instead a result that brings all together and stands for all.

Women's lack of full equality in American society has many dimen-
sions: lack of equal pay; continuing obstacles to full political representation; the huge, gnawing problem of care labor and its unequal
distribution in families across our nation; the stubborn problem of wom-
en's vulnerability to domestic violence. Each of these deserves a book.[2] In
this particular book I have chosen to focus on sexual assault and sexual
harassment, in part because these issues are current flash points for wom-
en's demands for justice, for resistance to those demands, and for occasional retributive overreach. (This topic clearly overlaps with the topic
of domestic violence, but that issue has separate importance and will not

be my focus here.) I believe that a good approach to the difficult issues of sexual assault and sexual harassment will indicate a spirit in which other issues might be constructively addressed. The issues on which I focus, furthermore, are issues for which law has long been a culprit, giving women inadequate protection, and for which recent legal work has begun to undo that history of wrong. So they provide a valuable theater in which to study the interplay between legal and institutional change and underlying societal struggles.

In Part I I dive immediately into the attitudes and emotions that brought Americans to this crisis and that impede a lasting peace. I look first at the key concept of "objectification," treating a person as a mere object, which illuminates much of the path before us if the concept is itself dissected with sufficient clarity. I then focus on a trait that fuels the longstanding denigration of women's full equality: the trait of pride, which underlies so much abuse of power—along with its relatives, greed and envy. The proud treat others as objects because they see only themselves. They neither listen nor see. Because pride plays a pernicious role in racism and class inequality, as well as sex discrimination, it offers us a way of understanding how one form of abuse is related to others, and especially, at this time in our national life, it invites us to reflect on how an unacceptable racial subordination and an unacceptable sexual subordination are intertwined aspects of a diseased national culture.

Life would be simpler if victims were always undamaged psychologically and had only constructive and helpful emotions. In Chapter 3 I argue that this is not necessarily the case, considering emotions of victims that may fuel a barren retributivism.

In Part II I turn to history and law. I give a brief account of the gradual revolution in criminal law that has led to more adequate standards for rape and sexual assault and to better treatment of victims. Because in our country most criminal laws are state laws, this revolution has of necessity been plural, messy, and complex. Meanwhile, at the federal level, feminists have pursued a different strategy, seeking protection against workplace sexual harassment by using Title VII and, later, Title IX of the Civil Rights Act of 1964. The key theoretical move was to secure agreement that sexual harassment constitutes discrimination on grounds of sex. Sexual harassment is a civil offense in which the defendant is not the individual perpetrator but the institution. But a plaintiff can succeed if she can show either that some type of "quid pro quo" was demanded of her in the employment context or that the harassment created a "hostile work environment"—and that her repeated complaints brought no redress. I examine the theory of sex discrimination that led to these legal developments and trace the main outlines of the case law. Sexual assault and sexual harassment can overlap, in fact, since harassment often includes some type of assault, although it need not. But the two involve altogether different legal strategies, standards, and concepts, and one of my aims is to dispel prevalent confusion about these distinctions. Finally, in an Interlude, I more briefly inspect the current atmosphere of controversy and uncertainty surrounding sexual assault on college and university campuses, suggesting how we may, going forward, strike an appropriate balance between accountability for victims and due process for the accused.

#MeToo is neither the beginning of a feminist revolution in law nor is it the end. As a result of hard legal and political work over the years, law has become far more responsive to women's voices. In the recent outpouring of #MeToo voices, credible reporting by many women has encouraged still other women to come forward and has made it much more likely that they will be believed when they do. Even though many of the reported offenses can no longer be prosecuted because of the statute of limitations or evidentiary problems (lack of forensic evidence, for example), reporting has prompted many states to begin removing these barriers to accountability. We need to think how to encourage yet more rapid reporting, because of the many ways in which information helps others.

#MeToo has helped win accountability. But the fact that so much of the #MeToo movement is social rather than legal creates a problem: how to secure justice and protect equal dignity when punishment is meted out not by impartial legal institutions but by shaming and stigmatization.

These forms of group behavior have a long record of not obeying limits of proportionality and due process.[3] Ironically what began as a movement against objectification can at times yield a reverse type of objectification.[4] My analysis of the emotions of victims in Part I prepares us to grapple with this problem.

The fundamental issue is not sex; it is power. Sexual abuse and sexual harassment, as feminists have long contended, are abuses of power by people encouraged to believe that they are above others and that others are not fully real. Culturally, men have been the dominant group in hierarchies of power, so the abusers this book considers are male. But people lower in the power hierarchy may be victimized whether male or female, and this book considers some cases in which the victims are male. My approach through "pride" has three important consequences: First, sexual abuse and harassment should be seen as closely akin to other abuses of power—abuses on the basis of race or class. Second, at times sexual abuse itself targets males lower in the power hierarchy. Third, women are especially vulnerable to sexual abuse when they are also targets of a racialized or class-based abuse of power. This book is in a sense about women, but it is really about hierarchies of power and the abuses they engender in people who are raised to think that they are above the law and that other people are not fully real.

Part III turns to recalcitrant areas of our national life. In some areas, despite #MeToo, powerful men remain above the law. When men are shielded by long-lasting institutional structures that give them enormous power, they may continue to do wrong with impunity. These "citadels of pride" insulate men who objectify and demean women from accountability. I examine the federal judiciary as one example of this problem. Impunity is heightened by greed, a frequent ally of the vice of pride. As examples of this problem I look at big-money college sports and the culture of celebrity in the arts, suggesting remedies for each. In all of these analyses I draw on Part I's discussion of the vices of domination, focusing particularly on pride and greed.

This will be a tough book, one that does not allow the "tender emotions" to become an excuse for weakness or retreat from accountability. But it is also a book committed to finding a path forward. Part III will argue that retributive emotions, attitudes, and demands do not provide that way forward. The only genuine opening to a shared future involves tough-minded insistence on accountability—combined with a spirit of constructive work, generosity of spirit, and what we might call "affirmative love." Wounded people become retributive easily, and we should sympathize with this reaction to genuine trauma. But sympathy is not a justification. Parents who have lost a child to criminal violence often become obsessed with capital punishment, but that understandable response does not justify capital punishment, or make the parents' attitude healthy or helpful. In criminal justice more generally, victims often become obsessed with revenge in an unhealthy way, and "victim impact" statements often taint a criminal trial with retributive overreach, jeopardizing the fairness of the criminal justice process. Just because a victim says something does not make it right or good. Creating a culture of accountability-with-reconciliation involves much more than emotion. But, as Martin Luther King Jr. knew and taught, getting the spirit and the emotions right is essential in guiding our more specific efforts.

At the end of the U.S. Civil War, Abraham Lincoln condemned slavery in the strongest possible terms, and committed our nation to moving beyond that hideous injustice. (We are not beyond it today, obviously, but full racial equality is a goal toward which the nation has been inching its way, with some long overdue commitments emerging in the wake of the murder of George Floyd in May 2020.) Lincoln did not, however, crow in triumph over the victory of his side. Instead, he recommended a spirit of constructive work and positive love as the only way to move beyond the egregious sins of the past:

> With malice toward none; with charity for all; with firmness in the right, as God gives us to see the right, let us strive on to finish the work we are in; to bind up the nation's wounds; . . . to do all which may achieve and cherish a just, and a lasting peace, among ourselves, and with all nations.

Lincoln asks for a justice free from malice, a vigilant firmness of judgment animated by a spirit of love for the potential for goodness in our fellow human beings. Many years later, Dr. King took up the task anew, in light of the nation's failure to deliver on its promise of equality and respect, and he continued and deepened Lincoln's call for a revolution of the heart that would put aside retribution to create a world of peace.

Women and men, too, need such a peace. This book, by studying the causes of our gender "war," proposes some strategies, both structural and emotional, to get there.

What has led me to engage with this topic at this time? First of all, over thirty years of feminist teaching and scholarship. Since around 1990, I have regularly taught a course called "Feminist Philosophy," attempting to deal respectfully and fairly with all the major varieties of feminism, and I have learned from all the writings I teach. I have learned even more from my successive generations of students, especially from their critical challenges. I have also had the good fortune to spend the past twenty-five years at one of the nation's premier law schools, where I have been steeped in conversations about criminal and civil law and have had daily conversations with some of the best legal thinkers about these issues—including Catharine MacKinnon, the creator of our current legal theory of sexual harassment, who used to teach regularly in our law school; and Stephen Schulhofer, one of the great progressive critics of sexual assault law, with whom I taught a class called "Sexual Autonomy and Law." I've also had as colleagues two judges—Richard Posner, now retired from the U.S. Court of Appeals for the Seventh Circuit, and Diane Wood, until recently chief judge of that same circuit—both of whom have made important legal contributions in this area. Although I am a philosopher and not a lawyer, then, I have learned from some of the best legal minds, and as a result have published articles on rape law and sexual harassment law.

I am also a woman. And like so many women in our society, I have been a victim of both sexual harassment and sexual assault. In an article about my graduate education at Harvard, I described the sexual harassment that I (along with many others) encountered from two noted professors.[5] And in a piece in the *Huffington Post*, right after the indictment of Bill Cosby, when so many were treating his crimes as the sui generis work of a singular "bad apple," I described my own sexual assault by another well-known actor with a similar reputation for rectitude, similarly insulated from accountability by power and the way his talents made money for others—Ralph Waite, the "daddy" on TV's *The Waltons*.[6] I have also, in an unrelated incident, suffered date rape. I see no value in narrating these experiences again, since my purpose in narrating them at all was to show that the Cosby case was not unusual; by now we all know that such things happen to many women. I also don't want this to be a narrative of victimhood, and I am seeking a perspective that is fair to all involved, as I believe we should always do in life.

Instead, let us turn to the stories of many women, to the law's obtuseness, and to courageous efforts toward change.

PART I

SITES OF STRUGGLE

CHAPTER 1

Objectification

TREATING PEOPLE AS THINGS

> It is true, and very much to the point, that women are objects, commodities, some deemed more expensive than others—but it is only by asserting one's humanness every time, in all situations, that one becomes someone as opposed to something. That, after all, is the core of our struggle.
>
> —Andrea Dworkin, *Woman Hating*

"Someone as Opposed to Something"

Sexual violence is not just a problem of isolated "sick" individuals. It is fed by pervasive features of American society. Along with virtually all societies, the United States has long nourished a culture of entrenched male privilege that defines women as subordinate, as not counting as much as men count. But things are yet worse. As I'll argue, this background culture—even when covered up with claims of respect and affection (many of which may be sincere)—denies women key features of full and equal humanity, treating them, in certain ways, as commodities or objects for male use.

Two central features of a full human being, as our major religions and a broadly shared secular culture have long, and rightly, taught, are *autonomy* and *subjectivity*. Human beings, in other words, are centers of choice who should, in consequence, be enabled to make certain important life-defining choices for themselves, rather than having their lives dictated to them by others.[1] And they are also centers of deep inner experience, whose feelings and thoughts matter greatly—to them, and, if things go well, to others who deal with them. Good social and political institutions, in modern democracies, are understood to have the job of protecting both autonomy and subjectivity. A healthy democracy protects autonomy by giving people opportunities to choose for themselves in key areas such as religion, speech, political opinion, occupation, association, sex, and marriage. It protects subjectivity by recognizing that people need spaces for their beliefs to take shape (freedoms of religion and speech, again) and for their emotions to seek fulfillment (freedom of association again, rights to marry and form friendships, and, crucially, protection of sexual consent).

These key norms have implications for many areas of social life that have been abridged for women in the past—including voting, education, and marital choice. But they have special urgency when we contemplate our current theme.

Sexual assault and harassment violate autonomy and subjectivity in profound ways. They typically ignore or ride roughshod over a woman's capacity for consent—or extort a pseudo-consent by threat—treating women as convenient objects, whose decisions don't really matter, for male gratification. At the same time, sexual violence treats women's emotions and thoughts as irrelevant, as if only the desires of the dominant male are real and important. Sometimes, worse yet, the neglect of women's thoughts and feelings is so profound that a bogus subjectivity is imputed to a woman, one that neatly dovetails with male wishes—for example, the notion that "no means yes," that women really enjoy their enforced sexual submission.

Worse still, at times male domination of women takes the form of nudging them into pliant submissiveness. As John Stuart Mill puts it in *The Subjection of Women*,[2] men—whom he calls the "masters of women," to reinforce an analogy with slavery—were not content with controlling women's physical being. They wanted willing obedience. "They have therefore put everything in practice to enslave their minds" (15). Women, he continues, are accordingly taught from an early age that their ideal character is "not self-will, and government by self-control, but submission, and yielding to the control of others" (16). They learn that the only sentiments proper to a woman are those involving abnegation of self, and that the only way to be sexually attractive to men is to cultivate "meekness, submissiveness, and resignation of all individual will into the hands of a man" (16). Women may thus develop what we might call an anti-autonomy mindset, and, in a sense, an anti-subjectivity subjectivity, telling themselves that their own experiences and feelings don't fully count, that it's not right to protest or assert themselves. This makes protest against unequal sexual conditions far more difficult. Sometimes women even turn themselves into commodities, pleasing objects for the male gaze. A proper Victorian, Mill does not explore the implications of his insight for sexual violence (although in a subsequent chapter he assails the absence of laws against domestic violence and marital rape). Later feminists, as we'll see, have taken up the challenge of extending these insights.

Most men of Mill's time, like most men in ours, would have vehemently denied that they dominated their wives and daughters. And yet: these men created, held in place, and perpetuated, for these women they allegedly loved, a lopsided legal regime in which rape in marriage was no crime, in which married women had no property rights, no right to vote, and no right to divorce, even on grounds of cruelty.[3] Even today, when these rights have been secured and when women are able to hold independent jobs, and when many men genuinely support women's equal autonomy, the law, as we'll see, contains many recalcitrant vestiges of this denial of equal autonomy and subjectivity, and our informal culture contains far more.

Women never really become things, of course. Personhood, however neglected, remains alive beneath the corset of conformity. As Mill knew, many women resist efforts to subjugate their minds. Even when minds are to a degree "enslaved," the baneful self-transformation he describes is reversible: a suppressed desire for full human self-assertion, which, as he emphasizes, has already caused many women to rebel against the status quo, can be awakened in all women—to the benefit, as he sees it, of both women and men.

A long tradition of feminist reflection has explored this contrast between full human personhood and mere thinghood. With some further analysis and elaboration, this tradition guides us well.

Elizabeth Cady Stanton Addresses Congress

Invited along with other prominent feminists to speak in 1892 before the House Committee on the Judiciary, Elizabeth Cady Stanton (1816–1902) delivered a speech that must have surprised the other feminists as much as it did the representatives. Stanton had long been somewhat isolated within the feminist movement for her uncompromising radicalism, especially her defense of women's access to divorce. Biographer Vivian Gornick rightly sees her as a precursor of the radical feminism of the 1970s.[4] One might then have expected a speech about specific feminist demands, pushing the envelope on both suffrage and divorce rights.

The speech that Stanton actually delivered was altogether different. It became very famous: feminist Lucy Stone published the entire text in the *Women's Journal*, and in 1915 the U.S. Congress reprinted it and sent 10,000 copies around the world. Stanton herself was very proud of it. But the speech is not radical in the expected way, focusing on concrete political demands. At first it seems oddly irrelevant to politics: for it is all about the isolation of each individual in the journey through life, "[t]he isolation of every human soul."

• The speech is poetic rather than crisply analytical. We must work to reconstruct it. Initially, Stanton depicts the solitude of each soul as alarming: each of us lives and dies alone. "Rich and poor, intelligent and ignorant, wise and foolish, virtuous and vicious, man and woman, it is ever the same, each soul must depend wholly on itself." Solitude is at times painful, a "march" and a "battle." It is, however, inevitable. Therefore, concludes Stanton, women need self-development through education and political opportunities to make their own choices, so that they will be equipped to direct their life's course well.

But there is another, apparently different, picture of solitude in the speech, one that seems in tension with the first. Every human life, Stanton suggests, contains a precious inner world, one that no other person can fully see, an inner space that is rightly called "conscience" and "ourself." Conscience includes both a power of autonomous choice and a rich subjectivity, and these powers are now seen as deeply precious, though "more hidden than the caves of the nome." This conception of solitude, which Stanton explicitly links to American Protestant traditions,[5] yields further reasons why women should be given education and political rights: because this inner world is precious and sublime, and demands respect. Respecting it means developing it. Here Stanton speaks of a woman's "right of individual conscience and judgment," her "birthright to self-sovereignty." Thus, even if women could depend utterly on men, she seems to argue, it would still be an egregious offense to fail to give them freedom of choice and a chance to develop their thoughts and emotions.

How should we fit the two parts of the speech together? Clearly, its normative center is its argument about the duty to respect the precious core of each human self. What work is done by the earlier passages? Superficially, they seem at odds with the later sections, in that they portray solitude as painful, rather than a hidden zone of precious selfhood. Solitude can, of course, be both. I believe the earlier passages fulfill a purpose: they head off a defensive male response. We can imagine many men in the audience thinking: Sure, women have conscience, but they are immature, like children, so they need constant male supervision to exercise it well. Respecting women, on this male view, does not entail higher education or political rights—just the opposite: it entails close paternal protection. The earlier part of the speech heads off this response by reminding the audience that nobody can spend an entire life under another person's care. According to the Protestant tradition, each person's journey to salvation must be made alone. The primary reason to educate women and give them political rights comes from the normative importance and preciousness of conscience, its powers of choice and subjectivity. But to anyone seeking to inscribe conscience within a society of patriarchal non-independence for women, the inevitability of solitude should be a salutary warning: women will face their necessarily solitary death and judgment unprepared.

In short: men deny women full autonomy and subjectivity. Put to the test, however, they must concede that women have souls like them (at least their religion says so). So they should face up to the consequences of that admission: they should no longer deprive women of the opportunity to cultivate faculties of choice and to deepen their inner world through education.

This same type of analysis is familiar in the American tradition of argument for freedom of religious choice: Stanton and Roger Williams (founder of Rhode Island and prolific writer about religious liberty) are cousins.[6] (Williams argues that to deny freedom of religious expression to those with whom one disagrees is "soul rape.") So Stanton's audience would likely have been well prepared, culturally, to listen to her appeal.

Like many leading feminists, from Mary Wollstonecraft to Catharine MacKinnon, Stanton over-generalizes, failing to note examples of respectful men who do respect women's equality. However, there are two good reasons for this strategy. First, she wants to show that this male bad behavior is the norm, not the rare exception; it's all too easy to neglect the magnitude of a problem when our eyes are constantly directed to exceptions. Second, even when men are exemplary, they live in, and do not insist on changing, a pernicious legal regime in which women have grossly unequal rights. So how exemplary are they, really? This will be a persistent question in this book, since even men who did not harass women in the workplace still thought it was extreme to make sexual harassment a legal issue. And so forth.

Stanton focuses on voting rights and higher education. She does not speak, here, of sexual violence. That concern, however, is central to her life's work, as her audience would have been sure to know. One of the main considerations she always pressed in favor of granting women divorce rights was marital cruelty. And in 1868, in one of her most famous speeches, she urged in favor of women's suffrage, the claim that male domination has heretofore had a very bad record of violence: "The male element is a destructive force, stern, selfish, aggrandizing, loving war, violence, conquest, acquisition, breeding in the material and moral world alike discord, disorder, disease, and death."[7] While her language here is sweepingly rhetorical and vague, and her tendency to essentialize the natures of male and female unfortunate, her intention is pretty clear: male violence is a deep empirical fact that law must confront. And in letters, she uses unambiguous language: marriage without rights against nonconsensual sex is "nothing more nor less than legalized prostitution."[8] Stanton worked consistently to reform marriage laws. Combining the two speeches, we are invited to look for denials of autonomy and subjectivity in sexual violence, not only in men's more polite denials of university education and the right to vote. The twentieth-century feminists who were Stanton's heirs would make this link explicit.

Interlude: Sexism and Misogyny

At this point we need to introduce a distinction. Denial of rights and privileges to women may be motivated in two different ways: by what I shall call *sexism* and by what I shall call *misogyny*. I use these terms in the specific sense defined by feminist philosopher Kate Manne in her recent book *Down Girl: The Logic of Misogyny*,[9] whose analysis I accepted, up to a point, and extended, in my own recent *The Monarchy of Fear*.[10] (The point is to nail down two distinct and useful concepts, not to capture the ordinary meaning of words, so the definitions alone will tell us what the two terms, in their special technical usage, mean.) *Sexism* is defined as a system of beliefs holding that women are, in specified ways, inferior to men. A sexist will use that belief system to deny women voting rights, higher education, and so forth. *Misogyny*, by contrast, is an enforcement mechanism: the misogynist digs in on behalf of entrenched privilege and is simply determined not to let women in. (The misogynist needn't hate women, as some ordinary uses of the term suggest: his strategy is most often motivated by selfishness and sheer unwillingness to admit women to the world of male privilege.)

The two approaches to women's demands are often combined: in order to keep women out, the misogynist will often appeal to sexist arguments. But if we probe more deeply we can usually figure out which approach is primary. Sexist beliefs are fragile, and they tend to be refuted by evidence. Consequently, people rarely rely on them too far. As John Stuart Mill had already remarked in 1869, sexists must lack confidence in their own judgments of female incapacity, since they work so hard to stop women from doing things that, by their own account, women are unable to do: "The anxiety of mankind to interfere in behalf of nature, for fear lest nature should not succeed in effecting its purpose, is an altogether unnecessary solicitude. What women by nature cannot do, it is quite superfluous to forbid them from doing."

Indeed, Mill continues, if we examine all the prohibitions and requirements society has organized, we would rationally conclude that men do not believe that "the natural vocation of a woman is that of a wife and mother." Rather, it seems that they must believe that this vocation is not attractive to women: "that if they are free to do anything else—if any other means of living, or occupation of their time and faculties, is open . . . there will not be enough of them who will be willing to accept the condition said to be natural to them." Mill is saying that the denial of basic rights to women (including divorce, suffrage, and access to higher education, but also including the right to refuse sex, even within marriage) is allegedly motivated by sexist beliefs about female inferiority, but on deeper inspection it is a power play: men use sexist rhetoric to put up barriers to women's full entry into society and to keep them available for their own service and use, however politely and gently they speak about women's need for shelter and protection.

Mill's insight (developed further in Manne's distinction between sexism and misogyny) will help us think about sexual violence and harassment. Most men will deny that they are complicit in such crimes, and insist that they love and respect women. However, to the extent that they support and profit from a legal and social power structure that systematically denies women a full measure of consideration for their autonomy and subjectivity, they are passive misogynists, enforcing an inequality of power and privilege out of which these abuses grow.

Objectification

This brings us to the key feminist concept of objectification, a linchpin of feminist analysis during the past fifty years. It may seem a long distance from Stanton's poetic speech to the stern evangelism of radical feminists such as Catharine MacKinnon and Andrea Dworkin, but in reality there is great continuity of thought and analysis. This chapter's Andrea Dworkin epigraph could have come right out of Stanton, and recent feminists make explicit the connection to sexual violence that is clearly a major, if under-analyzed, concern in Stanton as well.

Sex-based objectification has become a familiar concept. Once a relatively technical term associated primarily with the work of MacKinnon and Dworkin, "objectification" has now become a term of normative assessment in common parlance, used to criticize advertisements, movies, and other cultural representations, but also to criticize the speech and behavior of individuals. It is almost always pejorative, designating a way of speaking and acting that the speaker finds objectionable, usually, though not always, in the realm of gender and sexuality. Thus we hear of women "dehumanized as sexual objects, things, or commodities,"[11] and this sort of dehumanization is taken to be a salient social problem, both by feminist theorists and by many women describing their daily lives. It's a problem that is rightly seen to lie at the heart of feminism.

MacKinnon insists on a further point: objectification is so ubiquitous that for the most part women cannot help living surrounded, even suffused, by it. In a striking metaphor, she states that "All women live in sexual objectification the way fish live in water"—meaning by this, presumably, not only that objectification surrounds women, but also that they have become such that they derive their very nourishment and sustenance from it. (Here she agrees with Mill, and with Mary Wollstonecraft, who made the same point earlier.) But women are not fish, and for MacKinnon objectification is bad because it cuts women off from full self-expression and self-determination—from, in effect, their humanity. The connection of this normative concept to the radicalism of Stanton is evident. But we still need more clarity: what is objectification, and what lies at its heart?

To objectify is to treat as a thing. But to treat a desk or a pen as a thing would not be called "objectification," since desks and pens just *are* things. Objectification means *converting into* a thing, treating *as* a thing what is really not a thing at all, but a human being.[12] Objectification thus involves a refusal to see the humanity that is there, or, even more often, active denial of that full humanity. But we need to dig deeper, asking what is involved in the idea of treating someone *as a thing*, since the concept has not always been analyzed with the requisite clarity and complexity. For twenty-five years I have argued that we need to make a series of further distinctions.[13]

There are many ways in which full humanity may be denied, so objectification should be viewed as a cluster concept, involving (at least) seven distinct ideas, seven ways to treat a person as a thing:

1. *Instrumentality*: objectifiers treat their object as a (mere) tool of their purposes.
2. *Denial of autonomy*: objectifiers treat their object as lacking in autonomy and self-determination.
3. *Inertness*: objectifiers treat their object as lacking in agency, and perhaps also in activity.
4. *Fungibility*: objectifiers treat their object as interchangeable with (a) other objects of the same type, and/or (b) objects of other types.
5. *Violability*: objectifiers treat their object as lacking in boundary integrity, as something that it is permissible to break up, smash, break into.
6. *Ownership*: objectifiers treat their object as something that is owned or ownable by someone, that can be bought or sold, or otherwise treated as property.
7. *Denial of subjectivity*: objectifiers treat their object as something whose experience and feelings (if any) need not be taken into account.

These different ways of objectifying a human being can be seen both in the context of sexual relations and in other contexts (slavery, labor relations, and so on). The seven are distinct notions, giving rise to different types of objectification, interrelated in a variety of complicated ways. We should think of the concept as involving a family of interweaving conceptually independent criteria, rather than as having a single set of necessary and sufficient conditions. However, while conceptually independent, the notions are causally linked in many complicated ways. For example, one may certainly deny women autonomy and subjectivity without treating one woman as fungible with other women. They still differ in the way they look and move. But once one denies a woman those core aspects of her full humanity, differences between her and other women (similarly denied) become superficial, mere matters of outer appearance, so we are on the way to the idea that one may be substituted for another. Again, one may deny autonomy and subjectivity to a woman without thinking of her as ownable, a market commodity. Once again, however, once those denials are made, reasons for not treating that putative shell of a human being as able to be bought and sold seem weak.

Along with feminist Rae Langton, we may add to my 1995 list

8. *Silencing*: objectifiers treat their object as unable to speak.[14]

Silencing is really an aspect of autonomy-denial, but it is so ubiquitous that it is useful to single it out.[15] And, again with Langton, we should insist that there is a distinction running through several of the items on the list, especially items 2, 7, and 8, that parallels my distinction between sexism and misogyny. That is, one might fail to believe that women are capable of autonomy; that they are capable of articulate thought and speech; that they have thoughts and feelings worthy of notice. Or, as the list suggests, one may actively *deny* or *thwart* a woman's search for autonomy, for speech, and for recognition of her inner life. One may even take pleasure in *subjectivity-violation*, invading and colonizing a woman's inner world.

According to Stanton, most men, most of the time, are active deniers of women's autonomy and subjectivity, much though they may cover their behavior by an apparent rhetoric of paternal guardianship. Lest imputing to men this active denial of women's full humanity, this misogynistic enforcement of a subhuman status, should seem excessive or paranoid, let's remind ourselves that John Stuart Mill analyzed the phenomenon of women's subjection in precisely this way: the "masters of women," not content with physical domination, contrived to invade and dominate women's autonomy and subjectivity.

The eight features of objectification are not equivalent and are not always co-present. So a question arises: What is the centrally bad move, the key to the harmfulness of objectifying women? Let's focus for now on just three features: denial of autonomy, denial of subjectivity, and instrumentality, or treatment as a mere means. In 1995 I said that treating someone as a mere means rather than an end was the core of the harm of objectification: It was the sort of failure Immanuel Kant diagnosed when he insisted that it was always wrong to treat humanity (in oneself or in another) as a mere means rather than an end. This still seems right to me, but more needs to be said about how this failure relates to the other members of my list. Clearly, if one sees another person as a mere means, denial of autonomy and denial of subjectivity naturally follow. If the person is seen as there to do what *you* want, to serve *your* ends, to that extent her own choices will be cut off in favor of yours (denial of autonomy), and her feelings won't be fully taken into account (denial of subjectivity). But we still must contend with the fact that sometimes we deny full autonomy without instrumentalizing, or denying subjectivity— namely when we have good and accurate reasons to believe that the other being is not, or not yet, capable of full human choice. Thus very small children are denied full autonomy, as are people with very severe mental disabilities and most domesticated animals, but all may be loved as ends, and we may care a great deal about their feelings, insofar as we are able to grasp them. In short, if sexist claims of women's incapacity were true, denials of autonomy and subjectivity might be compatible with treating women as ends.

At this point we are thrown back to the Stanton argument: insofar as such men pay lip service to a religion and a culture that recognize that women have souls and a destiny that must be pursued by one's own choices, the sexist fiction that they are like very young children rings false, and is best understood as a misogynistic shoring up of the dominator's privilege.

Why would men engage in the pretense that women are like young children—a view at odds, Stanton plausibly claims, with other things that men believe? One plausible answer is: because at heart they see women not as full ends, but mainly as servants, beings who are there to do things for them. Thus their denials of autonomy are closely bound up with their interest in making women into their instruments. They want to force women to make the choices that suit them. As for denial of subjectivity: a dominant male may protest that of course he cares greatly what the women in his life feel and think—but only up to a point. So long as what they think is agreeable to him, and does not threaten his position, well and good. Anything else is likely to be actively ignored or silenced. Slaves, similarly, are not always denied subjectivity; masters may imagine them as beings mentally well suited to their lot. Masters may also think with a limited empathy about slaves' pleasure or pain.

On the other hand, once again, the very decision to treat people as not ends in themselves, but as mere tools, leads rather naturally to a failure of imagination. Once one decides to use a person as a tool, it is very easy indeed to stop asking the questions morality usually dictates, such as, What is this person likely to feel if I do X? What does this person want, and how will my doing X affect her with respect to those wants? And so on. It seems likely that monarchs have also played this game: while in a sense thinking of the lower classes as human, they have denied them key features of full humanity because a fuller acknowledgment would threaten the useful arrangement whereby these people exist to serve the monarch's interests.

Needless to say, feminists who accept this analysis need not believe that there are no countervailing tendencies in men. Indeed the evangelism of many feminists, including MacKinnon's very optimistic teaching in law schools over the years, presupposes that men hold other, better, beliefs as well and are capable of self-criticism and change. Their point is that these better voices have little chance of prevailing so long as law and the larger social script are written by the bad voices. That is why legal reform is as central for today's radical feminists as it was for Stanton.

Objectification and Sexual Assault

• So far I have said nothing about violence. But once a woman is seen as a mere valuable instrument, her full autonomy and subjectivity denied, then it is more or less a matter of chance and circumstance whether she will be treated gently or harshly. Just as slaves, seen as useful tools, were sometimes treated gently and fed well—because that was useful to the master's household, perhaps also to his self-image—so too with the "masters of women." In this analysis, the difference between the gentle loving male who nonetheless accepts and profits from legal and social structures of subordination and the violent male who rapes and beats women is a matter of circumstance and degree, not a total difference of character. In more or less the same way, collaboration with any evil cause is different only in degree from the active commission of its evil acts. It simply doesn't usually suit a middle-class married man to rape his wife. The useful arrangement of marriage works better when he gets what he wants without struggle, by gentler means. BUT: if and when his interests so dictate, there is no barrier. (John Galsworthy's *The Forsyte Saga* [1906–21] is a profound exploration of just such a flipping of the switch, as it suddenly occurs to Soames that his "honor as a man" requires raping his wife Irene, for her obstinate refusal to be the pliant helpmeet he wants her to be.) Such a man, of course, will vehemently oppose legal reform.

Once again, we need to add that there are also good voices in most men, opposing violence and urging love and respect. To the extent, however, that the law is on the other side (in Soames's case, telling him that he can rape his wife with impunity), they have little chance of prevailing society-wide against pride and self-interest.

Let's now consider how such connections seem to play out in the sexual culture of the United States, where violence in intimate relationships is not rare, and, indeed, most violence takes place within some type of relationship. The most recent National Intimate Partner and Sexual Violence Survey, published by the Centers for Disease Control and Prevention, puts the incidence of sexual violence even higher than previous studies did.[16] Nearly one in five women surveyed said they had been raped or had experienced an attempted rape, and one in four reported having been beaten by an intimate partner. One in six women have been stalked. Sexual violence is, of course, not only directed toward women, but it affects women disproportionately. One-third of women said they had been victims of some form of sexual assault. One in seven men have experienced sexual violence, and one in seventy-one had been raped (usually when very young). More than half of female rape victims were raped by an intimate partner, and 40 percent by an acquaintance.

Nor are these numbers unconnected to traditional patriarchal attitudes: Edward Laumann, one of the great sociologists of our era, found some highly disturbing facts in his exhaustive survey of American sexual attitudes and experiences, published in *The Social Organization of Sexuality*, and the more popular *Sex in America*.[17] Laumann is no radical, and not even a feminist, but a very conservative quantitative scholar of impeccable respectability.

First, American men widely share a picture of male sexuality as easily aroused then uncontrollable. Once aroused, a man just "can't stop." Women are commonly seen as temptresses whose very presence and physical allure makes men lose control; after that, they just aren't responsible for what they do. Men combine this belief with a related myth about women: that they really want sex even when they say they don't, even when they fight against it. Laumann came to the following conclusion about how these attitudes lead to problematic acts of aggression:

> Although, clearly, sexual interactions between men and women are fraught with ambiguity and potential conflicts, there is something more going on than a few misunderstandings. There seems to be not just a gender gap but a gender chasm in perceptions of when

sex was forced. We find that large numbers of women say they have
been forced by men to do something sexually that they did not want
to do. But very few men report ever forcing a woman. The differences that men and women bring to the sexual situation and the
differences in their experiences of sex sometimes suggest that there
are two separate sexual worlds, his and hers.[18]

Specifically, Laumann found that 22 percent of women said they were
forced sexually at some time after age thirteen (and only 0.6 percent were
forced by another woman). Only 2 percent of men were forced. All but 4
percent of these women knew the man who was forcing them and nearly
half said they were in love with him.

Men, by contrast, overwhelmingly denied using force: only 3 percent
said they forced a woman and 0.2 percent said they forced a man. Some
may be lying, but Laumann and his co-authors plausibly hold that the
huge disparities cannot be explained away in this manner. They suggest
that a more likely explanation is that "most men who forced sex did not
recognize how coercive the women thought their behavior was."[19] They
imagine the husband who comes home drunk from a night out with the
boys, wanting sex now and thinking it his due; the young man on a date
with a sexy woman who makes and accepts some advances but says no
to intercourse. Laumann and his co-authors summarize: "He thinks the
sex they have was consensual. She thinks it was forced."[20]

Let's now connect Laumann's findings to our interest in objectification. The basic fact about these interactions is a male sense of entitle-
ment, connected to a half-conscious idea that women are there to do
something for men (the husband thinks sex is "his due"; the young man
who pays for a date similarly thinks it is a transaction at the end of which
the woman should serve his needs). These men don't even think of themselves as using force because they just think they are claiming their end
of a useful social bargain. Because of this background sense of entitle-
ment and this background instrumentalization, it is all too easy to deny
full autonomy (ignoring non-consent) and subjectivity ("no means yes").

Fungibility is lurking in the margins as well: if this woman doesn't serve my interests, I'll just find another who will.

Our internet and social media culture magnifies these problems, making it astonishingly easy to deny both autonomy and subjectivity to the women one imagines. Internet porn makes available a seemingly endless number of pliant woman-representations, fully fungible, whose every movement and expression serve to heighten a male sense of control and power. These woman-representations are devoid of autonomy: they exist only to gratify male wishes. And they have a bogus subjectivity crafted to male specifications. This clearly has spillover effects on "the real world," even if one disputes their magnitude (and even if one insists that some pornography has value even for feminists).[21] Internet culture is not really different in kind from the longstanding depiction of women in advertisements, print pornography, and other media. But it is disturbingly different in degree: it is a whole world—a world in which the viewer, utterly immersed, sees nothing but women-representations ready to do his bidding. Many men today spend many hours in this world.

Thus, although there have always been men who cannot attract a female partner, it is only today, in the internet era, that we find the "incel" (involuntary celibate) movement, itself spread through the internet and social media, in which large numbers of men who believe women have denied them a gratification that is theirs by right support one another in feeling that when a woman in the "real world" doesn't behave pliantly, like a woman in the internet porn world, it is all right to punish her in a violent way.[22]

The feminist concept of objectification, together with its ancestor concepts in Stanton, Mill, and Wollstonecraft, helps us to understand the *what* of sexual harm: what is going on and in what ways it matters. We still need to understand the *why*: the underlying formations of emotion and desire that lead to this sort of behavior.

CHAPTER 2

Vices of Domination

PRIDE AND GREED

You know, I was a superstar when I was a little kid too.
—NFL player and sexual predator Jameis Winston
in a homemade video from his home trophy room,
which he calls the "Boom Boom Room"[*]

"**O**bjectification" is at the heart of sexual violence—as well as other harms. But objectification is behavior. It emerges from underlying character traits, enduring patterns of action, vision, and emotion. Emotions are an important part of character, as Aristotle and many subsequent philosophers have emphasized; but emotions may be short-lived, and they may sometimes not represent enduring traits. My focus here is on syndromes fostered in our society (and others), especially in men. For it is pride—the character trait, not the related momentary emotion—that is key to understanding the prevalence of sexual objectification in our society.

Pride is a trait that involves habitually thinking oneself above others and thinking that others do not fully count. Pride has many forms, and some people have one form without another. (Thus, people who have race pride may lack class pride, or may even cling to race pride as a substitute for their lack of class pride.) Wherever males are situated in other American hierarchies, however, long-standing traditions have nourished

[*] See Chapter 8 for context.

gender pride in them—the view that women don't fully count and that it's acceptable to look down on them. Pride is abetted by some other bad traits, especially greed and envy. But these other traits become socially toxic above all when they are combined with pride.

Pride is a deep cause of the subordination of women in general. But this chapter's analysis will also prepare us to understand, ultimately, why gender-pride has run rampant in areas of unusual male privilege such as sports, the media, and the judiciary: the prouder you are across the board the easier it becomes not to listen to or look at women in your sphere. Injured pride, and consequent shame, is also damaging, playing a large role in much domestic violence.

But first, let's look at the proud, guided by the imagery of an insightful philosopher-poet, Dante Alighieri (c. 1265–1321). Dante's poetry delves deeply into human virtues and vices, attaining through poetic imagery a rare degree of human understanding. The souls in Purgatory, in the middle work of his great trilogy, aren't damned, because they repented, although many more with similar vices did not repent, so they are in the Inferno. But these souls have bad habits of character, and they have to change them by laborious practice in good actions and suitable attention to others, thus changing their habits. Dante, whose tour of Purgatory is conducted by another poet, the great Latin poet Virgil, learns that he has lots of the vices he encounters; hopefully, before death, he can get rid of at least some of them. Dante's self-critique is, I claim, a poetry we need in our time, helping our society to see itself.

Ascending the Mount of Purgatory, Dante and Virgil find themselves on a desolate terrace, where a small number of souls struggle to correct themselves and ascend. (Readers know already from the *Inferno* that the reason for the small number is not that the bad trait corrected here is rare, but rather that very few of those who have this trait manage to repent and change, thus ending up in Purgatory rather than Hell.) They now see a strange sight: quasi-human forms, but bent in on themselves like hoops so that they cannot look outward at the world or other people. Since their faces don't look out, but only inward at themselves, they can neither see nor be seen. Consequently, exclaims the puzzled Dante, they "do not look like people" (*non mi sembian persone*, x.113). Virgil tells him that it is the "heavy condition of their punishment" (*la grave condizione di lor tormento*) that doubles them over to the earth. But of course, as is usual with Dante, their punishment does not express something external, added to who they are or were. It is an apt expression of their stunted ethical condition. Although human, they never looked other humans fully in the eye, acknowledging their full humanity. They gazed only at themselves.

Who are these unfortunate souls? We could call them narcissists, but the name that Dante gives to their weighty vice is "pride." He makes it clear that this vice is closely linked to other common forms of narcissistic self-preoccupation, such as resentfulness, chronic envy, and greed. But pride's self-absorption is the most complete, and it is in that sense a master-vice, bad by itself and making other vices worse. It is also ubiquitous in Dante's highly competitive Florentine society, and he becomes aware that he himself has that trait, at least in the context of literary competition. When that letter *P* (for *peccatum*, "sin" or "vice") is removed from his brow, all the other *P*'s become immediately fainter. (Dante's picture is religious, but it embodies a human insight that transcends religion.)

I shall speak of virtues and vices, but the language of sin is also resonant in this context, since Christian discussions of the deadly sins are, in fact, an extremely valuable source philosophically, as well as influential in American culture.[1] (My use of the word "sin" does not imply any particular religious picture, nor does it imply any religious notion of original sin.) The traits considered here are socially encouraged and shaped, from many different viewpoints—although they are also supported, very likely, by some innate evolutionary tendencies in human beings, prior to any particular socialization, such as a propensity to form hierarchies and to compete with others for ranking. This means that they will be easy to encourage and hard to extinguish.

Pride the Emotion

• Before we can understand pride as a bad character trait, however, we need to examine pride the transient emotion. Pride is a common emotion, but it is rarely analyzed by secular philosophers. One philosopher who does analyze it, and brilliantly, is David Hume, for whom pride—along with its opposite, which he misleadingly calls "humility"—is the first of the emotions to be analyzed in the middle book of *A Treatise of Human Nature*, entitled *Of the Passions*.[2] As philosopher Donald Davidson noted, Hume's discussion of pride ascribes to it a rich cognitive content, despite his project of shoehorning all emotions into his simple framework of impressions and ideas.[3] Hume's discussion of pride contains many insights, but his basic claim is that pride involves a combination of pleasant feeling with a double directedness of thought: toward an object (the thing you are proud *of*), and toward the self (the reason why *you* are proud of that thing). He calls the former the *object* of the emotion and the latter its *cause*. Thus, a person who has a beautiful and expensive house feels *proud of* the house, but the reason is that it belongs to *him*. In other words, the house is just an occasion for the emotion, if it is pride and not aesthetic feeling. It causes the pleasing emotion, but it is not what the emotion focuses on or is all about. The object or real focus of the emotion is the self. So pride is distinct from admiration or love.

Hume adds that there are many possible causes of pride, but typically they are things that already stand in some close relation to the self: personal characteristics, bodily appearance, possessions. The very same characteristics, when we imagine them in some other person or that person's belongings, will not excite pride. Moreover, the cause is typically something that is not hugely common, but "peculiar to ourselves, or at least common to us with a few persons." The reason he gives is that pride is not focused on the intrinsic quality of the object: its point is essentially comparative. It's all about you, but you will not feel it if the item in question is something that belongs to everyone. Social judgments in his view are in any case more comparative than intrinsic, and the whole point of pride is raising oneself up above others. Thus, if there are hundreds of guests at a delicious feast, they may all feel *joy*, but it is only the "master of the feast" who will feel pride, since only he will have "the additional passion of self-applause and vanity." Moreover, the cause of pride, for this same reason, must be conspicuous and obvious to others. Pride, for Hume, has roots in pre-social human nature, but is strongly influenced, as well, by contingent social rankings. It flourishes most conspicuously in a highly competitive and positional society.

Pride the emotion might be fleeting, hence harmless, but it already embodies a skewed way of seeing the world and the self in the world. Instead of loving your house because it is beautiful or comfortable, you see it as a thing that brings *you* social distinction. Instead of loving your companion animals for their affectionate nature and their skill, you see them as all about *you*. Think, too, about parents whose main emotion toward their children is pride—a phenomenon we know all too well. Such parents have a hard time loving their children at all, since they see them as tools of their own prestige. And although it is clear that husbands through the ages have often felt pride about their wives, that attitude, too, is not likely to be compatible with a steady acknowledgment of the woman's autonomy and subjectivity. Just as in Homeric times a woman was a literal trophy to be won in battle, so in our times we know all too well the "trophy wife," object of pride because her beauty (or other wifely virtues) brings prestige to the masculinity of the man who "won" her.

In short, pride the emotion already involves instrumentalization, hence objectification, with its tendency to deny full autonomy and subjectivity. This mindset already teeters on the verge of violence. Consider again Galsworthy's character Soames Forsyte, whom we met in Chapter 1. A charmless but wealthy man, he gains prestige in the world's eyes by successfully wooing the beautiful Irene. He views her with pride rather than with love. When, then, she defies him and refuses to sleep with him—conduct threatening a humiliating public breach—there is no barrier in his emotions to proving his masculinity and his domination of her by marital rape. (This is one example of the way in which the shame that follows injured pride leads to domestic violence.)

Pride the Trait; Gender-Pride and Its Opposite

Let's consider, now, pride solidified into an ongoing trait of character—a complex of emotions, beliefs, and action-tendencies. This trait is brilliantly expressed in Dante's depiction of the proud: they really are like hoops, bent over on themselves, so that they can see only self and not the outer world. As we turn from the pleasant emotion to the enduring character trait, we observe that pride as a trait does not always feel pleasant. Since it is a habitual way of being in the world, we should not think of pride as a sudden upsurge of delight, but rather as a steady state of self-involvement—so habitual that the proud person is often unaware of it. This self-involvement is often a type of self-satisfaction, although, as in the case of Soames Forsyte, it has an edge of anxiety: any threat to the proud person's superiority would definitely be felt as a painful wound.

If, with Dante, we think of people as all pursuing the good with some type of love or striving—a part of the Catholic tradition that I think brilliantly right—we should also agree with him that pride represents a very fundamental deformation of love. By love he means a longing and reaching-out for the good that is basic to our humanity. For the proud, nothing is real outside the self. Pride, more than any other sin, robs a person of a very fundamental relationship to external reality, thus a basic attribute of personhood. The proud don't even get to the point of making a wrong choice of external objects, since they can't see distinct objects at all, only the self. All their dealings with the world are forms of instrumentalization. Dante insightfully sees that the proud in this way do not simply become objectifiers; they also become less than fully human: because their faces don't turn outward: "they don't look like people."

Some people are proud globally, seeing only self in all their worldly dealings. Thus they totally lack compassion for those they see as far below them. Dante shows people whose pride is global but focused on one attribute: power, noble birth, or artistic excellence (his own sin). Because these people also think their own excellence the most important thing their pride quickly tends toward the global.

But we can also imagine people who are proud only locally, seeing the reality of some parts of the world and not others, seeing real humanity in some dealings and only self plus the instruments of self in others. Probably rulers who thought of their subjects as mere things did love members of their families and showed concern for their well-being. And in most cultures where males dominate, they have horizontal, friendly and respectful, relationships with other males, while failing to see the humanity of those "below." Even the construction of who is "below" can vary, giving rise to different types of group pride.

Thus, white people, male and female, have for centuries had white race pride, often without having class pride: U.S. racism crosses all social strata. White women, moreover, have often had white race pride without gender pride. Elizabeth Cady Stanton fought for a full human vision of (white) women while retaining some deplorable racist attitudes. Some people may have class pride without race pride: some white abolitionists were from the upper strata, and fought for the equal rights of educated African Americans while looking down on and instrumentalizing manual laborers and farmers. Some may totally reject male gender pride while retaining white race pride and class pride: such a rare one was John Stuart Mill, who fought for the acknowledgment of women's autonomy and subjectivity (in both theory and practice) while writing about the racial inferiority of the people of India and while retaining attitudes indicative of class pride: thus, he depicts domestic violence as if it occurs only in the lower classes.

As Dante indicates, pride is a general tendency of the mind; nonetheless, people compartmentalize, and they can look some groups of people in the eye while treating others with deplorable narcissism. And they often justify their compartmentalization with lots of arguments about the inferiority or even the bestial quality of those on whom they look down. Sometimes—remember our distinction between "sexism" and "misogyny"—these arguments are flimsy stratagems to justify conduct that is motivated by the sheer love of domination. Sometimes, however, the beliefs involved are sincerely held. (Most people today sincerely believe that non-human animals are inferior and use those beliefs to justify treating animals as mere things.)

Sometimes people cling to one type of pride all the more intensely when they feel insecure with respect to a different type. And there is one type of pride to which all males can cling, even when they feel vulnerable with regard to class, race, political power, employment, and other positional advantages: male gender pride. Male gender pride is taught in all societies and all groups within societies, and it gives a place of superiority for males who may have no other claim to positional advantage. Mill puts it very well:

> Think what it is to a boy, to grow up to manhood in the belief that without any merit or any exertion of his own, though he may be the most frivolous and empty or the most ignorant and stolid of mankind, by the mere fact of being born a male he is by right the superior of all and every one of an entire half of the human race: including probably some whose real superiority to himself he has daily or hourly occasion to feel. . . . [Such men] are only inspired with pride, and the worst sort of pride, that which values itself upon accidental advantages, not of its own achieving. Above all, when the feeling of being raised above the whole of the other sex is combined with personal authority over one individual among them. . . . (86, 88)

Mill believes that this lesson is taught ubiquitously, though not exceptionlessly. And for the most part Mill is correct—until very recently. In the final sentence he links male pride to a baneful form of personal authority over an individual woman—and he has already linked that authority with a tendency to use sexual violence in marriage. Most men don't turn in that direction. They prefer to deny women full autonomy while treating them well, like beloved children. But objectification, once present, offers no hard and impregnable barrier to violence, emotional or physical.

Gender pride is cheap and easy in a culture that subordinates women legally and/or socially. To have other forms of pride you need to have something to show off, and, as Hume rightly says, it must be something recognizable to all as a comparative status advantage. Perhaps people who have those comparative advantages more easily become proud over-all, like Dante himself (although we'll later see, from Dante's example of the emperor Trajan, that he knows that one may have many advantages without being proud at all). But just show up with male secondary sex characteristics, and, as Mill says: you can claim unearned privilege over half the world's people.

Rulers who want docile subjects understand the appeal of this easy type of pride. Historian Tanika Sarkar describes the way in which the British rulers of India reinforced traditional male forms of authority over women, against indigenous Indian reform efforts—keeping the age of marriage very low for women (it was then twelve!), refusing to consider marital rape a crime even when the bride was a child. Her cogent analysis of British rhetoric concludes that defending Indian male gender authority was a savvy ploy to give the subject male a sphere of absolute rule, thus (it was hoped) diverting him from rebellion against the Raj.[4]

The virtue opposed to pride is usually called "humility." This name is misleading if it means that you think with pain that you are below others. (That was Hume's definition of an emotion that he misleadingly calls "humility.") A general tendency to inferior self-positioning does not seem particularly virtuous. Nor does it correct pride's error, since people obsessed with their own inferiority are not especially outward-focusing or inclined to respect the autonomy and subjectivity of others. Indeed that tendency is narcissistic in its own way, cherishing comparative status competition above all else. But Hume is not using the word "humility" the way the Christian tradition uses it; indeed, he probably should have used the word "shame." Nor does he call this shame a virtue.

The Christian virtue opposite to pride, as Dante depicts it, is, basically, non-narcissism and human decency: a tendency *not* to plume your-self on positional advantages, but rather to look outward toward others, seeing and hearing them with sympathetic attention. Dante gives three examples, two of which involve religious doctrine, so I focus here on the third, the emperor Trajan. Trajan is approached by a poor widow whose son has been killed, and she is asking for justice.[5] Trajan promises to heed her request as soon as he returns from his journey. She is skeptical and in pain, so he urges her to take comfort; he will take care of this before he goes away: "Justice wants it, and compassion keeps me here" (x.93).

Trajan really sees this poor, defenseless woman as a full human being and really listens to her. He does not think of her as an inferior, much less a mere instrument. He cares about her feelings, feels compassion (*pietà*) toward her, and honors her capacity for choice by becoming her faith-ful agent, thus giving her an autonomy she would otherwise lack in that culture. He might have been totally different—indeed, most men in his position would have been different, out of rank-pride, gender-pride, and sheer busy self-preoccupation. His salient virtue is that he drops the self for a time to look and listen; we might call it respect combined with com-passion, or even love of humanity. It's being uncurled, facing outward, and looking the world in the eye.

Once again: people compartmentalize. Abolitionists, both Black and white, usually had gender-pride while decrying race-pride. Women were not even allowed to enter the room at abolitionist meetings: thus Eliz-abeth Cady Stanton was refused, but her mediocre husband admitted. But we have at least a rudimentary sense by now of how pride operates and how gender-pride comes to be one of its most insidious forms. And certainly, just as the habits of pride tend to spread from one domain to another, so, often, do the habits of virtue: once you're in the habit of treating other people decently and openly, you are more easily led to do that in some domain where your attitude has previously been prideful.

Purgatory is a place where souls gradually lose their vices. How might they do this? First, they come to understand what is defective about their trait: the proud confront their own narcissism and see how it has cut them off from seeing others. Second, they see examples of the opposed virtue. What Dante calls the "whip of pride" is really like a whip: a sharp awareness of a better way of meeting the world that goads the souls to work harder. Instead of being punished with grim retributive pain, they are reshaped and reformed, and reform begins by study of historical and contemporary examples of virtue. Third, they ultimately practice the virtue. Dante, like Aristotle, thinks of virtues and vices as patterns of emotion and choice formed by habit and repetition—not mindless repetition, but intelligent practice, informed by their awareness of the difference between the virtue and its opposite. Thinking of Trajan, we see that this practice would involve open and respectful dialogue, and, especially, hearing the complaints of victims whom the social system has wronged. In my conclusion I'll describe a picture of reconciliation based on this idea.

Let's now turn to our own nation, and to a characteristic American combination of pride and greed that, for upwardly mobile men (and who, really, in America, is not trying to move upward?) blots out love and joy—and sows seeds of abuse.

Dante in America: Pride and Greed

American masculinity is dominated by a type of comparative status competition focused on money-making. We don't have titles of nobility, so for us, comparative superiority is determined, largely, by money and the things money can buy. In his influential book *The Darwinian Economy*, economist Robert Frank argues that all modern societies are caught up in a quasi-Darwinian struggle for competitive advantage focused on money and possessions.[6] Frank has, I think, a deficient sense of historical change (aristocratic and monarchical societies aren't like that), and, even where modern capitalism is concerned, a lack of interest in social differences (Finland is markedly different from the United States). So he really shouldn't use Darwin to name his theory, since Darwin found universal mechanisms that operate across populations and eras. However, Frank does give an insightful description of the American national character, if there is such a thing. In Dantean terms, he sees American pride as closely linked to another trait: greed.

Frank is not the only writer who sees American life as dominated by status competition for money. Sigmund Freud, who spent some years teaching in the United States, never liked the place, but was always tactful when journalists asked him why not. After his death, however, friends reported his true view. In a speech at the New York Psychoanalytic Society in 1947, Viennese analyst Paul Federn reported that Freud used to say that there was not "enough libido actually to be found and felt by him."[7] And what had become of all that energy? Had it gone into the creation of art, poetry, or philosophy? No, said Freud; all that libidinal energy had gone into money-making. As analyst Ernest Jones reports, Freud felt "that commercial success dominated the scale of values in the United States."[8] Polite as he always was, on one occasion Freud himself told an audience at Clark University that it seemed irrelevant to lecture on dreams in America, a country "devoted to practical aims."[9]

Greed was all too familiar in medieval Florence too, and Dante positions it close to pride. Unlike other traits involving the obsessive and excessive pursuit of one thing, such as gluttony and sexual excess, greed, in Dante's view, doesn't point beyond itself to something more like love. The gluttonous and the hypersexual have at least something right: they have their eyes on a genuine good, even if their conception of that good is superficial. They can be educated to value the good more deeply. Because they do see a genuine good, they have abundant energy to do many other good things, such as having friends and writing poetry. (Dante is in the group of the sexually promiscuous, and has many friends among the "foodies.") Greed, by contrast, has little continuity with higher things: money is inert, just some stuff, not a person or people, or a life-giving good like food. It is merely a competitive token, with no intrinsic value. And greed can become remarkably obsessive, eclipsing all other pursuits.

Like the penalty for pride, the penalty that purges greed is a representation of the sin itself: "What greed does is here made plain for the purgation of the converted souls" (xix.115–16). The greedy are stretched out on the ground face down, "just as our eyes did not lift themselves upward, fixed on earthly things" (118–19). Just as in life they gazed raptly at some inert stuff, so now they are unable to see people or nature or the beautiful light of day. Like the proud, the greedy are visually impaired: the difference is that the greedy at least look at the earth (read: their money and possessions), while the proud are bent double and see only themselves. However, because money is merely a token of status, this is a distinction without a difference. Greed and pride go very well together, and pride makes greed less open to change.

Pride and greed deform eroticism, leading to the all-too-common view that a woman is a token of money and status. This attitude involves, as Dante says, a failure to look outward, so it has a kind of infantile narcissism about it. As we ponder the vicious career of apparent suicide Jeffrey Epstein and the history of his pedophilic enterprises, in which numerous other rich men allegedly participated, we see pretty clearly the link between their pedophilia and their obsession with money and status. Pedophilia involves a need not to recognize adult autonomy and subjectivity in a sexual partner, and is thus a quintessential form of sexual objectification.

In short, Freud's Dantean insight: proud American males, obsessed with status competition, are unable to see a woman's full humanity, and simply don't know how to love. A sex partner is a mere token of wealth and social position.

How could a society be different? Narcissism has to be undone early. Dante would say that eros must be turned outward toward other people by an education that focuses on their separateness and their real value, and on the value of their own feelings and choices. It would involve continual practice in listening and seeing, as the souls in Purgatory learn very late. It would then involve imitating the example of Trajan, becoming capable of supporting another person's autonomous choice and imagining another person's subjectivity.

Dante had extraordinary luck: divine intercession set him on his journey when he was right "in the middle of the path of life" (thirty-five!). He was also, importantly, a poet, someone who had cultivated his imagination—although in Chapter 7 we'll see that great artists are not immune to pride-deformation in their sexual lives.

People whose gender-pride is combined with a high degree of other forms of American competitive success may prove more recalcitrant, more overweening in their pride, believing that they can bend the whole society, even the law, to their use. Remember how few of the proud Dante places in Purgatory; most Florentine "big shots" are in Hell because they expressed no remorse. This will be my theme in Part III, where we will study failures of legal and ethical accountability in three high-success areas of American life.

Other Cousins of Pride: Envy, Resentfulness

Dante links two other sins very closely to pride, claiming that they share pride's narcissism. With envy, the connection is easy to understand. The envious (those who are envious as an ongoing character trait, not just a momentary emotion) are focused on the good fortune of others, which, as they see it, puts them in the shade. They thus seem to be obsessed with competition and their own relative status. However, caution is needed. In *The Monarchy of Fear* I pointed out that some forms of envy involve inequality in access to the genuine goods of human life. Thus, for example, if we think, as I do, that access to adequate health care is an important good, necessary to a life worthy of human dignity, we must also notice that some societies, including our own, put this good off limits for many people. The envy of such a person for the adequate health care of the rich is not linked to narcissism, nor is it without awareness of intrinsic goods. This sort of envy needs to be addressed by adequate policies that bring these genuine goods within the reach of everyone. Is this sort of envy even a sin? Insofar as it focuses on the wish to blight the happiness of those who enjoy the good in question (rather than to bring about political change so that everyone has the good), it is certainly defective; but if it motivates striving to bring a genuine good to all, it is surely virtuous.

The envy that is closely linked to pride is the sort that is focused only on relative status, with no or only a faint awareness of genuine intrinsic value. But in times of social change there is often great confusion about values and entitlements. Consider the rapid advancement of women in higher education worldwide and in many professions, and the envious male reaction to these competitive successes that is all too common.[10] When society as a whole defines success in terms of relative status, and its high positions are, as usually they are, limited in number, the sudden influx of a previously excluded group is likely to be viewed, by at least some, with envy, even though it should be welcomed as progress in inclusiveness and justice. When males are brought up to think that places in universities and in the professions are theirs by right, and to expect that women will be below them and support them, thoughts of justice are difficult to come by. Understandably enough, the sudden success of women has given rise to confused reactions, some of them suffused with envy. A virtuous claim, "I deserve a university education," gets conflated with an envious status claim, "They are taking the places that are rightfully ours." This confusion is augmented by the fact that our society as a whole is a greedy status-focused society, and by the fact that too few people have access to this important good.

The more life's good things are viewed purely in competitive status terms, the more room there is for envy to fester. When people clearly see an important good, such as health care or higher education, as an intrinsic good that should be securely possessed by all, they typically support social movements of greater inclusion, rather than seething with envy of others. When they react, instead, with envious resentment of the new claimants (as in much opposition to movements to expand access to university education and other important goods), this is a sign that they view the competition for these goods as a zero-sum game. This is why envy is akin to pride: it is whipped up by obsession with the thought that other people's achievement is a threat to my ego.

Status envy takes many forms, but one form it takes is sexual objectification and even violence. Men unsuccessful in social competition sometimes retaliate by depicting desirable women as mere "sluts" and trying to ruin women's social lives. The purest and most overtly violent form of sexual envy is probably the "incel" movement, in which males who see sexual conquest as a competition, and see themselves as the losers in this contest among males, act out violently against the women who (as they see it) cause them shame by refusing them. (Often these women are not even aware of the man in question.) Whipped up by online exchanges, they sometimes act out violently toward a woman or women. As with all violent sexualized representations, it is difficult to know how much actual violence the online world engenders, but the conclusion that represented violence is a cause of real-world harm is at least as strongly supported by evidence as many other causal claims we accept.[11]

Incels might seem merely pathological, but they represent, in an extreme form, a broader tendency to retaliate against women by sexualized denigration as a result of some type of status envy.[12] In that case, the imagined competition seems to be for social status, and it focuses on the relative success of other men. A different type of case, in which the competition is professional and the envy is directed at the women themselves, is that of the website AutoAdmit. This website originally purported to give advice about getting into law school. The site quickly degenerated into real-world porn: anonymous male students writing on the site named and clearly described female law students as "sluts," acting out pornographic scenarios. The point was not simply to depict a high-achieving classmate as a mere "whore," thus proclaiming superiority over her, but also to do real-world damage to the women when they applied for jobs, since even if prospective employers didn't believe the pornographic tale, it still tainted women in their eyes. The site even offered advice about how to get the fake story onto the first page of Google under the woman's name. So the site not only produced stress in the classroom (the writers of the anonymous posts knew the women's names and physical traits), but also did real harm. Two women, high-achieving Yale law students, sued for defamation and infliction of emotional distress. A huge obstacle was internet anonymity: only three men of the many involved could be tracked down, and others were named in the suit under pseudonyms. Eventually there was a settlement whose terms are undisclosed.

Dante also links resentful anger to pride. At first the link appears mysterious. Isn't anger about another party's wrongful action and about justice? Why might anger be linked to narcissism? The cornice of the "wrathful" is filled with a dark smoke. Dante is unable to see people or objects. The "wrathful," like the proud, are unable to see anyone else, wrapped in the acrid smoke of their own resentment. Moreover, what they lack, and what they need if they are to reform, is the spirit of love; it is here that we find the famous speech about love and compassion that is the heart of the entire poem. What Dante has in mind is the way in which the habit of resenting injuries (resentment as a trait) can easily make people obsessive about their own entitlements and who has slighted them. In that state of mind, they do not see other people. Their anger says "me me me," and other people become mere means to salve the wounded ego. In Purgatory they learn examples of Christian reconciliation, which is forward-looking and seeks community rather than solitary vindication. We don't have to believe that all anger is narcissistic in order to see the truth in Dante's claim that it often is.

All this is poetic imagery, but even before we engage in a more extensive analysis of anger, we can see its pertinence to male-female relationships in a hierarchical society in a time of transition. Men feel entitled, and women aren't cooperating. They feel entitled to jobs, and all of a sudden a lot of those jobs go to women. Worse yet, they used to be able to treat women as helpful pliant adjuncts of their search for positional success: acquiescent sexual objects, useful housekeepers, and child-rearers. After all, even law for much of U.S. history made a woman a kind of property, with no right to refuse intercourse in marriage, no independent property rights, and so forth. And now, lo and behold, the old world is crumbling. Women are refusing to play by the old rules. You expect a pliant object, and suddenly this object makes demands and tries to be recognized as a full person. In such a situation there is indefinite scope for an anger that is obsessive (everything is about the wounded ego), highly retributive (women deserve a "smackdown" for slighting male demands), and focused on shoring up the ego rather than creating a new world of shared recognition and responsibility.[13]

Objectification is a well-known phenomenon in social life. The instrumentalization of people, involving denials of autonomy and subjectivity, has a deep inner source: the vice of pride, in which other people (or at least some groups of them) are not fully real, and the self is the focus of practical vision and effort. Envy and resentfulness are cousins of pride because they replicate its tendency to refuse a loving vision of humanity and to bend the self in upon itself.

Projective Disgust as Pride

One further cousin of pride, not recognized by Dante, plays a significant role in our diseased gender dynamics. This is the trait akin to the emotion of disgust.

As I've said in *The Monarchy of Fear* and elsewhere,[14] disgust is of two varieties. *Primary object disgust* focuses on waste products such as feces and urine, on the decaying corpse, and on animals that share similar properties (bad smell, decay, ooziness and sliminess). Although in evolutionary terms primary object disgust is probably linked to avoidance of danger, it is well known experimentally that disgust does not accurately track danger. Experimental scientists find that disgust is linked with a shrinking from substances that are "animal reminders," tokens of our animal weakness and vulnerability (not our equally animal beauty or strength!). This being the case, the craftiness of the human psyche has spawned a further type of disgust that projects these same disgust properties (bad smell, hyperanimality, hypersexuality) onto a group of subordinate humans against whom the dominant group can define itself, representing itself to itself as having transcended the merely physical. If those allegedly subhuman humans embody the stench and smell of the body, that is because they are beneath us, and we are not like that.

The eighteenth-century satirist Jonathan Swift, obsessed with disgust in much of his work, suggests repeatedly that human society is a fragile set of stratagems to conceal the disgusting fluids and smells within. Thus Gulliver finds himself well received by the clean and beautiful horse-like Houyhnhnms only because he wears clothing, and his hosts assume that these clean coverings are part of his body. The Yahoos, unclothed humans, disgust them, and, eventually, Gulliver himself. Swift also knew that although disgust is humanly universal, and ultimately aimed at the disgusting in oneself, its ruses particularly target women, onto whom men initially project ideal qualities of purity, and then find themselves revolted when, as with the disappointed lover in Swift's poem "The Lady's Dressing Room," they discover the animal body behind the façade.[15] As the lover uncovers the tokens and smells of his mistress's bodily reality (earwax, snot, menstrual fluids, sweat), he at last exclaims in horror that "Celia, Celia, Celia shits"—repeating three times the heavenly name of the mistress (Celia derives from the Latin *caelum*, or "heaven"), and then the allegedly repulsive reality.

The operations of *projective disgust* vary in each society, since different societies use the projection to subordinate different groups: racial subgroups, "lower" castes, sexual and religious minorities, aging people. And each disgust formation is subtly different from others.[16] In all societies, however, women have been disgust's targets, as males define themselves as capable of transcendence, women as inexorably linked with birth, sexuality, and death. One way of keeping women in their place is therefore to make insistent reference to the alleged disgustingness of female periods, breastfeeding, sexual fluids, and simple excretion. President Donald Trump is fond of this trope.[17] But projective disgust, though learned, is real, and to those who truly feel disgust at women's bodies (a disgust often mingled with desire), that disgust is one further reason to keep women subordinate and separate (from the workplace, the political arena, etc.).

Projective disgust is a prominent source of resistance to women's testimony about sexual violence: women must be "sluts," they must be "asking for it." As we'll see, a repeated way of evading women's search for legal justice is to portray them in such ways, as mere dirt and slime.

Projective disgust is a narcissistic cousin of pride. People who represent a group of human beings as subhuman, animal, disgusting, while thinking of themselves as transcendent, clean, and pure, are lying to themselves and refusing to look at the world as it is. We are all animals, and it is a narcissistic lie to say that I am not an animal and you are. But disgust is subtly different from Dante's pride. The proud look only at themselves, like hoops doubled over. The disgusted refuse to look at themselves. They don't look clearly at the world either, but as to themselves, they look into a magic mirror that represents the self as angelic and non-animal.

Being born into a dominant group is good luck, in a sense, opening many opportunities of self-cultivation and political, workplace, and social participation. Now, however, we can see that it is also very often a piece of moral bad luck, nudging the young person toward some very serious vices involving the objectification and use of others. At an extreme the door to violent behavior is open. A member of the dominant group need not heed the siren song of pride: Trajan cultivated the virtue of looking and listening, acknowledging the full humanity of a woman "beneath" him in class and gender. But hierarchical societies make it difficult for the dominant to be virtuous in this way.

The behavior that pride engenders is bad, and people deserve blame for these bad actions. Actions are the domain of law, and we must push for greater accountability. Part II will tell the story of these efforts to date. But we should remember, too, that people are not fully to blame for their bad character traits: they did not make the society that made it hard not to be that way. If we think back to the young boy who had multiple possibilities, who might have been a Trajan with the right education but became instead a defective person, we might begin to feel that mercy and, if possible, reconciliation and reform, would be better responses than plunging all these people into a frozen hell.

Purgatory is tough. Nobody is let off the hook for their vices. But the process of moral change focuses throughout on the image of the childlike loving soul, "like a child at play, crying and laughing, the simple little soul that knows nothing, but . . . turns happily to what delights it" (xvi.86–90)—and then becomes distorted by various pressures of a vicious world.

These souls have to open their eyes and relearn love. But Dante has to learn something too: not to hate them, but to see their vices as deformations of human possibility for which they are not fully to blame. Purgatory is a lesson in mercy and in the vision of human possibility. Today we could do worse than to ponder that lesson.

CHAPTER 3

Vices of Victimhood

THE WEAKNESS OF THE FURIES

Thus did every type of bad practice take root in Greece, fed by these civil wars. Openness, which is the largest part of noble character, was laughed down; it vanished. Mistrustful opposition of spirit carried the day, destroying all trust. To reconcile them no speech was strong enough, no oath fearful enough. All of them alike, when they got the upper hand, calculating that security was not to be hoped for, became more intent on self-protection than they were capable of trust.

—Thucydides, *The Peloponnesian Wars*, III.82–3

And what happens to victims of wrongdoing? Do they sail through life unblemished, or does injustice at times exact a moral, as well as an emotional, cost?

It is the end of the Trojan War. Hecuba, the noble queen of Troy, has endured many losses: her husband, her children, her fatherland, destroyed by fire. And yet she remains an admirable person—loving, capable of trust and friendship, capable of combining autonomous action with extensive concern for others. She then suffers a betrayal that cuts deep, traumatizing her entire personality. A close friend, Polymestor, to whom she has entrusted the care of her last remaining child, murders the child for money. That is the central fact in Euripides's *Hecuba* (424 BCE), an anomalous version of the Trojan War story, shocking in its moral ugliness, and yet one of the most insightful dramas in the tragic canon.[1]

From the moment Hecuba learns of Polymestor's betrayal, she is a dif-

ferent person. Unable to repose any trust in anyone, unwilling to be persuaded by anyone, she becomes utterly solipsistic, turned in on herself.
She decides to dedicate herself henceforth entirely to revenge. She murders Polymestor's children and puts out his eyes—symbolizing, it would
seem, the total extinction of their former relationship of mutuality and
care, as well as her own refusal to see him, and even his children, as fully
human. Polymestor comes onstage blind, crawling on all fours like the
beast he always was. As the play ends, it is prophesied that Hecuba will
be transformed into a dog—an animal associated by the Greeks with
rabid pursuit of its prey and a total lack of interpersonal concern.[2] As
Dante summarizes her story, "deranged, she barked like a dog: so far had
anguish twisted her mind" (Inf. xxx.17–18).

Hecuba is not just grief-stricken: she is stricken, as well, in the very
core of her moral personality. She becomes unable to sustain virtues that
used to define her as human being, friend, and citizen. In depicting her
downward transformation, Euripides clearly alludes to, and inverts, the
mythic creation of citizenship and human community depicted in the
final drama of Aeschylus's Oresteia (458 BCE), by then a famous creation story of the Athenian democracy. There the Furies, grim goddesses
of revenge, begin as dogs, sniffing after their prey, incapable of love or
justice. But at the end of the play they agree to trust the promises of the
goddess Athena and to adopt a new way of thinking characterized by
"mildness of temper" and "a mindset of communal friendship." They
stand up, receive the robes of adult citizens, and celebrate the law-abiding
justice of the city.[3]

Aeschylus's moral is that a political community must abandon the
obsessive pursuit of revenge and adopt an idea of justice that is both law-
governed and welfare-oriented, focusing not on hunting one's prey but
on deterring future bad behavior and producing future prosperity. Euripides's moral is the inverse: moral trauma can cause the collapse of trust
and the other-regarding virtues, producing a revenge-obsessed parody of
real justice.

Euripides's grim drama is part of a long tradition of reflection, in the

Greco-Roman world, about the damage that events beyond people's own control can do to them as they aim to lead a flourishing human life, a life that includes acting in accordance with all the major virtues. The most prominent conclusion of this tradition is that events people don't control can block them from acting in many valuable ways. By removing political citizenship, friends, family, and the wherewithal to act in society, such events may prevent a person's life from being completely flourishing or *eudaimôn*. Just having the virtues inside, as Aristotle and others stress, is not enough for *eudaimonia* ("human flourishing"), if one is radically cut off from acting. But in *Hecuba*, Euripides delves within and suggests a more radical conclusion: such events can also corrode the virtues themselves, producing moral damage of a long-standing sort. The first type of damage is easily reversed: a person who was an exile can be restored to citizenship, the friendless can acquire new friends. But Hecuba's damage lies deeper, in long-standing patterns of action and aspiration that form part of her character. Particularly vulnerable are the relational virtues, patterns of friendship and trust. Bad treatment at the hands of others, removing trust, can actually make people worse.

How can this be? How can the crimes of Polymestor undermine Hecuba's virtue? Aristotle appears to deny the possibility, holding that a good person will be firm in character and will "always do the finest thing possible given the circumstances," amid the blows of fortune, although perhaps, in extreme circumstances, falling short of full *eudaimonia*.[4] Most tragic dramas agree, showing people still noble under fortune's blows. The character Hecuba in Euripides's play *The Trojan Women* is just such a noble figure, showing love, leadership, and the capacity for rational deliberation in the midst of disaster. His *Hecuba*, virtually unique, displays tragic events in all their potential ugliness, showing us that their cost is often greater than our stories reveal. For this reason the play has been undervalued through most of the modern era, dismissed as repugnant, a mere horror-show. As scholar Ernst Abramson observed in 1952, it came to the fore again in the light of the grim events of the twentieth century, which have shown that good character is more fragile than we like to think.[5]

Immutable Virtue?

It is attractive for feminists to believe that victims are always pure and right—women and other victims of injustice. Often people who take this view are inspired by a prevalent modern philosophical view: the good will is not affected by contingencies beyond people's control. Immanuel Kant is one of the most influential sources for this view, although it has ancient Greco-Roman antecedents in Stoic ethics (which influenced both Christian ethics and Kant), and it also corresponds to some strands within Christian thought. Kant says that even if the good will has no chance at all to accomplish anything, "yet would it, like a jewel, still shine by its own light as something which has its full value in itself. Its usefulness or fruitlessness can neither augment nor diminish its value."[6] The jewel image clearly implies, further, that the will cannot be corrupted by those same external circumstances. People may also be inspired by a well-known psychological tendency known as the "just world" hypothesis: If there is misery, it must be deserved. If no desert, no deep harm.

Early in the feminist tradition, the Kantian view was effectively called into question. Mary Wollstonecraft analyzed the damage that women's personalities and aspirations suffer under inequality. She claimed that women all too often exhibit servility, emotional lack of control, and lack of due regard for their own rationality and autonomy. These, she argued, are morally bad traits that women have been nudged into by their dependence on the good will of men. Criticizing Jean-Jacques Rousseau, who praised the coy and submissive Sophie as a norm for female character, she insisted that women, just as much as men, should have the opportunity to grow into fully autonomous agents, winning self-respect and the respect of others for their dignity and self-authored choices.[7] When they are denied this opportunity, they suffer damage at the very core of their being.

In a similar vein, albeit within a very different philosophical tradition, John Stuart Mill insisted that one of the worst aspects of the male "subjection" of women is its mental and moral aspect. We have seen parts of this passage in Chapter 1, but let's now see Mill's whole argument:

Men do not want solely the obedience of women, they want their sentiments. All men, except the most brutish, desire to have in the woman most nearly connected with them, not a forced slave but a willing one, not a slave merely, but a favourite. They have therefore put everything in practice to enslave their minds. The masters of all other slaves rely, for maintaining obedience, on fear: either fear of themselves, or religious fears. The masters of women wanted more than simple obedience, and they turned the whole force of education to effect their purpose. All women are brought up from the very earliest years in the belief that their ideal of character is the very opposite to that of men; not self-will, and government by self-control, but submission, and yielding to the control of others. (*Subjection* 15–16)

Because women are brought up this way, and because, in their socially and legally powerless condition, they cannot obtain anything except by pleasing men, women think that being attractive to men is the main thing in life.

And, this great means of influence over the minds of women having been acquired, an instinct of selfishness made men avail themselves of it to the utmost as a means of holding women in subjection, by representing to them meekness, submissiveness, and resignation of all individual will into the hands of a man, as an essential part of sexual attractiveness. (16)

These insightful observations have been taken up in recent times by social scientists working on the deformation of preferences under conditions of inequality. Jon Elster's *Sour Grapes* used the idea of "adaptive preferences" to explain the long persistence of feudalism, and the fact that the revolutions of the eighteenth century required a revolution in consciousness before a change in rights could be achieved. Elster took his title from the Aesop's fable in which a fox, learning quickly that the grapes he initially wants are out of reach for him, quickly schools him-

self not to want them and to call them "sour."[8] Other scholars working on these phenomena have emphasized that deformed preferences
can be found even earlier in life, so that people learn never to want
the attractive thing in the first place—thus echoing Wollstonecraft and
Mill's observations about women. Economist Amartya Sen has found
deformed preferences in subordinated women even where their own
physical strength and health is concerned. For example, his study of
widows and widowers in India showed that widows (told by the culture that they had no right to continue living) failed to complain about
their health, even when suffering from malnutrition and other diseases,
while widowers (used to having a submissive partner to wait on them,
and deprived of that assistance) were full of health-related complaints. I
have developed the same idea about higher education and political participation: women who are told that higher education, or running for
office, is not for them often fail to complain when they do not have
access to these important things.[9]

But modern feminists have some strong reasons for sticking to the
Kantian view. Victim-blaming is ubiquitous as a strategy of subordination. It comes easy to the proud to construct fictions of their own moral
superiority, portraying the subordinated as in some sense deserving their
subordination because of intellectual and moral inferiority. Colonial
domination was "justified" with arguments alleging that the dominated
people are like children, needing firm control. Even the usually clear-
eyed John Stuart Mill said this about the people and cultures of India
(while in the employ of the British East India Company). In our own time
we have all heard such denigrations of African Americans, especially
those living in poverty, and of their culture, as ugly excuses for white
dominance.[10] Indeed such victim-blaming is a virtual trope of recent conservative thought about race. As philosopher Lisa Tessman says of one
such critic, "His account leaves no space for implicating the oppressive
social systems that cause moral damage."[11] A substantial feminist literature raises doubts about the concept of adaptive preferences as applied
to women, for similar reasons.[12] There is no subordinated group that has

not been systematically charged with inherent moral deficiency, denying the extent of the damage domination does to the subordinated.

Sometimes these denials involve utterly unrealistic denials of basic facts: for example, the deliberate fracturing of African American families under slavery, or the current reality of over-incarceration (including both the bail system before trial and punitive sentencing after conviction), which results in the absence of a large proportion of the nation's African American men from their homes.[13]

It seems crucial for people seeking justice not to put a rosy light on these grim facts and their moral toll. There are delicate issues here: Up to what point is a social damage merely a source of unhappiness, and at what point does it eat into the moral personality? How far do subordinated peoples really internalize and act out the negative image of themselves purveyed by their dominators, thus (as Wollstonecraft and Mill argue) failing to achieve key moral virtues? One must approach the complexity of these issues subtly and yet frankly. It does no good to pretend that everything is rosy when people are schooled to servility and deprived of encouragement for autonomy. Indeed such a pretense plays into the hands of dominators by implying that the damage inflicted by domination is merely superficial.

In general, here's how the world looks to me. First, dominators usually have a defective moral culture that rationalizes their domination in many ways, not least by its victim-blaming. Second, one thing dominators typically do in order to maintain their power is to encourage servility and an absence of autonomy and courage in the subjugated. They also inflict trauma by cruelty, one purpose of which is to break victims' spirit. Sometimes they fail: people have great resources of resilience and insight, and can indeed shine like jewels in the worst of circumstances. But sometimes they succeed, and that success is the dominator's deepest moral crime.

Women are especially likely to exhibit a complicated mixture of moral overcoming and moral damage. Unlike most subordinated groups, they live in intimate proximity to their dominators. This is good for them in a way, since it means that they may be well fed, cared for, even educated.

But it is also bad for them: the intimate context contains depths of cruelty that are not always present outside of intimacy. In an article titled "Racism and Sexism," African American philosopher Laurence Thomas predicted that sexism would prove more difficult to eradicate than racism, because males typically have a stake in the domination of women (expressed, for example, in the phrase "a real man") that whites do not typically have in the domination of Blacks (the parallel phrase "a real white," does not exist, or so he said).[14] Thomas's article received a lot of sharp critiques, and, forty years later, it does seem that he is wrong about the depth of racism in U.S. culture. But what he said is surely true of sexual orientation prejudice as compared with sexism/misogyny in U.S. society. Sexual orientation prejudice has dropped away with startling rapidity—in part because dominant straight society has no stake in it. There is no concept of the "real straight" that entails ongoing subordination of LGBTQ people. Meanwhile, with gender, given the frequently intimate context, the stake proud males have in producing pliant women remains high.

Moral Damage in Feminist Thought

Feminist philosophers have not typically been uncritical Kantians. Kant and white male Kantians did not need to wrestle with sexual violence, domination by a spouse, or the myriad problems that child care and domestic work pose for women's aspirations. They, and their twentieth-century followers, casually asserted things about virtue that were false: for example, that two valid moral claims could never conflict. One way luck influences virtue, as the Greek tragic poets knew well, is precisely by producing such conflicts, in which it seems that whatever one does, one will be slighting the claims of some important commitment or virtue. Kant simply denied that this ever happened, and many followed him.

Female philosophers of my generation questioned that denial. Juggling child care and work, we knew that the claims of the different virtues often did conflict, particularly in an unjust society. We had allies among leading male philosophers—particularly Bernard Williams (who actually did a lot of child care and, in general, understood women's demands with a rare sensitivity).[15] But it was far more difficult for powerless young women to make bold countercultural claims than it was for a dominant male, who had, in addition, served as an RAF pilot during his national service.

We did persist, however. And although outstanding female philosophers have worked in the Kantian tradition (often showing its complexities and tensions)—women such as Onora O'Neill, Christine Korsgaard, Barbara Herman, Marcia Baron, and Nancy Sherman (also an Aristotelian)—on the whole, women doing explicitly feminist philosophy have rarely been Kantians, because they have felt that Kant denied truths of their experience. Barbara Herman did show surprisingly, and cogently, that Kant has important insights about the urge for domination inherent in sexual relations.[16] But hers was a late attempt to show feminists who had dismissed Kant that he actually had something to offer them, as indeed he does. My own approach to the topic of objectification is infused with Kantian ideas, and I have learned a lot from the views of Herman and Korsgaard—as well, of course, as the great (Kant-inspired) John Rawls. For the most part, however, feminist philosophers from a variety of perspectives have been drawn to other sources and have used their insights to craft views that take the damages of domination seriously.

A pioneer in this area was Sandra Bartky. Already in 1984, in her essay "Feminine Masochism and the Politics of Personal Transformation," she insisted (as had Wollstonecraft before her) that many of women's emotions and character traits have been shaped by a system of domination to serve its ends. She insisted that views that deny the possibility of such damage are highly superficial:

> Those who claim that any woman can reprogram her consciousness if only she is sufficiently determined hold a shallow view of the nature of patriarchal oppression. Anything done can be undone, it is implied; nothing has been permanently damaged, nothing irre-

trievably lost. But this is tragically false. One of the evils of a system of oppression is that it may damage people in ways that cannot
always be undone.[17]

In another valuable article, "Foucault, Femininity, and the Modernization of Patriarchal Power," Bartky described in a way similar to Mill's,
but with far greater specificity, the production of an "ideal body of femininity" that serves male interests, being slender rather than massive,
weak rather than muscular.[18] I would add that this was an era when
women were forbidden to run in marathons on the grounds that this
could tax their frail reproductive organs, and when female tennis players were upbraided for looking muscular. (Chrissie Evert represented the
"good" woman; Martina Navratilova, who introduced serious weight
training to the tennis regimen, the "bad" woman.)

My own work on "moral luck," in *The Fragility of Goodness* (1986),
was not explicitly feminist, but was inspired both by life and by discussions with other women. And valuable work on moral luck began to
crop up all over the profession. Claudia Card took aim at the ideal of
women as caring helpmeets in the work of such people as Carol Gilligan
and Nel Noddings.[19] Making eloquent use of Friedrich Nietzsche, she
argued that the valorization of self-abnegation is a kind of slave morality:
women, feeling themselves powerless, give the name of "virtue" to traits
that powerlessness has imposed upon us. It's worth noting that related
insights were developed already in 1973 by a male Kantian, Thomas
Hill, in an important article, "Servility and Self-Respect," which explicitly discusses the way in which a male-dominated society requires servile
behavior of women.[20]

In a related vein, Marcia Homiak, a distinguished Aristotle scholar,
argued that real virtue requires enjoyment of one's own activity and a
type of "rational self-love" cultivated in confident relationships with
others—and that sexism has all too often robbed women of that joy and
that confidence.[21] Her insights have been too little heralded, and feminists should make them central.

In 2005, Lisa Tessman contributed an important systematic study on

the whole phenomenon of moral damage in the context of feminist struggle and resistance.[22] Following the example of those who draw on ancient
Greek thought, but with valuable contemporary elaboration, Tessman
argues in *Burdened Virtues* that, in a variety of ways, sexism damages
the subordinated self. She concludes that thinking seriously about equality means thinking, as well, about the need to repair the damaged self,
supporting the cultivation of virtues that domination has made difficult.

Thinkers in this tradition can still stress, as many do, that we must
listen to the narratives of victims and give their account of their own
experience some degree of priority. That epistemic correction is important, since members of subordinated groups have typically been denied an
equal status as knowers and givers of testimony.[23] Listening never means
listening with no critical questions. The possibility that moral damage is
distorting the narrative—often in an "adaptive" direction, denying real
wrongs—ought to be with us always as we listen.

Is Retributivism a "Burdened Virtue"?

Tessman makes a further valuable point about the virtues. The struggle
against systematic wrongdoing, she argues, requires a specific battery of
traits that are virtues in the context of the struggle, advancing its goals,
but not so good as elements in the overall life of an agent striving to
live well. A type of uncritical loyalty and solidarity, for example, may be
required in a political struggle, and yet it may not equip us for the best,
most reciprocal types of friendship. We can think of many further cases.

Consider two cases, closely related, that point us back to Euripides's
play. The first is the denial of trust and friendship to those on the "other
side"; the second is a focus on retributive anger. Tessman explicitly gives
the latter as an example: she says that victim anger is useful to the political struggle, but that it can also become excessive and obsessive, deforming the self. So, she concludes, people have a tragic choice before them:
either to fail to fit oneself maximally for struggle, or to do so but lose
some of the richness of a fully virtuous personality.

I agree with Tessman that in both cases there is distortion of the personality, but I don't agree that this distortion is useful in a struggle for freedom and equality. We don't have a tragic choice after all, although we do have the extremely arduous task of waging a difficult struggle without poisoned weapons. If we want reconciliation and a shared future in the long run, however, we had better figure out how not to rely on traits that ultimately poison the search for a decent political community.

Let's think first of mistrust of all people on the "other side." Hecuba had learned that Polymestor was untrustworthy. But she concluded that all men are untrustworthy. This is a common move in feminism (as in other struggles for equality). In my younger days, heterosexual women were often charged with disloyalty to the feminist cause, and the phrase "woman-oriented woman" was used to mean both "feminist" and "lesbian." Some otherwise admirable feminist groups even advised their members not to collaborate professionally with males. (The same tendency can be found in other movements for equality.)

I gave my book chapter on *Hecuba* as a Eunice Belgum Memorial Lecture in 1983, several years after her tragic suicide in 1977. Eunice, a gifted PhD classmate of mine, had gotten a good job at a liberal arts college. Once there, she co-taught a class on feminism with a male (feminist) faculty member. At a meeting of the Society for Women in Philosophy (SWIP), of which Eunice was a member, Eunice was denounced for betraying the cause by cooperating with a male faculty member. Her parents told me that she had made many phone calls the day she committed suicide, prominently including calls to female students in that class, to apologize for corrupting their consciousness by trusting a male faculty member. I felt and feel that Eunice was (originally) correct and that SWIP was wrong. If we can't form cooperations with well-intentioned people on the "other side"—not in *blind* trust, to be sure, but after careful scrutiny—we have no hope of eventual reconciliation. Thus the refusal of trust is not a "burdened virtue" in Tessman's sense: it is not useful, and it retards the progress of the struggle.

Indeed, sometimes a struggle requires trust even without solid evidence of intentions. Nelson Mandela was no credulous weakling. His ability to trust others was combined with a secure and advanced critical capacity. Throughout the struggle in South Africa, he formed close bonds with white allies (including Dennis Goldberg, a Rivonia Trial co-defendant, and Albie Sachs, later a distinguished judge). These friendships were carefully developed and scrutinized over the years, partly through Mandela's close ties to the South African Jewish community. Here, trust was well-founded. But Mandela also took some risks in the trust department. During coverage of his funeral in 2013, I remember seeing a mature policeman recall, with tears in his eyes, a moment during Mandela's inaugural parade as president in 1994. Mandela got down from his car to talk to a group of young police recruits, all white as of course they were. He shook their hands and said "Our trust is in you. Our trust is in you." They had expected only hostility and retribution from Mandela, and he offered them trust.[24] In this case, unlike those of Sachs, Goldberg, and so many others, the trust had not been earned or scrutinized. But the men were young and malleable, and Mandela proposed to leverage friendship and trustworthiness by behaving in a friendly and trusting manner. I think this is the right direction, as I'll elaborate in my conclusion. The *Hecuba* reminds us that without trust (which is never perfectly secure) there is no hope of community.

Let's now think about anger. The feminist case for anger imagines it as vigorous protest, the opposite of servile inactivity. As such, anger looks strong, indeed essential. However, we must begin by making a distinction. If we analyze anger into its component parts, as a long philosophical tradition in both Western and non-Western thought has done, it includes pain at a perceived wrongful act that is thought to have affected either the angry person, or some people or causes she cares a lot about. Here we already have lots of room for error: the person may be wrong about whether the act was inflicted wrongfully rather than just accidentally; she may be wrong about its significance. But let's suppose that these thoughts withstand scrutiny: then anger (thus far) is an appropriate response to wrongdoing. It expresses a demand: this is wrong, and it should not happen again. It alludes to the past, but it faces forward and proposes to fix the world going into the future.

This is the type of anger that I have called *Transition-Anger*, because it registers something that has already happened but turns to the future for a remedy. This type of anger may be accompanied by proposals to punish the offender, but these proposals will understand punishment in one or more future-directed ways: as reform, as expression of important norms, as "specific deterrence" for that same offender, and as "general deterrence" for other offenders contemplating similar crimes.

Transition-Anger is indeed important for a struggle against injustice. It is outraged protest, and protest is important to draw attention to wrongs and energize people to address them. This type of anger doesn't "burden" the personality by deforming it. It is exhilarating and liberating to face forward and imagine solutions to problems. Nor does this type of anger risk becoming obsessive or distorted.

However, let's face it: this is not all that people usually mean by anger. Anger is rarely free from contamination by a further element (present in all philosophical definitions of anger, including Gandhi's): the wish for payback, for commensurate pain to befall the aggressor. I've already said that Transition-Anger has uses for punishment—for reasons of deterrence, education, and reform—so it's tricky to distinguish the future-directed type from the purely back-directed retributive type. But people are usually not pure in their orientation to future welfare. When struck, their impulse is to strike back. They so easily imagine that a counterbalancing pain on the other side annuls or undoes their pain or wrong. Hence the widespread support for capital punishment among relatives of homicide victims. Capital punishment has never been shown to have deterrent value. People go for it because of its alleged fittingness as proportional retribution. Your child's death is made good by the criminal's death, or so it is all too easy to think.

We all know victims who focus obsessively on retributive fantasies and plans toward those who have wronged them. Virtually the entirety of divorce and child custody litigation is retributive in spirit, rarely aimed at equity and general welfare. Our major religions nourish retributive fantasies: the Book of Revelation, for example, deserves Nietzsche's judgment that it is an ugly revenge-fantasy. And a study of the way "victim impact" statements have figured in criminal trials, when admitted, shows that they serve largely to ramp up the demand for harsh punishment of a retributive sort.[25] Past injuries, however, are past. Pain creates more pain and does not repair the original injury. The proportionality of pain to past pain is by itself never a reason for a harsh punishment, and it typically distracts from the task of fixing the future.

Both Western and Indian philosophical traditions[26] (the only non-Western ones I know enough about to speak) judge that ordinary anger is retributive; what I've called Transition-Anger is exceptional. Studying the breakdown of marriages and friendships, one is inclined to agree (although these days most parents aspire, at least, to an anger at their children that is non-retributive, aimed at future well-being). However, the numbers don't matter: it is the distinction that matters, and this distinction has simply not been clearly made, throughout the whole philosophical tradition. Transition-Anger is useful in a struggle and does not burden the personality. Retributive anger burdens the personality—and is not very useful in a struggle for freedom. Martin Luther King Jr., the one distinguished Western philosopher who did recognize and emphasize this distinction, spoke of the way in which the anger of people in his movement had to be "purified" and "crystallized." In a statement of 1959, he vividly characterized the two types:

> One is the development of a wholesome social organization to resist with effective, firm measures any efforts to impede progress. The other is a confused, anger-motivated drive to strike back violently, to inflict damage. Primarily, it seeks to cause injury to retaliate for wrongful suffering . . . It is punitive—not radical or constructive.[27]

I'm with King: the retaliatory sort of anger is not useful to the struggle. Nor is it really "radical" in the sense of creating something new and better. King wanted accountability, legal punishment, and the public expression of shared values. He rejected pain for pain as easy, weak, and stupid.

The Weakness of the Furies

Feminism today needs a similar distinction. Anger is strong and valuable if it expresses well-grounded outrage and faces forward—with constructive ideas, a refusal of payback retributivism, and, let's hope, a radical trust in what we may create by joining together. It is not strong and valuable if it indulges in easy retributivism, and we all know that getting stuck in retributivism is a common human weakness. If we see clearly the weakness of retributivism in the capital punishment context—and I believe most feminists do see that—it seems odd to defend retributive anger as essential to feminist struggle. Strangely, however, even when the distinction between retributive anger and what I call Transition-Anger has been announced and made central, as it was by King and as others have done in his spirit, feminist discussions of anger's value tend to ignore this distinction and ride roughshod over it—so hard it is to get one's mind around the fact that there is an anger that eschews retribution.

We need to address the future, and for that we need an uncertain trust and a radical type of love.

PART II

LAW STARTS TO CONFRONT THE ISSUES

The Domain of Legal Action

L aw speaks to all. Even if it is uneven and flawed in implementation, and even if it urgently needs major structural reform, it speaks the language of citizenship and of rights. A woman can *plead* not to be raped. She can *hope* that her workplace has no harassment. But law says: you don't need to plead and hope; these things are yours by right. If you don't have them where you work, you have a right to go to court and demand them—not because you are someone special, but because everyone has this right. So it's a major goal of concerned women to bring sexual offenses into the domain of law and to make laws that are adequate to protect women from abuse.

Law and individual behavior interact in many ways. Law expresses society's norms, announcing what we think good and bad. It also aims to *deter* bad conduct by announcing that bad conduct will be punished and by following through reliably. Law hopes to deter the delinquent individual from committing a similar act again (what is called "specific deterrence"), and also to deter other people from committing that type of bad act ("general deterrence"). The *expressive* aspect of law can add to its deterrent function: by announcing a fundamental social commitment, law puts people on notice that we mean what we say. Law may also *reform* criminals, although this goal has been achieved only rarely in the U.S. penal system, where prisons are so gruesome that they rarely promote improvement. But law also achieves reform in a more global way: law educates people about what is right and wrong—and this teaching has been evolving. (For millennia people have grown up knowing that murder is wrong, but until recently they often didn't know that sexual harassment is wrong.)

Law is always highly general, since it needs to give instructions for dealing with a wide range of individual cases. At the same time, however, our legal system aspires to be fair to the individual—largely through the mechanism of indictment, trial, resolution (conviction or acquittal), and (if there's a conviction) sentencing. Under U.S. criminal law, an individual who is tried before a jury or judge (i.e., someone whose case has not been disposed of by a plea bargain) must be convicted by the very exacting "reasonable doubt" standard, which is not used by most non-common-law nations (Japan is an exception), but is preferred in the common-law tradition (Britain and former British colonies), because of the high importance thinkers in that tradition have typically attached to avoiding the punishment of innocents. Under U.S. civil law, by contrast—of which discrimination law is one department—the standard is the weaker "preponderance of the evidence" standard. This standard is also used when a civil suit is brought in connection with a criminal matter. Thus a defendant acquitted of a criminal charge (for example O. J. Simpson) may subsequently face and lose a civil suit for damages (as Simpson did) without inconsistency. The traditional thinking is that depriving someone of liberty is a very grave matter, requiring a more exacting standard than is required in a civil matter, where the usual penalty is financial. (Simpson was ordered to pay $33.5 million in civil damages.)

In yet another way, the general and the particular interact in our tradition, since we are a common-law country. The basic idea in common-law legal traditions is that law is a repository of wise ideas built up over time, always supplemented by and adjusted to the new particular. In other words, law is incremental and not fixed. There will naturally be texts also—statutes and in some cases a written constitution—but they are understood to form part of this evolving yet relatively stable body of wisdom. Though statutes are highly general to begin with, they develop specificity and thickness over time through adjudication of cases and respect for the principle of *stare decisis*, "standing by what you have decided," which typically applies the interpretation of law in a prior case to new cases. Both statutes (laws passed by a representative body) and constitutional principles are shaped this way in the U.S. tradition, and both may play a role in the sphere of sexual abuse.

Our common-law idea of law is Janus-faced, looking both backward and forward. In order to be both expressive and deterrent, law is, or ideally ought to be, forward-looking, trying to shape a better future. And yet, in a common-law system, law is also understood to be an accretion of past judgments and beliefs, and this accretion is given some normative significance, since it is seen as a source of both stability and wisdom. For women, so long excluded from full membership in this "wise" tradition, there's a problem in that idea. Critics of the common law, especially the British Utilitarians, beginning with Jeremy Bentham in the eighteenth century, felt that for this reason the common law was typically "backward" in the pejorative sense as well, not keeping up with the times and a drag on progress. They therefore sought to replace the gradualism of the common law with a regime of ideal statutes designed to promote maximal future social welfare.

By now we can see that there was considerable arrogance in the idea that a group of elites can design social welfare once for all, and at least some truth to the idea that principles evolving over a long time contain wisdom. However, in the criminal law especially, where the utilitarians were bold reformers—opposing capital punishment and torture, and crusading, already in the eighteenth century, for the decriminalization of same-sex acts and for women's suffrage—we can see the value of building into the common-law process a role for the critique and for the voices of outsiders. Utilitarians saw that the "wise judgments" of the past had been made by a narrow elite and expressed upper-class male norms, including the norm that women and poor people should remain subordinated. They have much truth on their side: law based on past elite judgments cannot do its job well unless other voices enter the conversation. Sexual violence is such an area: the traditions that the common law has long upheld have been male traditions, and the voices of women—and of men who care about gender equality, and of LGBTQ people—have all too rarely been permitted to shape emerging norms.

Now let's move from these highly general observations to the specific configuration of U.S. law in the twin areas of sexual violence and sexual harassment. Our system has some unique features, often misunderstood or simply not grasped at all, that we need to confront before we can understand how protest and legal change have worked in the past and how they might be directed in the future. Some recent books that claim to inform the public simply don't offer this very basic factual information.[1]

First, then: in the United States—unlike many other nations—sexual assault and sexual harassment are dealt with extremely differently, through different parts of the legal system—even though people understand that there is much overlap between the two offenses. (One thing a sexual harasser may do is to threaten or even commit a sexual assault; and sexual assault can both function as part of a "quid pro quo" and create a "hostile environment," the two major indicia of sexual harassment.)

Sexual assault is dealt with under the criminal law, as a specific criminal act. This means that the accuser is the government, bringing a charge, usually after a complaint by an individual victim, who will likely be a key witness. The defendant is usually an individual, who has rights to legal counsel and other constitutional rights, and who must be found guilty beyond a reasonable doubt (if there is no plea bargain).

Sexual harassment, by contrast, is dealt with as a civil offense under Title VII of the U.S. Civil Rights Act of 1964. Title VII is a general civil rights non-discrimination statute, and sexual harassment, like racial harassment (neither of which is mentioned in the statute itself), has come to be recognized as a category of objectionable discrimination on the basis of sex. We'll follow that story in Chapter 5. Here the defendant is not an individual; it is the firm or workplace that is being accused of negligence for not stopping sex discrimination. Although specific acts of named individuals may be important in the case, the prosecution typically also has to show that the workplace has failed to address the problem when given the opportunity to do so. The plaintiff, by contrast—as is usual in the civil law—is typically an individual, rather than the government, although there are sometimes group plaintiffs. An individual malefactor may in addition face criminal charges, but typically in harassment cases the disciplining of individuals is left to firms or companies, and the accountability of these organizations is a key aspect of the law. Indeed the deterrence aspect of sexual harassment law is aimed largely at organizations: if they don't prevent or root out such behavior they face a daunting financial penalty.[2]

Yet more complicated: sexual harassment is uniformly defined throughout the United States because Title VII is a federal statute, which federal courts in turn progressively interpret in the usual incremental common-law way. Typically defendants are tried first in federal district court, and any appeal goes through the federal appellate system and, eventually, if an appeal is accepted, to the U.S. Supreme Court. Sexual assault, by contrast, is for the most part covered by state-level laws. If a conviction is appealed, the appeal typically goes through the state appellate system, though if the case raises a constitutional issue it may ultimately be appealed to the U.S. Supreme Court.

There is such a thing as federal criminal law, but it is reserved for issues that have an interstate aspect. Most federal criminal law deals with fraud, corporate and securities malfeasance, and the like. Some sexual offenses, however, are federal: the Mann Act of 1910, which prohibited taking a woman across state lines for "immoral purposes" (the law under which boxer Jack Johnson was convicted of traveling with his white wife), was such a federal law. One salient federal law today is the Child Protection Act, which deals with child pornography and the online exploitation of children. This extremely tough law, signed by President Obama in December 2012, is at odds with state regulation of sexuality in some striking ways, particularly in regard to the age of consent. (Under the federal law, circulating a nude photo of someone under eighteen is a federal crime. So, even though in most states teenagers can legally have sex at sixteen or seventeen, they will be breaking a federal law if they send nude photos to one another, and the statute has sometimes been interpreted to prohibit even having a nude photo of *oneself* on one's phone.)

Similar tensions exist at present between federal and state policies toward the regulation of marijuana: behavior that is legal under state law may, in cases involving transport and sales, be illegal under federal law. A new fixture at Chicago's O'Hare airport, since the recent legalization of recreational marijuana in Illinois, is the bright blue "cannabis amnesty box": before going through airport security into a federal law zone, passengers who have substances legal under Illinois law but illegal under federal law are invited to leave them behind!

The difference between sexual harassment and sexual assault affects reform strategy and the role of academic theory within reform movements. In the evolution of the federal tort of sexual harassment, which has been highly centralized, with a sequence of high-profile Supreme Court cases, a key role has been played by academic legal theory. Catharine MacKinnon's 1978 book *Sexual Harassment of Working Women* and, in addition, her work as a lawyer on two of the key cases have made a huge difference.

With the criminal law, things are very different. Although all U.S. criminal law can raise constitutional issues (concerning rights to legal representation, adequate police warnings, rights to confront the accuser, etc.), most of the action is at the state level, and state criminal laws vary greatly, both in the way different offenses are divided up and in the specific elements of each offense. This means that most of the action for the reformer must also be at the state level. Of course states do consult one another, and sooner or later reforms of rape law tend to make their way through the states, but there is no necessity here. There remain significant variations, and states that are more and less receptive to progressive reform. The Model Penal Code developed by the American Law Institute in 1962 was an attempt to introduce uniformity in both categorization and sentencing, and it was put forward largely by progressive reformers, but it has had a checkered history and has been heeded more by some states than by others. (For somewhat obscure reasons, New Jersey has stood out as a poster child for progressive sexual assault reform.) Criminal law is taught to law students under large general rubrics, but a good casebook will always cite the specific state statute and show how its wording influences the outcome.

In this situation we should not expect to find well-known heroines and heroes. Academic writings have certainly pushed the law of sexual assault in valuable directions. In Part II, I shall be drawing on, and supporting some key arguments of, Stephen Schulhofer's *Unwanted Sex*,[3] for example, and I was lucky enough to co-teach with him as I began to learn in this area. Earlier, the work of lawyer and academic Susan Estrich, especially her book *Real Rape*,[4] made a salient contribution, and she is rightly seen as a leading proponent of the "no means no" standard. A lot of the work, however, went on in the trenches: in state legislatures where statutes were reconsidered, in trial courts where lawyers fought for justice for victims of assault, in jury deliberations where ordinary people thought well and hard about the legal arguments, in judicial chambers where both trial and appellate judges decided to think for themselves rather than to follow convention uncritically.[5] Chapter 4 traces some high points of this incremental, plural, and incomplete reform movement.

Accountability for Sexual Assault

A BRIEF LEGAL HISTORY

Before the feminist challenge to U.S. criminal law that began in the 1970s, a woman complaining of rape was required to show that the man involved had used physical force, and force beyond the force requisite to consummate the sexual act itself. The threat of death or grave bodily injury was usually sufficient—but not the "mere" threat of force. Usually, too, the woman had to show that she had resisted, even in the face of force or the threat of force, since only this resistance was taken to give evidence of non-consent. Some states made resistance a formal statutory requirement, but more often it was read into statutes as a requirement implicit in the notions of force and/or non-consent. The old requirement was that the victim resist "to the utmost"; later this phrasing was replaced by terms such as "reasonable resistance" or "earnest resistance." Typical of its period was a New York statute of 1965 saying that rape is committed only when the man uses "physical force that overcomes earnest resistance" or makes a threat of "immediate death or serious physical injury."[1] A woman who did not resist physically, or who succumbed to lesser threats, was treated as consenting, and the man's conduct was not criminal at all.

The standard produced bizarre results. In one case, the victim said she submitted to intercourse because the man threatened her with a knife or box cutter. She got the weapon away from him, then submitted to intercourse a second time when he choked her and told her he could kill her.

A 1973 New York appellate court set aside the man's conviction, saying, "[R]ape is not committed unless the woman opposes the man to the utmost limit of her power. The resistance must be genuine and active. It is difficult to conclude that the complainant here waged a valiant struggle to uphold her honor."[2] In another case, a petite Illinois woman who had stopped along a secluded bike path submitted to oral sex when a man, almost twice her weight and a foot taller than her, put his hand on her shoulder and said ominously "This will only take a minute. My girlfriend doesn't meet my needs. I don't want to hurt you."[3] Understanding this as an implicit threat, the woman did not fight back. Nonetheless, an Illinois court set aside the man's conviction, saying "the record is devoid of any attendant circumstances which suggest that complainant was forced to submit."[4]

These requirements were criticized by law enforcement professionals, who believe it unwise for women to fight back in situations of attack. But even in 1981, in a case in which the defendant took away a woman's car keys in a dangerous area of town, "lightly choked" her, and made menacing gestures, a lower court concluded that the woman had not resisted sufficiently to establish non-consent.[5] Although the conviction was reinstated on appeal, a three-vote minority, in the 4–3 decision, said of the victim, "She must follow the natural instinct of every proud female to resist, by more than mere words, the violation of her person by a stranger or an unwelcome friend."[6] In another case, a high school principal coerced a female student to submit to sexual intercourse multiple times by threatening to block her impending graduation.[7] Nonetheless, the case was dismissed because the principal did not threaten the victim with physical force.

Notice the strange asymmetry between this treatment of sexual crime and our standard attitudes to property crime. If I remove your wallet without your express permission, I am committing a crime. I cannot defend myself by pointing to the fact that you failed to put up a fight. But if a man had intercourse with a woman, invading her intimate bodily space, our system thought it a crime only if she offered physical resistance, frequently in the face of danger. A conviction of theft does not require a demonstration that the thief used more force than was necessary to accomplish the theft itself (although such force may be an aggravating factor). But it was only in 1992, in an unusual ruling, that a New Jersey court held (explicitly rejecting prior tradition) that the element of "force" in rape was established simply by "an act of non-consensual penetration involving no more force than necessary to accomplish that result."[8]

Let's return to objectification, which I analyzed in Chapter 1 as involving, above all, a denial of autonomy and a denial of subjectivity, both resulting in treating a person as less than a full person. Both of these denials are evident in the old legal tradition. Autonomy is denied when a woman's ability to choose is slighted. There is really no autonomy when the only options are submitting to unwanted intercourse and facing bodily risk. Joseph Raz, a leading theorist of autonomy, imagines a "hounded woman" being chased by a carnivorous animal on a small island: this woman has free choice in a very thin sense, in that she can run this way or that way. But nobody would conclude that she had freedom of choice in a meaningful way: "Her mental stamina, her intellectual ingenuity, her will power and her physical resources are taxed to their limits by her struggle to remain alive. She never has a chance to do or even to think of anything other than how to escape from the beast."[9] Nor (and this is Raz's point) should we conclude that a political system that puts a person in that situation and does not problematize it has shown respect for autonomy.

Furthermore, the old legal regime does not show respect for subjectivity. The woman's fear, her reluctance, her lack of genuine affirmative consent—none of this is taken seriously. Not surprisingly, such laws derive from an era in which women were by and large legally defined as property, therefore as person-shaped things.

Law's denial of subjectivity went even further: a woman who brought a rape charge would typically be subjected to humiliating questioning about her sexual history. It was oddly assumed that the fact that a woman was not chaste was evidence of consent to the particular sexual act in question. Why would such an assumption be made? When we encounter friends dining at a fine restaurant, we usually do not infer that they would love to have a plate of rancid broccoli rammed down their throats. And yet it is just this sort of "reasoning" that pervaded most rape trials. It would appear that the inference reflects an underlying picture of women as divided into two groups: either chaste, fighting to the death against nonmarital sex, or whores with whom anything is permitted. These pictures of women have deep roots in our culture, coloring the ways in which we see, or mis-see, particular events. As eminent a cultural authority as Samuel Johnson once said to James Boswell—in response to Boswell's inquiry regarding whether it was "hard that one deviation from chastity should so absolutely ruin a young woman"— "Why no, Sir; it is the great principle which she is taught. When she has given up that principle, she has given up every notion of female honour and virtue, which are all included in chastity."[10] That idea is surely at work in the perception that a woman who does not struggle, at some risk to herself, has consented and has no right to complain. These beliefs are greatly reinforced by pornographic depictions of women. Women whose non-chastity implies consent to anything and everything exist in pornography, but they do not exist in reality—except in the limiting case of a person whose selfhood is so broken down by repeated ill treatment that she can no longer assert choice and selfhood at all.

Given our ugly history of racism, African American women have been disproportionately likely to be viewed as mere whores or animals (whether they have ever had sex or not), leading to the widespread view that there could be no criminal assault of a Black woman. Sometimes this view had its source in the myth that all African Americans had an unrestrained animal type of sexuality; sometimes in the view that they were mere property; sometimes in both.[11] And poor women were also subject to demeaning stereotypes, such as the view that they had no womanly "honor" and would have sex with anyone.

Distorted judgments about women also colored the interpretation of the mental element of rape. Men who hold stereotypical views of women may actually come to believe that a woman who says "no" is consenting to intercourse. The question the law typically had to face, as we have seen, is whether such beliefs were reasonable. The standard of the "reasonable" is notoriously elusive, and frequently serves as a screen onto which judges project their own (generally male) ideas of appropriate social norms. Many will recall the rape trial of Mike Tyson, at which he claimed (unsuccessfully) that the willingness of D. W. to accompany him to his room was sufficient to make his belief in her consent reasonable, despite the evidence of her vigorous objections and her attempts to escape.[12] Such beliefs about consent were not found reasonable in 1993; earlier they probably would have been.

By the early 1980s, criticism of these antiquated and demeaning views of women was spreading. In a 1982 case, a group of Boston doctors stood trial for taking a nurse bodily to a car, driving her up to Rockport, and repeatedly raping her over her repeated protests. Justice Frederick L. Brown of the Appeals Court of Massachusetts (the first African American appellate judge in the state) commented that it was high time to reject the defense of "reasonable mistake" as to consent in cases such as this:

> It is time to put to rest the societal myth that when a man is about
> to engage in sexual intercourse with a "nice" woman, "a little force
> is always necessary." . . . I am prepared to say that when a woman
> says "no" to someone[,] any implication other than a manifestation
> of non-consent that might arise in that person's psyche is legally
> irrelevant, and thus no defense. . . . In 1985, I find no social utility
> in establishing a rule defining non-consensual intercourse on the
> basis of the subjective (and quite likely wishful) view of the more
> aggressive player in the sexual encounter.[13]

As Justice Brown recognizes, men often indulge in wishful thinking about women's wishes, and (whether hypocritically or sincerely) convince themselves that aggressive behavior is what the situation calls for. If we interpret the "reasonable" in "reasonable mistake" in line with prevailing male social norms, we encourage this sort of wishful thinking. Justice Brown announces a truly radical conclusion: when a woman says "no," it is never reasonable in the legal sense to believe that she means "yes."

False beliefs informed men's sexual desires and sexual behavior—as when knowing that a woman was not chaste led to the assumption that she would "do it" with anyone,[14] or when being aroused by a woman's clothing, gestures, or kissing was understood to license the use of sexual force. False beliefs also shaped the preferences and choices of women, in many harmful ways. Women who had been raped, however violent and non-consensual the incident, often felt shamed and sullied, and frequently did not even consider turning to the law for help. Often guilt about their own sexual desires, or about having consented to kissing or petting, made women feel that they had "asked for it," even when the rape involved violence and substantial physical damage. In addition, women who had consented to intercourse, but who had not consented to acts of violence within intercourse, also felt it impossible to complain, since the reigning view was that a woman who said yes to intercourse had no right to complain about anything that happened next. Such a woman would surely have been treated with mockery and abuse by the police had she complained of assault.

These frequently tragic reactions were caused by a kind of distortion in belief and desire that the feminist movement of the 1970s exposed, arguing repeatedly that female sexual desire and attractiveness are not a way of "asking for it," and that the only thing that counts as "asking for it" is a woman's expressed consent to the acts in question—just as the only way of "asking for" someone to take your wallet is to take it out and give it to that person, without intimidation or threat, either explicit or implicit. Yet even though these falsehoods have been exposed and are no longer taken for granted by the legal system, they remain prevalent in popular culture. Even those who work in the law have more work to do in order to achieve a legal system that adequately protects women's choices.

The regime in which "no" does not mean "no" does not merely neglect a woman's autonomous choice. It creates a fiction: a woman who wears sexy clothing, who dances with men, who, in short, does not behave like a cloistered Victorian maiden, is expressing a choice to have sex with any and every man with whom she associates. This is a pretty ridiculous fiction, gratifying to the male ego but totally implausible. Women are not either sheltered virgins or "sluts" who say "yes" to all sex with all men.

Most women today wish to walk around in attractive clothing, to flirt, to dance, to date, while retaining control over their own sexuality. Indeed, even prostitutes do not say "yes" to all sex with all men. Wherever they retain any control over their working conditions, they say "no" to men who seem dangerous or abusive, to men who refuse to use a condom, and of course to those who can't pay. Prostitutes can be raped, and often are. A simple neglect of women's autonomy would be bad enough; worse is the embrace of a fiction (often encouraged by pornography), in which a woman's very existence means "yes."

With subjectivity the same is true: it is not just neglected, it is replaced by a bogus subjectivity. Instead of searching for the woman's real desire, many men grew up living in a fictional world in which all women want sex with all men, or at least with them. And the more the real world threw up obstacles to this perception, in the form of indifferent or reluctant women, the more the male would be tempted to retreat into the fictional world of "no means yes."

A further barrier to women's autonomy and subjectivity was the refusal to recognize rape within marriage. Under the British common law, rape by a husband was conceptually impossible, since marriage was taken to convey consent to sex thereafter, and indeed to annul a married woman's separate legal being. Although marital rape was harshly criticized by John Stuart Mill in *The Subjection of Women* and by other reformers, and widely recognized as morally bad—and although nineteenth-century feminists spoke often of a married woman's "right to control her own person"—a wife had no legal recourse until the 1970s. In 1976, Nebraska became the first state to abolish the "marital exemption" to rape. Other states followed. In 1984, in a typical progressive judgment, the New York Court of Appeals claimed: "The various rationales which have been asserted in defense of the [marital] exemption are either based upon archaic notions about the consent and property rights incident to marriage or are unable to withstand even the slightest scrutiny."[15] But as we'll see later, the revolution announced in that judgment remains incomplete.

No Means No

A watershed moment in the feminist legal struggle was the 1983 case of Cheryl Araujo, subject of the 1988 film *The Accused*, starring Jodie Foster, which I would rank as one of the very best films about law.[16] The film is reasonably faithful to the case with one large change: the male rapists were working-class Portuguese men, but in the film they are college fraternity boys. The choice—wise, I think—was to avoid denigrating men of a particular class or ethnic origin, but to portray rape culture as universal, as indeed it is.

Cheryl Araujo, age twenty-one, 5'5", 110 pounds, walked into Big Dan's Tavern in New Bedford, Massachusetts, to get cigarettes on the evening of March 6, 1983. I now quote from the trial record. "While there, she ordered a drink and engaged in a brief conversation with another woman patron. The two women also conversed with and observed the pool game of codefendants John Cordeiro and Victor Raposo."[17] There were approximately fifteen men in the tavern. "Sometime after the other woman left Big Dan's, the victim also prepared to leave. Cordeiro and Raposo offered to give her a ride home, which she declined. While the victim was standing in the area of the bar, [Daniel] Silvia and [Joseph] Vieira approached her from behind, knocked her to the floor, and removed her pants as Cordeiro and Raposo tried to force the victim to perform fellatio." She was then dragged, "kicking and screaming," and hoisted onto the pool table, where she was gang-raped by the men, each in turn, while the others restrained her. "Eventually, clothed only in a shirt and one shoe, the victim escaped and ran into the street where she flagged down a passing truck."[18]

The bartender on duty testified at trial that Araujo was "lying on the floor screaming" as two men forcibly removed her clothing, and two other men could be heard boisterously shouting "Do it! Do it!"[19] The defendants testified that she led them on, dancing with them and returning their kisses. Despite the court's efforts to shield her, Araujo's name was repeatedly broadcast on cable TV. Leading feminists gathered to talk about the case, and it became a national cause célèbre.

In the end, four defendants were convicted of rape. Two others were acquitted. One of the jurors said: "She wasn't the greatest of women. She probably egged them on to some degree and they lost control. But after she said no, she was violated. That's how they broke the law."[20]

The juror's utterance is confused. It includes the time-honored idea that when men are led on they will "lose control." But then, it veers around to a different idea: she said no, and that means that when they went ahead she was violated and they broke the law. Many years later, one of the witnesses who picked up Araujo after she fled into the street echoed this idea: "So many things came out with the case, so many lies— that she was a whore, and things like that—but my thoughts were always that a woman, no matter what, has the right to say no. And frankly, even if she was a whore, it doesn't matter, because she said no."[21]

Like both of these remarks, the case was a true turning point in U.S. law, and a major occasion of public education. It established that "no" means *No*. A woman's sexy dancing or revealing clothing is not an invitation to sexual intercourse, when she says she does not want that. Men were on notice: they should take women at their word and stop when told to stop.

No doubt in the confusion of that cultural moment some women often did say "no" when they really wanted the man to go ahead. There is some empirical evidence to this effect.[22] But there's no problem in using the new standard; at the worst, some women who actually want sexual intercourse will need to wait until they are less confused about how they present themselves to men. This consequence can only be good. Women should respect their own autonomy while asking others to do so. "No means no" is not yet the law of the land: twenty-three states still require force more than is necessary to complete the sexual act, or the threat of such force.[23]

Where We Are and Where We Need to Go

Under the pressure of this feminist critique, rape law has changed considerably, increasingly reflecting the insights that (1) a woman's "no" means that she does not consent, and does not mean that she is "playing games" and "asking for it"; and that (2) her prior sexual history is irrelevant to the question of consent on a particular occasion. Change has been slow, and there are many problems to solve, on the way to creating a legal culture that truly protects women's equal autonomy and acknowledges their genuine subjective wishes and feelings (as opposed to bogus projections), while at the same time protecting due process for the accused.

Nonconsent Without a "No"

The longstanding emphasis on "no means no" does not yet enable the law to grapple well with cases in which the victim is silent out of fear (as in *Warren*, the case of the small Illinois cyclist). There remains a tendency to suppose that silence expresses consent. But we would never think that a patient's silence in response to a question about whether he or she wanted a medical procedure was evidence of consent to that procedure; a doctor who simply went ahead and did the procedure, claiming that the patient had expressed consent by silence, would be culpable.[24] Indeed the major revolution in medical ethics in the past hundred years has been a new emphasis on patient autonomy. Doctors used to think that they needed only to consult their own view of the patient's best interests. Now the norm is explicit informed consent.[25]

Why should a doctor's decision to go ahead with a colonoscopy or another medical procedure require explicit informed consent, while the intimate choice of a woman to engage in sex is not treated with the same respect and courtesy? The old attitude of doctors expressed a disregard for patient autonomy and subjectivity, a know-it-all attitude of superiority that is similar in many ways to the attitude of domineering males toward women (with the difference that doctors are typically working for the good of their patients, as they perceive it). So why have Americans successfully replaced the know-it-all regime with a regime of respect for autonomy in the medical sphere, while we lag behind in the sexual sphere?

Sometimes this asymmetry is due to the legacy of the societal myth that good women will fight to the utmost: thus if there is no fighting there is ipso facto consent. Sometimes it is due to a view of women as children who don't know their own minds. A further problem is that sex is romantically thought of as a matter not of decision but of being "swept away." Although many campuses and at least some state laws now insist on an affirmative expression of consent, by either words or gestures, there is no consensus as yet that this is the wisest course in the sexual domain, even though there has long been unanimity that affirmative consent is necessary if taking someone's property is not to count as theft. Many people fear that passion will be dampened by an insistence on a "yes" of some type. And yet, what deeper expression of personal autonomy is there than sexual intimacy? Even if sex is not like surgery in many ways, it is, ultimately, an expression of personal values, where respect for choice seems not unromantic but respectful and appropriate.

It seems difficult for law to articulate the idea of consent in a manner that protects a woman's autonomy in cases like *Warren*, without some type of affirmative consent requirement. This obviously needn't be a formal contract. But, given the high likelihood of misreading and misunderstanding in this domain, a "yes" is not too much to require, and there's no need to fear that passion will flag. Or rather, if the passions of those who like to go ahead without a "yes" were indeed to flag, that would not be a bad thing. And yet very few states have adopted an affirmative consent standard; even the revised Model Penal Code, due out in 2020, seems unlikely to include it.

Sexual autonomy and subjectivity are complex. However, there seems little chance, in our current hyper-sexualized culture, that sexual desire will be banefully stifled by legal attention to affirmative consent. As with informed consent in medicine, this norm, once promulgated, can be internalized, so that everyone is on notice that only "yes" means "yes."

The Extortionate Use of Power

"No means no" also does not enable us to deal well with the extortionate use of power. Sometimes there is actually a kind of "yes," but it is tainted by asymmetrical power. Recall the case of the high school principal who demanded sex in return for graduation. In this case, unlike *Warren*, the student didn't fear physical force, and did actually "agree" to sex. But she submitted to an extortionate demand that would have been clearly illegal in the financial arena. Sexual extortion is hard to theorize. Law cannot look at each scenario on a case-by-case basis, asking whether there is an asymmetry of power here. What it must do is to ask which relationships have an inherent power asymmetry.

Asking such questions is at the heart of sexual harassment laws, as we shall see; but it is relevant in the criminal law of sexual assault as well. All states have laws against sex with minors ("statutory rape"), defining such sex as per se illegal no matter whether or not there is a "yes."[26] Most states make further distinctions: sex between two teenagers close in age is less problematic than sex where there is a wide age difference. The vast majority of states make sex between a corrections official and a prisoner illegal. In addition, the Prison Rape Elimination Act of 2003 is a federal law aimed at deterring sexual assault in prisons. Many states also criminalize sex in other contexts of authority and trust: education, medicine, psychiatry. Others have left this responsibility to the regulatory bodies of these professions.

An evolving area of law is that of mental disability, whether age-related or not. Gradually states are developing flexible standards of competency that fit the complicated situation of an aging population, where often competencies vary within the same person: thus a person who is capable of consent to sex may be incompetent to manage decisions about property. All of these issues are extremely complicated, since law needs to balance respect for sexual autonomy and subjectivity with the need to protect a vulnerable individual from exploitation.

The marital rape exemption has been undone in many states. As of 2019, twenty-eight states have completely abolished the exemption. But what remains is a patchwork of specific exemptions at various levels: thus some states eliminate the exemption only where the husband uses force or the threat thereof, and not where there are other types of extortionate coercion that are recognized as criminal in non-marital contexts, such as the extortionate use of financial threats. There is clearly a lot of work still to do.

The Statute of Limitations

The #MeToo movement has raised, rightly, many questions about the statute of limitations for rape and sexual assault. As women (and men, including many sexually abused in childhood) decide to come forward, supported by a new climate in which women's testimony is believed, they often find that they are unable to bring a formal complaint because it is too late. This is a matter in which there is great variety among the states. Only thirty-four states have a statute of limitations for rape at all, and these states include some traditionally conservative states (Alabama, Arkansas, Louisiana, Wyoming, Idaho) as well as some traditionally liberal states (Maryland, New York, New Jersey—the last being the most legally progressive in general). Complicating the matter further is the huge variation in how rape and sexual assault are defined, and the different degrees of these crimes that are recognized, each of which may have a different statute of limitations. Some states have longer periods for child victims. Some have DNA exceptions: if a match is found in a DNA database, a charge may be brought after the usual statute of limitations has elapsed.

Why do states impose a statute of limitations? First of all, there is the sheer difficulty of prosecution after a lapse of time. Witnesses may disappear or die, essential evidence may be impossible to gather (DNA evidence, for example) or may have become degraded. States plausibly are reluctant to saddle their detectives with a large flood of hopeless tasks, and the knowledge that there is a statute of limitations is supposed to incentivize prompt reporting. Even when a crime has been promptly reported, the difficulties of rape kit testing and storage are large. Given these problems, even states with no statute of limitations rarely prosecute long-ago rapes.

There are, however, more theoretical reasons. One salient idea is that the suspected or real perpetrator should not be on the hook forever: after a time of heightened anxiety, he or she should be able to go about life again on a par with everyone else. However, there is no statute of limitations for murder, so we agree in thinking that a murderer should never be able to sleep in peace, so to speak. One thought behind the movement to abolish or at least lengthen the statute of limitations for rape is that rape is actually a life-altering and terrible act, not the same as murder but closer to murder than many state legal systems suggest. On the other hand, it's hard to avoid the conclusion that many states have no statute of limitations for rape out of zealous determination to be "tough on crime," and that some of these "tough on crime" policies have a racial tinge.

In the wake of #MeToo, there has been a widespread call to remove statutes of limitations, at least for felony sex crimes. In 2017 my own state, Illinois, removed the statute of limitations on a list of sex crimes involving victims under the age of eighteen, and in 2019 the limit was removed for all cases of felony sexual assault and sexual abuse. An odd statute is California's 2016 law, which removes the statute of limitations for rapes committed after January 1, 2017. Although it's easy to understand the potential expressive and deterrent value of this law, it seems to get the situation almost backward. What we seem to need is the ability to prosecute rapes committed back when women had good reason not to come forward and rarely did come forward. Now, difficult though it remains to come forward, it is much easier than it used to be, and women have a real choice in the matter (for the most part).

What should we say here? I am inclined to support the movement to remove the statute of limitations, on the grounds that it is still very difficult for women to come forward, and also on the grounds that lifting the per se restriction gives prosecutors broad discretion to consider the circumstances of each case—including the nature of the evidence and the reasons why the victim did not come forward promptly. We must grant

that very few older sex crimes will, in fact, be prosecuted—for evidentiary reasons. And we must be vigilant against discrimination by race
and class when long-ago crimes are prosecuted. (Discrimination might
be on both sides: both favoring, for example, wealthy white victims and
ignoring poor and/or minority victims, and also choosing not to prosecute wealthy or powerful men for long-ago crimes but prosecuting poor
and/or minority defendants for similar crimes.) But removing the statute
of limitations enhances women's autonomy and respect for the emotions
that still discourage prompt reporting.

Improving Evidence

One improvement in the nature and use of evidence is already under way,
and is a matter of social change more than of law: a woman's testimony
is much more likely to be believed than it used to be. Like other subordinated groups, women have been victims of epistemic injustice as well
as substantive wrongdoing.[27] At this point the tide has turned, in large
part because so many women have come forward, and people realize that
sexual assault is very common; that it happens in all parts of our society;
that it is particularly likely to occur in acquaintance relationships; that it
happens to people's friends, relatives, and neighbors; and that in the past
many of these abuses have gone unreported.

Now a woman who comes forward, even with an older complaint,
is far more likely to be found believable. Should the case go to trial, her
testimony is far more likely to be believed. As many observed after the
2018 Kavanaugh hearings, many convictions are achieved without external third-party corroboration (often difficult to obtain), simply because
the woman's testimony is found credible. (It helps if she told one or more
others at the time.) Law has helped in some measure, since a woman will
no longer face humiliating questioning about her sex life—something
that deterred complaints and, if there was a complaint, tainted the woman's testimony in the eyes of juries. But progress is as yet incomplete. The
public needs much more education about women's narratives and how
rape victims behave after a rape. Juries are too often, still, skeptical of
women's stories in part because they lack this education.

Another evidentiary issue urgently requires attention: the processing of rape kits. Most states have huge backlogs, and insufficient funds to ensure timely testing. Thus DNA evidence that would be crucial in a case, and often would prevent future crimes, sits there unanalyzed—sometimes until after the statute of limitations has passed (a reason why some states have created a DNA exception to the statute). It is in everyone's interest to ensure proper processing, and in the larger budgetary crisis facing many cities and states this issue has had too little discussion and visibility, often getting lost among the many other more sensational issues grabbing public attention. Especially given the very high cost of incarceration (upwards of $55,000 per prisoner per year), we should take into account the fact that there are other ways to use money to diminish crime. Mayors and governors should be required by public pressure to offer a plan for meeting this need, as part of their overall approach to criminal justice. Neglect of this issue in public debate sends women a powerful signal that the legal system does not rate their autonomy and safety very high, when we consider the many other things on which money is spent in cities and states today.

Incentivizing Information

Despite widespread social changes, there is still far too little timely reporting. The usual issues still have some weight: shame; fear that anonymity will not be protected despite "rape shield" laws; worries about how employers, friends, and intimate partners will react to a complaint. But social change is slowly eroding these barriers. There remains the sheer reluctance to get entangled in a lengthy legal process. When a woman has been raped, the harm has already been done. What can she hope to gain for herself by pursuing a complaint? Many people say "closure" and the satisfaction of asserting her rights, but these are often dubious benefits in an uncertain and protracted legal process where a woman knows that she will face vigorous cross-examination and a likely dearth of corroborating evidence. There is also just the sheer burden on her time. Some women are so traumatized by a rape that they can't move past it without seeking legal justice. Others feel that work, friends, therapy, and just getting involved in life are superior to a legal struggle. Victims of burglary definitely have something to gain by going to the law: the restitution of their property, or suitable compensation. For the victim of rape, by contrast, the only personal advantages are nebulous and fraught with stress.

However, when a woman does not complain, other women are very likely to suffer. Sexual assault is often a serial offense, and later victims have a justified grievance against earlier victims if they do not report. Therefore, both legal scholars and policy-makers have recently been advancing various proposals for inducing prompt reporting. One obvious approach is *mandatory reporting.* In areas such as child abuse and domestic violence, states have for a long time required certain personnel (medical, educational) to report evidence of the abuse. Title IX follows this model for what we might call "outcry witnesses" to sexual abuse, that is, people to whom a victim reports a sexual assault—not friends or family, but university personnel in some position of supervision or authority.

Thus if a student comes to me, a professor, complaining of rape, I am obliged to call the Title IX coordinator and give her name. This action then often incentivizes A herself to pursue a complaint. The coordinator calls her, offers to protect her anonymity, explains the complaint process, and asks her if she wants to make a complaint. Although some worry that this approach might discourage frank advice-seeking, in my experience it works well, and typically eases the victim's way into the process. But it is full of holes, since there is no mandatory reporting for other outcry witnesses, nor for actual witnesses of the crime itself—unless a victim names them as witnesses, in which case they will be contacted for a statement. Campuses can do a lot more than they are currently doing to convince everyone that going to authorities with an "outcry" report or a first-hand witness report is the norm of good behavior, and is not objectionable "snitching."

Whistleblowing is much in the news these days. Both the federal government in general (in the Whistleblower Protection Act of 1989) and the federal judiciary (in the reforms to be discussed in Chapter 6) have recently taken steps to protect whistleblowers and to defend them against the charge that they are violating an ethical norm (such as the norm against "snitching" in the student context or the norm of confidentiality in the judicial context). More, however, might be done. In some areas such as tax fraud, whistleblowers are rewarded, should their information prove correct. In a recent article, Saul Levmore and I have investigated this issue for sexual assault on campuses, in a manner that is deliberately exploratory and open-ended.[28] We survey many possibilities: reward by public celebration, penalties for non-reporting, and others. We conclude that reporting is best incentivized by carrots rather than sticks, and that mere public celebration of whistleblowers is too weak a signal, since it is bound to be generic and impersonal, given the large number of assaults.

One option that Saul and I considered is modeled on an insurance policy. A university might contract with a reputable third party, such as a law firm or professional investigator. This outsider, over time, would act as a kind of insurance company. The university then would require that every entering student be given an insurance policy. If the insured were sexually assaulted on campus and were to complain to a designated authority within one month of the occurrence (and the claim were found credible), the insurer would pay a specified sum. Over time the insurer would be able to build a history that identifies dangerous people or groups (fraternities, say) on the campus and would deny coverage to such people or groups. Insurers also would build a comparative record of universities and might increase charges if some have more sexual assaults than others, thus giving universities incentives to implement strategies to hold down the number of sexual assaults. Payments are envisaged not as compensation for the harms suffered by victims, but as a reward meant to encourage early reporting in the interest of other women who might suffer in the future.

There is much more to be said for and against this idea; one worry is that it could incentivize false claims. But new bold ideas are needed to incentivize prompt reporting. Our country is now ready to acknowledge that whistleblowers have an important role in serving the public good, not least when they themselves are victims. In Part III we'll see that whistleblowers have an especially crucial role to play in toppling "citadels of pride," zones of unusually well-insulated male privilege.

Rapes of Men and Boys
Our society has a hard time understanding that men and boys can be victims of sexual assault. Part of the problem is homophobia, which makes people simply not want to think about male-male sex (since most rapes of males are committed by other males). Another problem is the shame of victims, who feel themselves sullied and their masculinity impugned. They may also feel that being a victim of assault somehow makes them gay, whether they are or not. But rape is an abuse of power, as I've argued all along. It is not primarily an expression of sexual desire or attraction. It is questionable whether pedophile priests and prison rapists are gay in any meaningful sense. Their crimes are abuses of their position of power. In Part III we'll study some "citadels of pride," in which young men have routinely been abused along with women. The Prison Rape Elimination Act, passed unanimously by Congress in 2003, finally recognized this problem; it also established a commission to work on implementation. Haltingly, grudgingly, and imperfectly, churches and schools are beginning to address this problem as well. But far more needs to be done.

Sexual assault remains a tremendous problem in our society. Despite the considerable progress that law has made over the past fifty years, women's autonomy (and that of male victims) is all too often still held hostage to male abuse of power and privilege.

CHAPTER 5

Women in the Proud Male Workplace

SEXUAL HARASSMENT AS SEX DISCRIMINATION

> No woman had a voice in the design of the legal institutions that rule the social order under which women, as well as men, live . . . That women have voluntarily engaged law at all has been a triumph of determination over experience.
>
> —Catharine MacKinnon, "Reflections on Sex Equality Under Law"

Work matters. First, it is a source of needed income, and thus, for women, of independence from male support (or nonsupport). But for most people today it is more than that: work is what fills up a large part of our time. So, for better or worse, what happens there has a large impact on a person's sense of self. One perpetual issue, which no modern society has solved, is how work can be made fulfilling or meaningful for the vast majority of workers, who have little freedom to define their own tasks. But even when work is not very interesting or personally expressive, conditions of work can either protect the worker's human dignity or undermine it, and can give scope for personal autonomy—or deny it—in some especially crucial person-defining areas, such as control over one's body and sexuality. For women, winning protection of autonomy and dignity at work has been a long struggle, in which law, and legal theory, have played a defining role, and women have seized the reins of legal creativity.

In the peaceful postwar years that are sometimes romanticized as a time when America was just fine and the American family was whole, women who could afford to stay home rarely worked (meaning *wage labor*, since of course they did a huge amount of valuable work in the home). For women who did work outside the home, the world of work offered few avenues to empowerment, for the most part dooming them to low-level repetitive tasks for which men gave them instructions and expected deference. The workplace was configured by men and expressive of what men liked to do and how men felt like behaving. Men expected deference and, often, more. Sexual banter, sexual come-ons, and demands for sexual favors as a condition of employment—all this was ubiquitous.

There were always many men who respected women and would never have engaged in such behavior. But even these men were typically clueless about how to deal with male colleagues who made unwelcome sexual overtures, whose whole way of relating to women was full of sexual innuendo, who demeaned women by remarks alluding to other gender-based stereotypes (women's high voices, their shortness, or, even worse, their putative stupidity). Every workplace I've ever been in until extremely recently has had such men in it, and one or two are enough to pollute the whole place and make life a misery.

Good men disapproved of bad behavior, and sometimes even expressed shock—but they had no idea what to do about it, besides, perhaps, speaking to the malefactor (often giving, cluelessly, the complainant's name), which usually made things worse. The vacillating behavior of well-intentioned men brings to mind Yeats's famous line, "The best lack all conviction, while the worst/Are full of passionate intensity." Those lines, written as a prescient warning of the rise of fascism, express a general truth of human nature: few people will take a personal risk for justice. Usually, too, these well-intentioned men had conventional lives in which the woman was a "helpmeet," and they lacked interest in fundamental change.

The result? Malefactors suffered no penalty. The women almost always suffered a penalty. There was no grievance procedure anywhere—until the early 1980s, when law had already taken up the issue.

The absence of procedure and law conveyed a suggestion: this is personal. It is not an issue for which the employer has responsibility. It is not a matter of principle or policy. It is perhaps unfortunate, but there's nothing much to be done beyond (fruitless) personal suasion. And often even worse: this is what *will* happen when women enter the workplace, because their presence excites innate sexual urges and, after all, men will be boys. It's natural, but rather embarrassing to discuss. Sometimes too: we men like things this way. Pretty girls make us feel good, and feeling that they are available for propositioning and touching titillates us and gives us a sense of power.

With sexual assault, a lot of work had to be done to define the crime more appropriately and to extend the reach of the law, but law had been somewhere on the scene for over two millennia. With sexual harassment, by contrast, the behavior was an offense that did not even have a name until the term "sexual harassment" was introduced in the 1970s by women seeking legal change.[1] It took years of effort by many people before sexual harassment would be recognized as a social and political harm regulable by law: not merely personal, but, in Catharine MacKinnon's words, "A social wrong and a social injury that occurs on a personal level."[2] In those days, it was "just life."[3]

As a result of this obtuseness, every woman of my generation whom I know or know of has encountered some type of workplace harassment, with no recourse.

Here's something useful about law. It is impersonal. It gives cover to weak-willed people with good intentions. They don't need to get personally involved in the struggle for women's equality, they need only point to the obvious utility of conforming one's behavior to law. Today we can see that the turn to law has had very good effects in the area of sexual harassment, deterring a large amount of the behavior that used to exist, educating society about the importance of women's dignity, making an expressive statement about that dignity, and giving a "handle" to the well-intentioned but weak-willed when they wanted to criticize some of their peers.[4] Norms have changed, even though there is still a lot of bad behavior.

But how, back in the 1970s, might law actually incorporate women's experience, given that it had not done so previously, and who would take the lead? Clearly it would help if a hook could be found in existing law, since passing a new statute on a controversial topic is an uphill battle. And it would be better if the law were federal, since passing new criminal statutes in every state would be a gargantuan task. Who could take this on? It would clearly have to be women who took the lead, despite their virtual absence in the higher reaches of legal academia and the judiciary. And women did in fact step forward—as theorists, lawyers, and plaintiffs.

The Textual Basis: Title VII

The Civil Rights Act of 1964 contains a long, detailed section about discrimination in employment. It reads, in part: "It shall be an unlawful employment practice for any employer . . . to discriminate against any individual because of his race, color, religion, sex, or national origin" in an extensive list of employment contexts. (The statute shows the marks of its era: Communists are explicitly exempted from all protection.) The phrases "because of sex" and "on the basis of sex" are defined as including (but "not limited to") pregnancy and childbirth, although it is immediately stated that the statute does not require employers to pay for abortions, except where the life of the mother is endangered; but employers are also not prevented from paying for abortions. The section forbids practices that have a "disparate impact" on protected groups insofar as these practices are not "job related for the position in question and consistent with business necessity." The statute also created an administrative body, the Equal Employment Opportunity Commission (EEOC), which is charged with enforcing the law.

Title VII, as originally drafted, focused on race; "sex" was added during debate, as an amendment proposed by a segregationist, Democrat Howard W. Smith of Virginia. It is clear from the record that a salient motive for adding it was to undermine support for passage of the law as a whole. Another was to give a concession to white women, on the theory that they would be disadvantaged by new protections given to Blacks—an odd theory, since without the added word, African American women would have been protected against racial but not sex-based discrimination. African American lawyer Pauli Murray offered a different vision: she said the amendment was needed even more by African American women than by white women; without it, only Black males would benefit.[5] Because we should always remember that Congress is a "they" not an "it," there is no single answer to the question of what the drafters intended. But Murray was certainly right that African American women needed protection from sex discrimination even more than white women, and were more vulnerable to sexual harassment in the workplace.

As to what they intended by the word "sex" itself, this is left very open-ended by the words "not limited to." Explicitly, women may not be discriminated against because of pregnancy if they are similar "in their ability to work" to "others not so affected." But it is left open that other issues might be added in due course. Almost certainly, nobody was specifically thinking about what we now call "sexual harassment." But the law explicitly ruled out some things (forced payment for most abortions), and it didn't rule out the extension to sexual harassment that took place later.

There is a longstanding debate in law about the interpretation of statutes: should they be interpreted with reference to the intentions of the drafters? Or should we simply look to the plain meaning of the text? This is not a liberal/conservative issue. Justice Antonin Scalia was the Supreme Court's great foe of reliance on intention in statutory interpretation. And in this case, where there is an evident plurality of conflicting intentions, it seems almost impossible to disagree with him. (We'll see later that Scalia was in fact a strong defender of the use of Title VII to create a cause of action for sexual harassment.) Especially in this case, where the plain meaning of the text is that gaps are left to be filled in later, it is implausible to claim that the statute does not cover sexual harassment, by citing the fact that nobody was talking about it at the time. No such claim was made by the Supreme Court, which recognized sexual harassment as a form of discrimination covered by Title VII despite the fact that it is not mentioned explicitly in the text.

This is an important issue today, given that the Supreme Court held in June 2020 that "sex" in Title VII should be read to include employment protections against discrimination on the basis of sexual orientation and gender identity.[6] Indeed, the entire issue turned on the textualist approach to statutory interpretation, as Justice Neil Gorsuch made clear in his majority opinion. Clearly legislators were not *thinking about* those issues either in 1964. But to discriminate against A, a woman, because A chooses sex with women and not men is indeed in the most literal sense to discriminate *on the basis of sex*. Had the woman chosen sex with a man, she would not have encountered discrimination. I'll investigate this historic opinion later in this chapter. The bold feminist approach to sexual harassment law had a large role in the litigation, since it is a clear example of reading Title VII on its textual face, rather than looking to the mental intentions of Congress.[7]

In short, as Judge Diane Wood, until recently chief judge of the U.S. Court of Appeals for the Seventh Circuit, puts it in a new paper, parts of Title VII are still "works-in-progress" where sex discrimination is concerned, although one might have thought that fifty-five years "was long enough to work out the kinks and ensure that its protections are readily available to any covered person who needs them."[8] In the 1970s, this incompleteness was a serious defect—but it also offered an invitation for creative work.

Very quickly this work began. Catharine MacKinnon says that she began writing her landmark 1979 book late in 1974—while she was still a law student at Yale (JD 1977, PhD in political science, 1987). But she was not alone: already, feminist lawyers had begun to bring cases arguing for the inclusion of sexual harassment under Title VII, as a form of unlawful sex discrimination.

Between 1974 and 1976, the theory that sexual harassment is sex discrimination under Title VII was advanced in a number of cases, at first unsuccessfully. In the 1974 case *Williams v. Saxbe*,[9] however, a D.C. district judge ruled in the plaintiff's favor, finding that the supervisor's action (firing Williams because she refused his advances) counted as sex discrimination and that the employer had thus violated Title VII. Although the judge was overruled on appeal, his opinion proved influential at the appellate level, leading to several reversals in the opposite direction in other cases.[10]

An ultimately unsuccessful case that did a lot to advance the sex discrimination theory of Title VII through its impact was *Alexander v. Yale*,[11] the first use of Title IX, the education part of the statute, to advance the theory that sexual harassment constitutes sex discrimination in education. Brought by five Yale undergraduates and (in the first phase) one Yale faculty member, the suit alleged that the five had each suffered from sexual harassment, and the faculty member argued that the climate of harassment made it impossible to do his job in an "atmosphere of distrust." (The faculty member was the highly regarded classical scholar John J. Winkler, also a gay activist.) The New Haven Law Collective (a feminist group), and especially feminist lawyer Anne Simon, argued the case, while Catharine MacKinnon, by then a recent Yale Law graduate, advised the plaintiffs. The plaintiffs asked simply that Yale establish a grievance procedure to hear complaints of sexual harassment.[12] Meanwhile, MacKinnon and Winkler kept going to the media, who were eager for scandal about Yale; in this way they brought national attention to the issue.

The district court dismissed the claims of five out of six of the plaintiffs, but allowed one to proceed, saying that in her case "it is perfectly reasonable to maintain that academic advancement conditioned upon submission to sexual demands constitutes sex discrimination in education"—although after court-ordered fact-finding the court found that the student deserved a bad grade anyway, so there was no quid pro quo. Five of the six appealed (minus Winkler), but all but one had graduated by the time the court heard the appeal, so their injuries were declared moot. Nonetheless, probably because of the extensive unflattering publicity generated by the case, Yale did what the plaintiffs wanted, setting up a grievance procedure.

To illustrate my claim about the well-intentioned: at that time, a typi-

cal view of some well-behaved men in the Yale Classics Department was
that Jack Winkler was on a political crusade of a somewhat extreme and
implausible type. Much though these people disapproved of bad behavior, the idea that it violated existing law was to them almost comic.[13]

Not all work on sex inequality relied on Titles VII and IX. Just as
claims of racial discrimination had made progress under the equal protection clause of the Fourteenth Amendment starting in the mid-1950s,
so did claims about sex a little later. In 1971, the Supreme Court in *Reed
v. Reed*[14] recognized that inequality on the basis of sex could constitute
an equal protection clause violation. The case concerned an Idaho law
that mandated preference for males in administering estates. Two of the
co-authors of the brief for the plaintiffs were Pauli Murray and Ruth
Bader Ginsburg. It was only in 1976 that the Supreme Court held that
classifications involving sex deserved not simply the extremely deferen-
tial form of scrutiny known as "rational basis review," where the government virtually always wins, but rather something like the more rigorous
and skeptical form of scrutiny, or "strict scrutiny," that had already
been recognized for race—although for sex-based classifications they
recognized a slightly weaker type of review that they called "intermediate scrutiny."[15] Still, *Reed v. Reed* was a landmark of high-level feminist lawyering.

MacKinnon, then, was not a solitary voice crying in the wilderness.[16]
She was part of an extensive network of legal feminists who were determined, *inter alia*, to use Title VII to ensure protection against sexual
harassment. MacKinnon herself gives plenty of credit to others, though
she was certainly the most theoretically creative and analytically profound. To say this takes nothing away from MacKinnon's enormous
insight and lawyerly skill, nor does it deny her isolation within the legal
academy, where she did not get a tenured or even tenure-track job for
many years after her landmark book.[17]

Race and Sex

Title VII aimed above all at ending racial discrimination. A focus on race as a core instance of discrimination has informed all subsequent work on other types of discrimination, especially sex discrimination. In part the importance of race has been strategic: convincing people that something is like racial discrimination proves rhetorically valuable, helping them see the wrong. In part, too, race became central because of the key role of women of color, especially the feminist lawyer Pauli Murray and, later, the plaintiff Mechelle Vinson, in crafting and furthering legal approaches to sex discrimination, which Murray called "Jane Crow."[18] But at a deeper level the analogy to race also expressed and made graphic the idea that sex discrimination is about subordination, just as surely as racial discrimination is—even if with (sometimes) a more polite veneer.

In the area of sex, it was tempting at first to think that women should simply demand to be treated just like men—applying law's concepts to women in just the way they applied to men. In the area of race, however, that approach had already been found wanting. Consider education: "separate but equal" was always a lie, since the schools for African American children were never really equal. But it was also perfectly clear that even if they had been, the very separateness was asymmetrical: for whites, perhaps at worst an inconvenience and a denial of freedom of association, for Black children a badge of inferiority. *Brown v. Board of Education*, the famous Supreme Court case of 1954,[19] saw through the veneer of similarity to the reality of subordination, emphasizing the damage done to Black children by being forced to be in separate schools. Again, consider marriage. If a state forbids Blacks and whites to marry, in one sense the ban looks symmetrical: Blacks can't marry whites, whites can't marry Blacks. But of course in reality it was not symmetrical at all. It was expressive of an ideology of "White Supremacy," as the U.S. Supreme Court wrote in *Loving v. Virginia*, the famous case of 1967 that struck down state bans on miscegenation.[20] In short: laws can violate the equal protection clause even if arrangements are symmetrical, as long as they uphold a hierarchy that renders a group systematically subordinate.

This substantive anti-hierarchy way of thinking about discrimination (and the equal protection clause) did not meet with general agreement, at least at first. In one of the most cited law review articles of all time, "Toward Neutral Principles of Constitutional Law,"[21] federal appellate judge Herbert Wechsler argued, in 1959, that *Brown* was wrong to take into account the asymmetrical stigma separation imposed on Black children. Law, he insisted, must seek neutral principles that are not mere expressions of party politics. So far, so good. As his argument continues, however, Wechsler makes it clear that he believes that this search for articulable reasons demands that one stand so far away from present circumstances and their history that one will ignore many specific social and historical facts. Thus, he holds that judges deciding cases relating to "separate but equal" facilities should refuse themselves concrete contextual understanding of the special disadvantages faced by minorities, and the asymmetrical meaning of segregation for Blacks and whites. In other words, as judges they should forget some historical and contextual things that they clearly know.

Wechsler now offers a revealing aside: "In the days when I was joined with Charles H. Houston in a litigation in the Supreme Court, . . . he did not suffer more than I in knowing that we had to go to Union Station to lunch together during the recess."[22] Wechsler suggests, then, that the fact that a white man and a Black man cannot eat together in a white restaurant involves a symmetrical burden for both, a simple denial of associational freedom. Besides his strange omission of the fact that whites were always perfectly free to visit Black restaurants (a fact that the history of jazz clubs in Harlem would have made famous), his account of the example is oddly obtuse, given that he was a passionate opponent of segregation. For Wechsler, then, the denial is an inconvenience and, possibly, a source of guilt;[23] for Houston, it is a public brand of inferiority. To recognize this evident fact is hardly political bias, or a departure from general principles.

Wechsler's obtuseness extended beyond *Brown*. His paragraph on the case ends with two rhetorical questions: "Does enforced separation of the sexes discriminate against females merely because it may be the females who resent it and it is imposed by judgments predominantly male? Is a prohibition of miscegenation a discrimination against the colored member of the couple who would like to marry?"[24] These questions are supposed to receive a quick answer in the negative, and thus they are supposed to serve as a *reductio ad absurdum* of the mode of reasoning in *Brown*. But of course we might disagree with Wechsler. Then we would reject his *reductio*, concluding that thinking well about race (as in *Brown*) does indeed yield a productive way of thinking about sex discrimination.

Feminists took up Wechsler's challenge, using anti-hierarchy ways of thinking about racial discrimination to inform the law of sex discrimination. It's useful to think of Wechsler as MacKinnon's primary stalking horse in crafting her "dominance" theory of sexual harassment.

Race, then, was an important paradigm for thinking about sex discrimination. It is not, however, a perfect paradigm for sexual harassment, because it does not include the distinctive way in which demands for sexual favors are insulting and humiliating to both Black and white women.

Sexual Harassment of Working Women

In 1979, MacKinnon's long-awaited book was finally published. It stands today as one of the most influential books in the history of the legal academy. "It was a revelation," said Justice Ruth Bader Ginsburg. "And it was the beginning of a field that didn't exist until then."[25] She was not the only one. Left and right agree that the book has crafted the law in a virtually unique manner. A prominent federal judge usually regarded as on the right said often that it was the book by a law professor that had most influenced the federal judiciary.[26] MacKinnon is now thought of as a far-out radical, mostly on account of her work on pornography. It is important to recognize that her 1979 book was bold and daring then, but is now utterly mainstream.

What MacKinnon did was, first, to make amply clear to the clueless the ubiquity and harm of sexual harassment in the workplace—and then to articulate with detailed and cogent legal and theoretical arguments two distinct theories about why sexual harassment should be seen as sex discrimination under Title VII. Although MacKinnon has acquired a reputation as a passion-rousing evangelist, and sometimes, in public appearances, is so, *Sexual Harassment of Working Women*, albeit eloquent and vividly written, is careful, measured, and very closely argued in a first-rate lawyerly fashion. MacKinnon has always been a lawyer first and foremost, and she has aimed throughout her career to make law duly express equal respect for women. Preceded by her work in *Alexander*, the book was followed in 1980 by her work with the EEOC, advising on its sexual harassment guidelines, and by her brief in the landmark Supreme Court case *Meritor v. Vinson* several years later.[27]

Sexual Harassment of Working Women is often misremembered and misquoted. Frequently it is taken to repudiate what might be called the "difference" theory of discrimination and to favor the "dominance" theory. This interpretation is incorrect. MacKinnon shows that according to both of these theories of what discrimination is about, sexual harassment counts as sex discrimination. She also gives reasons why the "equality" theory, the name she uses in the book for what later came to be called the "dominance" theory, is a better theory to think with. But she gives no loophole to those not persuaded by these bold theoretical arguments: even the familiar "difference" theory is sufficient for the conclusion she wants.

The "difference" theory says that if two parties are similar they should be treated similarly, but if they are different they may be treated differently. It then supplies an account of *relevant* similarities and differences. Of course it's obvious that all the normative work of the theory is done in supplying the account of relevance. Think again of Wechsler: He and Houston are similar, both federal judges: so a law that forbids them to lunch together is treating similars similarly, says he, and is therefore permissible. But one should reply that Wechsler and Houston are not at all similar in an obviously relevant respect. Crucial historical and social factors differentiate them, making the denial of association totally asymmetrical. Thus the difference theory does not have to be obtuse, given its demand for relevance.

MacKinnon criticizes the difference theory as frequently applied in a Wechslerian manner that is willfully ignorant of history and context. She discusses a notorious case in which the denial of pregnancy benefits by insurance companies was upheld with just such bogus neutrality: all "non-pregnant persons" are treated similarly (given health benefits), and all "pregnant persons" are also treated similarly (denied health benefits). But the difference approach does not by any means entail this bogus neutrality: MacKinnon points to a case in which the Supreme Court held that it is sex discrimination to deny accumulated seniority to women returning from pregnancy leave but to grant it to an employee who takes leave for illness or disability (112).* The problem she finds is that the difference theory itself offers no clear account of which differences are relevant and which are not. Even at its best, the theory needs further filling out.

However, if we want to hang on to this theory, she continues, and preserve what is valuable in it, we can still show that sexual harassment is sex discrimination (192). Women, as employees, are being singled out, as a gender-defined group, for special treatment in a way that adversely limits women as men are not limited. "In so doing, it creates two employment standards: one for women that includes sexual requirements, one for men that does not" (193). MacKinnon does not deny that males can be sexually harassed (a fact that her later role in *Oncale v. Sundowner*[28] will dramatize). But, she continues, because most, though not all, sexually harassed people are women, we may still conclude that this behavior targets women as women. It would not have occurred (in most cases) had the victim's sex been different (195).

The theory MacKinnon prefers is called the "equality" theory in the book, the "dominance" theory later. It makes central historical and social facts about unequal power. One might see it as a type of difference theory with a very particular account of what a salient difference is for equality purposes. Thus MacKinnon observes that in reality the two theories overlap (120): the equality theory supplies depth and clear norma-

---

* Within this discussion, parenthetical citations are to MacKinnon's *Sexual Harassment of Working Women*.

tive argument where the difference theory is vague. It says that in asking whether a given situation is discriminatory or not (or, in the constitutional context, whether it violates the equal protection clause or not), we need to look at larger social structures of power and their history.

Let's return to *Loving v. Virginia*: to forbid Blacks to marry whites and whites to marry Blacks is not symmetrical and neutral, but discriminatory and an equal protection clause violation, because the historical and social meaning of the denial is totally asymmetrical. Just as denying interracial couples the right to marry has, in the words of the Supreme Court, "no legitimate overriding purpose independent of invidious racial discrimination" and is a measure "designed to maintain White Supremacy," so too, MacKinnon argues, an arrangement that positions female employees as potential sexual playthings for men, their employment contingent on submission, plainly has no legitimate purpose but to maintain a longstanding hierarchy of gendered power. This power structure has long escaped notice because it is thought natural, but, MacKinnon concludes, "[a] division which produces inequality may seem natural because of inequality so pervasive it has seldom been questioned or been rationally questionable" (109). The equality theory gives a deeper rationale for the prohibition, because it focuses on larger social structures.[29]

Here I also add that the equality theory captures a much deeper account of what the wrong is: the wrongs that I've tried to capture in talking about pride and objectification.[30]

Opponents (mostly male) immediately sought to portray MacKinnon's theory as anti-sex, saying that the workplace ought to be a place for erotic attachments, and she had taken this lovely opportunity away. No, not at all. If anything, I would say that her attitude to workplace relationships in the book is too permissive. Meeting the objection that her legal norm would prevent eroticism, she says "If the motive is benevolent, and no coercion is involved, one firm contraindication should suffice" (200)—and she leaves it at that, apparently permitting such relationships where there is no "contraindication." Apart from the difficulty of defining consent in situations of asymmetrical power, even the most mutually enthusiastic relationship may come apart, and the less powerful will be the one to suffer. Therefore most universities and many other work-places today wisely forbid sexual relationships in any situation of direct supervision.

Sexual Harassment in Law

MacKinnon's theory quickly became embodied in EEOC guidelines. The next challenge was in the courts, finishing the work that earlier cases had begun. The first landmark was the 1986 case *Meritor Savings Bank v. Vinson*, for which MacKinnon wrote the brief.[31] Mechelle Vinson was hired at Meritor as a teller-trainee in 1974. By May of the following year her supervisor, Sidney Taylor, had begun to harass her, demanding sexual favors. Fearing reprisal, she had intercourse with him many times, some-times consenting and sometimes being forcibly raped. He also touched her in public and exposed himself to her. Vinson charged that Taylor's harassment created a "hostile working environment," and that this con-stituted a form of unlawful discrimination under Title VII.[32] Eventually, she won. The case established that one type of sexual harassment—the type we now call "hostile environment," and that MacKinnon's book calls "conditions of employment"—is sex discrimination under Title VII: the employee reasonably believes that in order to remain employed she has to tolerate "unwelcome" sexual conduct. The Supreme Court help-fully distinguishes between the "non-voluntary" and the "unwelcome": Vinson often (not always) consented to the sexual conduct, but it was always deeply unwelcome to her. The right legal standard for workplace harassment, said the Court, is unwelcomeness, not non-voluntariness.

Notice, then, that the Court helpfully takes up a gap I've identified in the criminal law: the extortionate use of power. However we theorize sexual harassment, it is an abuse of power (as my analysis of pride pre-dicts). The two types of sexual harassment that have been recognized by the courts are the "quid pro quo" and the "hostile environment." Both involve asymmetrical power. In "quid pro quo" harassment, the plaintiff is given a sexual ultimatum. In the "hostile environment" type there is a more diffuse pressure to tolerate what is unwelcome, whether it involves pressure for sexual relations or a more diffuse sexualization of work relations. In both cases we can't really see what is wrong unless we see that the woman is, in effect, trapped: she tolerates an abusive situation because it is made a condition of her employment.

To constitute a hostile work environment, harassment, courts have said, must be "severe" or "pervasive." For a time, there were two different accounts of those key concepts. On one account, to be "severe," harassment must inflict grave psychological injury. On another, it must be deeply offensive to a "reasonable" person, imagined as in that situation. The first requirement is stronger (more difficult to meet) than the second, because it requires evidence of psychological injury, which is not always present even in situations of extreme offensiveness. And really, why should the standard be psychological injury? Unwelcomeness and offensiveness are what they are, even if a strong woman is not incapacitated by them. In the important 1993 case *Harris v. Forklift Systems*,[33] the Court decisively resolved this question in favor of objective offensiveness: conduct must be "severe or pervasive enough to create an objectively hostile or abusive work environment," but the plaintiff need not prove severe psychological injury, although that might of course be considered. Courts judging such cases are directed to look at all the circumstances, including "the frequency of the discriminatory conduct; its severity; whether it is physically threatening or humiliating, or a mere offensive utterance; and whether it unreasonably interferes with an employee's work performance."

By this legal standard, the conduct of Justice Clarence Thomas toward Anita Hill (whom he supervised first at the Department of Education, and later at the EEOC)—to which she testified in 1991—would be, under existing law, a somewhat unclear case. Assuming here the veracity of Hill's testimony, the conduct she described was not physically abusive or threatening, but it was offensive and somewhat pervasive, and she made a case that Thomas's discussion of pornography and his boasts about his sexual exploits were aimed at dating her (although surely no more counterproductive approach to someone with Hill's refined and discerning personality can easily be imagined!). Hill claimed that she reasonably feared retaliation for not responding. On the other hand, her situation lacks the extreme physical intimidation of Vinson's, and also the hostile bullying of Harris's (who was repeatedly confronted not only with sexual innuendo but also with sexist bullying such as being called a "dumb ass woman"). There's also a lot about pervasiveness that we don't know, since other witnesses were not admitted. Title VII focuses on individuals, not groups, so Hill would not need to show that Thomas harassed all or even many women; still, in a hostile environment case, where the result turns on both severity and pervasiveness, other testimony about the pervasive sexualization of the workplace would be useful.

In my view, if the case went to court (of course it was never litigated), Hill *should* prevail—not against Thomas, but against the Department of Education and the EEOC, because Title VII gives a cause of action against the employer, not against an individual supervisor—but she might or might not actually prevail: other plaintiffs with similar fact patterns have lost. The jury would have to be convinced that Thomas's conduct was both objectively severe and sufficiently pervasive. The EEOC guidelines say that "sexual flirtation or innuendo, even vulgar language that is trivial or merely annoying, would probably not establish a hostile environment." But what would actual judges and juries say of the Thomas case? It's in a zone where the record shows divergent results, as we'll see shortly with the case of *Baskerville v. Culligan*.[34]

In subsequent years some major gaps in existing law were gradually addressed. MacKinnon's theory and the related case law focused, reasonably, on sexual harassment that in some way involves sex or sexual relations. That was the sort that had been thought to be merely "personal," or "natural." But one can be harassed on the basis of one's sex without being pressured for sex, just as a member of a racial minority can suffer racial harassment by being singled out on the basis of race. Even the use of racial stereotypes is not required—only evidence that the targeting was reasonably understood as based on race. Because of the focus on sexual relations in early cases such as *Meritor* and *Harris*, courts at times got confused, denying a "hostile environment" claim when there was not much evidence of sexual pressuring.[35] A valuable corrective, and an extension of the doctrine, took place in 1994 in *Carr v. Allison Gas Turbine Division, General Motors*.[36] Mary Carr, the first female employee in the gas turbine division of General Motors at their plant in Indiana, was harassed in a manner both crude and threatening by the men working there, who seem to have feared that jobs for women would mean fewer jobs for men. By urinating at her from the catwalk, defacing her toolbox with obscenities, cutting up her overalls, and so on, they sought to make her life a misery and to drive her out. But they did not pressure her for sexual relations. Nor did their abuse focus on demeaning gender stereotypes. Clearly, however, they bullied her because she was a woman. Had she been male, she would not have had to endure this. Judge Richard Posner, writing for the majority, found Carr's a clear case of sexual harassment as sex discrimination, and ruled that GM's lack of response to her repeated complaints was sufficient for liability. He gave no sign that the absence of sexual propositioning was a doctrinal problem. (Posner also asserted the dominance theory as if it were unproblematic: he overruled the lower court judge on the findings of fact because that judge had not included the asymmetry of power in the workplace in his account of the facts of the case.)

The entire concept of sexual harassment focused on women's workplace experience and the domination of women by men. Nonetheless, by now it is clear that under some circumstances a man can suffer sexual harassment. The key case was *Oncale v. Sundowner Offshore Services*, in 1998.[37] Joseph Oncale worked on an eight-man oil platform in the Gulf of Mexico. He was repeatedly bullied and humiliated by the other men, threatened with rape, and once sodomized with a bar of soap—apparently because of his allegedly feminine characteristics. He claimed he was harassed "because of sex," and sought redress under Title VII. (As I've said, until 2020 the Supreme Court did not recognize discrimination on the basis of sexual orientation as a violation of Title VII, although some lower courts had done so. In any case all those involved in *Oncale* were heterosexual.) The district court and the appellate court rejected Oncale's contention, saying that as a male harassed by other males he had no cause of action. When the case went on appeal to the Supreme Court Catharine MacKinnon wrote an amicus brief in support of Oncale.

The Supreme Court unanimously ruled in Oncale's favor, with Justice Scalia writing the opinion. (Justice Thomas added a one-sentence concurrence.) Just as a finding of racial discrimination is not ruled out by the fact that both plaintiff and accused are of the same race, he wrote, so too a hostile environment "because of sex" may be found when all involved are male. Scalia insisted on his lifelong opposition to looking for legislative intentions behind a text: "statutory prohibitions often go beyond the principal evil to cover reasonably comparable evils, and it is ultimately the provisions of our laws rather than the principal concerns of our legislators by which we are governed." Harassing conduct, he continued, need not be motivated by sexual desire to create a hostile environment. *Oncale* is more important than it is clear; lower courts continued to differ about the parameters it establishes. But it is a welcome recognition that sexual harassment is a type of abuse of power that is independent of biology.

Sexual Harassment Today: Where Law Needs to Go

The law of sexual harassment has been an undoubted triumph of feminist theorizing and feminist lawyering. Still, as with sexual assault, a lot of work remains to be done. Here are three of the problems that still need addressing or are beginning to be addressed:

What Is a Hostile Environment?

The common-law tradition proceeds incrementally. New cases make vague boundaries increasingly precise. And yet, to this day, crucial parts of the idea of "hostile environment" remain so unclear that similar cases are treated differently, and individual judges and panels seem to have too much latitude. In an important article, Judge Diane Wood examines a series of sexual harassment cases in that circuit in which the plaintiffs lost, concluding that at least some of the outcomes were question-able.[38] Wood begins by pointing to a popular misconception that merely impolite and crude conduct is policed under Title VII. "The reality," she says, "is otherwise: the innocuous actions never get litigated, or, if they do, they are quickly thrown out of court, while even truly awful actions often fall outside the scope of the law . . ." Wood concludes that it is time to take stock and consider reforms.

Wood considers a range of problem cases, but let's look at *Baskerville v. Culligan*.[39] Valerie Baskerville was a secretary in the marketing depart-ment of Culligan, a manufacturer of water-treatment products. Over a seven-month period, she experienced acts of harassment at the hands of her supervisor. Judge Richard Posner, who wrote the impressive opinion in favor of Mary Carr's claim in 1994, wrote the 1995 opinion articulat-ing the decision against Baskerville. Posner enumerated the instances of the supervisor's conduct in a numbered list, one through nine—making them seem oafish and non-threatening by the very manner of his sardonic narration. (A typical example: once, when the PA system announced, "May I have your attention, please," the supervisor stopped at Basker-ville's desk and said, "You know what that means, don't you? All pretty girls run around naked.") Posner concluded, "We do not think that these incidents, spread over seven months, could reasonably be thought to add up to sexual harassment." Posner then added an analysis that appears to neglect his own insights in *Carr*. Sexual harassment, he said, is a concept "designed to protect working women from the kind of male attentions that can make the workplace hellish for women." Further, he divided such pressures into two categories: the grave (assaults, non-consensual physical contact, obscene language or gestures, etc.), and, on the other side, "the occasional vulgar banter, tinged with sexual innuendo, of coarse or oafish workers." Concluding that the supervisor's behavior fell into the latter category—it was "distasteful to a sensitive woman," but deeply distressing only to "a woman of Victorian delicacy"—he con-cluded that a harassment claim had not been established.

Nowhere, however, did he analyze the power dynamics in the Cul-ligan workplace, asking how the relevant asymmetries affected the meaning of the supervisor's words and gestures. "It is a little difficult to imagine a context that would render [the supervisor's] sallies threatening or otherwise deeply disturbing," Posner remarked, but without considering asymmetry of male-female power as an element in the context. (We don't even learn how many female employees there were, for example.) This is the type of thing Wood has in mind, and I agree with her: male judges may be too quick to see comedy where a reasonable woman might see a truly hostile situation. (Baskerville's experience is not unlike Anita Hill's situation, and I have just said that I think Hill ought to prevail on the facts she brought forward.) Moreover, as Wood points out, Posner used an outdated standard: a hostile environment exists only if the workplace becomes "hellish" for the victim—a standard rejected in *Harris v. Forklift Systems*. Further clarification of the standard is clearly necessary.

Getting Liability Right

Many confusions and uncertainties, throughout the history of sexual harassment law, have concerned employer liability. Title VII creates a remedy only against the employer, so the link to the employer is crucial. What sort of action does the plaintiff need to take to bring the offending behavior to the notice of employers, in order to have a cause of action against them? How timely does the complaint need to be? What sort of insulation, if any, do employers derive from an explicit harassment policy? What remedial steps on the part of employers are sufficient to put them in the clear? There are cases addressing all these issues, but there is still insufficient clarity, especially given notorious problems of underreporting and given the fact that, as Wood observes, more than 98 percent of civil litigation is resolved short of a trial. Wood herself has recently made a creative contribution to the understanding of liability, in the case of a lesbian woman harassed by other residents of a senior living facility.[40] The inaction of management, she held, is sufficient for liability. The case concerned the Fair Housing Act, not Title VII, but the two statutes use very similar language in defining sex discrimination, and they are often understood together.

Moreover, it may be time to reconsider the restriction of liability to the employer, and to discuss whether liability should be broadened to reach the guilty party.[41] The deterrent value of such a change would be great. Of course a plaintiff can also bring criminal charges against the guilty party, in cases where there is a physical assault, but pursuing two separate actions is difficult and costly.

Sexual Orientation Discrimination

Oncale broadened the reach of Title VII, finding discrimination in a case of same-sex harassment. Scalia's opinion grounded this result securely in the text, and in prior sexual harassment decisions. But in many workplace situations of discrimination and harassment, employees appeared to lack protection against discrimination on the basis of sexual orientation or transgender identity. The topic has always been important to feminists, who typically have made common cause with LGBTQ people in seeking justice. And as Oncale shows, the issues and arguments overlap. Scalia's opinion in *Oncale* was a harbinger of the Supreme Court's ringing textualist resolution of these further issues.

In June 2020, in *Bostock v. Clayton County*,[42] the Supreme Court declared unequivocally that "sex" in Title VII should be read so as to forbid employment discrimination on the basis of sexual orientation or gender identity. Three cases were before the Court, on appeal from appellate courts whose rulings had conflicted.

- *Bostock* concerned Gerald Bostock, an employee of Clayton County in Georgia, who began playing in a gay softball league and was promptly fired for conduct "unbecoming" a county employee. His suit for sex discrimination under Title VII was dismissed by the Eleventh Circuit, which held that Title VII does not prohibit employers from firing employees because they are gay.
- *Altitude Express, Inc. v. Zarda*[43] concerned Donald Zarda, a skydiving instructor. When a female client worried about being tightly strapped to him in her lesson, he tried to reassure her by telling her that he was "100% gay"—and was promptly fired. He too brought

suit under Title VII, and the Second Circuit found in his favor, allowing his suit to proceed.

- *R. G. and G. R. Harris Funeral Homes, Inc. v. Equal Employment Opportunity Commission*[44] involved the firing of Aimee Stephens, who was hired by the funeral homes as a man, but subsequently announced that she planned to "live and work full-time as a woman." Like Zarda, Stephens won her case at the appellate level, in the Sixth Circuit. This type of circuit split is a classic occasion for Supreme Court review.[45]

(By June 2020, both Zarda and Stephens had died—Zarda in a skydiving accident, Stephens after a long illness—but their relatives continued the litigation.)

Two intervening cases in addition to *Oncale* contributed to the Court's momentous decision.

- In *Phillips v. Martin Marietta Corp.*[46] a company refused to hire women with young children, but did hire men with children of the same age. Although the company maintained that they were not discriminating against women, since they preferred women overall, but only against motherhood, they lost, because a man in exactly the same situation as the woman who was refused a job would have been hired. In other words, the law is about the intentional treatment of individuals, not groups, and what needs to be shown is only that the plaintiff's sex is one factor involved in the hiring decision.
- In *Los Angeles Dept. of Water and Power v. Manhart*,[47] the employer required women to make larger pension fund contributions than men, citing the fact that women on the whole live longer than men and can therefore expect, as a group, to receive more from those funds. There was no evidence that the employer was biased against women or had negative views about their job performance. Nonetheless, a practice that looks reasonable at the group level can still be unfair to the individual, and, once again, the Court emphasized that Title VII concerns individuals, not groups. Any individual woman might make

the larger pension contribution and still die as early as a man. So the
employer could not "pass the simple test" of showing that an individual female employee would be treated the same regardless of her sex.

The three precedents established a clear framework for future cases:
(1) Title VII concerns individuals, not groups, and thus a pattern of
group discrimination need not be shown; (2) the factor of sex does not
need to be the only or main factor in the employment decision, just a
"but/for" cause, one without which the employment action would not
have happened; indeed, the employer might sincerely believe that they
were focusing on a totally different issue, such as "motherhood" or "sta-
tistical life expectancy"; (3) the test the employer must be able to meet is
this: would a person of the opposite biological sex be treated the same, in
the employee's same total situation?

The stage was set for Justice Gorsuch. Indeed his work was made
straightforward. "When the express terms of a statute give us one answer
and extratextual considerations suggest another, it's no contest. Only the
written word is the law, and all persons are entitled to its benefit."[48] In
going over the factors I've mentioned above, Justice Gorsuch dwells on
the importance of the first factor, individuality, for sexual harassment as
well as other forms of discrimination. To win a sexual harassment case
against an employer, a woman does not need to show that the employer
harassed all women or most women. She needs only to show that her
sex was a significant factor in the discrimination she suffered—that a
man in her exact position would not have been treated that way. Gorsuch then turns to the facts before him. They seem, and are, straightforward. "An individual's homosexuality or transgender status is not
relevant to employment decisions. That's because it is impossible to discriminate against a person for being homosexual or transgender without
discriminating against that individual based on sex." If an employer fires
a man for being sexually attracted to men, but would not fire a woman
for that trait, the male employee is being discriminated against on the
basis of sex. Or, in the transgender case: if the employer fires an employee

who was identified as male at birth but now identifies as female, while retaining an otherwise identical employee who was identified as female at birth, the employer is discriminating on the basis of sex. When an employer discriminates on the basis of sexual orientation or gender identity, sex is "necessarily a but-for cause." The employer may intend to discriminate on the basis of sexual orientation, but "to achieve that purpose the employer must, along the way, intentionally treat an employee worse based in part on that individual's sex."

The dissenting justices repeatedly allude to the beliefs and purposes of the legislators at the time Title VII was enacted. Indeed, although they make some weak attempts to defend their position on textualist grounds, the core of their position is a deference to legislative intent.[49] Here Justice Gorsuch again refers to Scalia's opinion in *Oncale*: "But, the Court unanimously explained, it is 'the provisions of our laws rather than the principal concerns of our legislators by which we are governed.'" And really: that principle is so solidly entrenched in the history of Title VII, particularly with reference to sexual harassment, that it is simply impossible to wave it away. As we've seen, the framers of Title VII were not all of one mind, but one thing that none of them had on their minds (very likely) was the issue of workplace sexual harassment.

Bostock is historic, for two reasons: first, on account of its result, and second, because it represents a triumph of principle over ideology—something our society badly needs at this time. Many people on both sides of the issue reported surprise or even shock at Justice Gorsuch's opinion. This reaction could just show that they had not been paying attention. For Justice Gorsuch, like Justice Scalia before him, has been an energetic proponent of a textualist approach, and he has even written a book in which he defends his views on this topic.[50] Justice Scalia, furthermore, had already taken a textualist step toward Gorsuch's reasoning. The reaction might, however, mean something that speaks sadly of our present moment: a belief that a conservative justice would vote on the basis of ideology rather than judicial principle, and would even diverge from long-articulated principles for the sake of ideology. It seems that many, both liberal and conservative, expected such behavior. Fortunately for our democracy, they did not get it. Instead, they got a ringing affirmation of principle, a welcome reminder that we live in a government of laws, not just a forcefield of contending interests.

Despite the importance of the case, however, it leaves issues unresolved, as Justice Gorsuch makes clear in his opinion. It does not decide cases about locker rooms and bathrooms, since it deals only with workplace discrimination in the form of firing or failing to hire.[51] Nor does it announce how far religious institutions may be exempt from the workplace nondiscrimination mandate. Finally (something not mentioned by Justice Gorsuch) it does not resolve the parallel issue raised by the Fair Housing Act, where the Seventh Circuit has held that the act's ban on sex discrimination entails a ban on housing discrimination on the basis of sexual orientation.[52] Title VII and the Fair Housing Act use similar language and are typically interpreted with reference to one another, but so far, there has been no decision on this matter at the Supreme Court level. Future years will bring future controversies, and in most of these, implicitly or explicitly, the law of sexual harassment will continue to play a guiding role.

As Justice Gorsuch wrote of Title VII: "Sometimes small gestures can have unexpected consequences. Major initiatives practically guarantee them."[53] *Bostock* follows the distinguished line of bold sexual harassment decisions in which textualist judges draw unexpected consequences from the open-ended language of Title VII.

Pride and Justice

Pride turns eyes inward. Equal respect requires looking one another in the eye, acknowledging one another's equal reality. For most of this nation's history, the criminal law declared that rape was a crime—albeit with inadequate criteria and blinkered definitions based upon stereotypes. Still, law understood that crime was somewhere in the vicinity, so law needed to be retooled and reformulated, not created where no prior law existed. It was otherwise with workplace sexual harassment. Where crime abounded, law simply did not see it: law itself, we might say, was proud. Males looked inward at other males, not at the experiences of women and ubiquitous denials of their workplace autonomy. And law looked inward with them.

If the reform of criminal law has been a signal accomplishment of dedicated lawyering and courageous intellectual protest, the achievement of sexual harassment law, albeit incomplete, has been something more amazing: the creation of a new domain of law, almost de novo, using only the abstract and open-ended text of Title VII. Where previous eras saw "nature," "eroticism," "flirtation," and perhaps, at worst, an "unfortunate personal situation," we now have a theory, a tradition of case law, and a set of ever-more-specific and refined problems yet to solve. It's a tradition to celebrate.

Nor does celebrating it require taking sides in bitter feminist turf wars. Linda Hirshman, for example, suggests in *Reckoning* that siding with MacKinnon and the courts on sexual harassment means questioning the sexual revolution and the legal availability of pornography. But if we keep our eyes on the key issues of domination and autonomy, we see that current sexual harassment law is neutral on those matters. The availability of pornography does not imply that it can't be one element in a hostile working environment. You don't have to ban hammers to treat assault with one as a crime.[54] And even more clearly, an embrace of newly free norms of sexual choice does not mean that men are entitled to deny women sexual autonomy by insistent workplace pressures.

To use a term from Rawlsian political thought, we might call current legal norms an "overlapping consensus" that can be embraced by people with various different "comprehensive" views of what gender relations ought to be—as is hardly surprising, given that key moments in the doctrine were articulated by Catharine MacKinnon, by liberal justice Ruth Bader Ginsburg, by moderate justice Sandra Day O'Connor, by textualist justices Antonin Scalia and Neil Gorsuch, and by libertarian pragmatist judge Richard Posner. What do all these figures have in common? They have all faced squarely the reality of women's (and men's) workplace situation, embracing the ideals of Title VII and courageously seeing in the vague text possibilities for extensions of the rule of law.

Thoughts about Sexual Assault on College Campuses

So far we have traced the evolution of legal standards for sexual assault and sexual harassment, and their current defects and challenges. There is, however, a significant area of our national discussion that is not fully covered by these discussions, because it involves a complex and uneasy mixture of federal law (Title IX, discussed in Chapter 5) and informal tribunals: sexual assault and harassment on college campuses. Because my previous discussions have covered the most salient issues in each area of law, I need not devote a full chapter to this case, nor do I wish such a disproportionate focus to suggest that women who attend college deserve more attention than women who do not. Unequal access to higher education is already a major problem of justice in our society, compounding other disadvantages based on race and class. There is no reason to perpetuate the injustice by paying more attention to the problems of those women who have managed to arrive at a college or university. One of the great strengths of the traditions I have described is the fact that working-class and minority women (for example Cheryl Araujo, Mechelle Vinson, Mary Carr) have been among their salient plaintiffs.

Yet, because the institutional structures are different, the topic of campus assault requires separate treatment, albeit briefly. Nobody knows exactly how large a problem this is, but one recent survey by the Association of American Universities found that around 20 percent of female undergraduates are victims of sexual assault or sexual misconduct at some point during their college life.[1] Other studies have found frequent sexual abuse of males as well, amounting to 6 to 8 percent. Although there are disputes over methodology and definition, there's no doubt about the severity of the issue. It would appear, however, that attending college does not make a woman *more* likely to suffer sexual assault.[2]

Sexual harassment and sexual assault have long included abuses of power between faculty and students, but on the whole, these cases have been understood as workplace abuses of power, and are dealt with under clear public rules, in much the manner of other workplaces. Thus, Chapter 5 has already basically dealt with these cases. In this Interlude I focus on student-student assault and harassment.

The literature on this topic is vast and controversies are heated, in part because the Obama administration guidelines have now been replaced by different guidelines developed by the Department of Education under the aegis of Secretary of Education Betsy DeVos. However, the controversies cross political lines. Thus the group of Harvard Law School professors who protested against the Obama guidelines as unfair to accused men, anticipating the DeVos critique (I'll describe their intervention as Stage Two below) included some conservatives, but also faculty from the left and even extreme left of the faculty.

I'll cover the salient issues briefly, without discussing all the ins and outs of all the controversies. Thus the intention of this brief discussion is to indicate, in a general way, how my overall view in this book's detailed chapters would approach campus cases, rather than to construct a comprehensive argument.[3]

Alcohol

A large proportion of sexual assaults and alleged sexual assaults occur when one party, or usually both parties, have been drinking heavily. Heavy drinking makes memory gappy and adjudication very difficult. In general campuses need to do much better with alcohol education and treatment. But one recommendation that most college administrators would support is: *lower the drinking age*. This approach seems counter-intuitive, but it is really sensible. Right now, if adults are present where there is under-age drinking (and most students are under twenty-one), they can be charged with contributing to the delinquency of a minor. So they refrain from providing badly needed supervision, including help for students who have passed out. If the drinking age were reduced to eighteen, adults could attend parties and be prepared to give assistance.

Another alcohol-related issue that needs addressing, in both education and adjudication: *sex with a person who has passed out or is close to that point is an assault*. This is a species of my point about affirmative consent, but it needs to be repeated again and again. The standard, however, is far from clear in application. Many cases before campus tribunals concern the thorny and as yet unresolved question of how impaired a person must be in order not to be capable of decision-making. Since the evidence comes, typically, from two impaired individuals, it is hard for them to remember how impaired they were. Third-party evidence is usually helpful, but is not always available.

Campus Tribunals

There is considerable confusion in the public mind over why campuses do not simply turn accusations over to the police. So it's important to point out that campuses have membership conditions, usually spelled out in the admissions contract, that go beyond the letter of the law and that need to be enforced by the campus itself. Plagiarism, not attending class, cheating on exams–all of these things are likely to be punished, sometimes with suspension or expulsion, even though they are not crimes. Similarly campuses may adopt sexual requirements that go beyond the law. Some of these are extreme: honor codes at some religious schools penalize all non-marital sexual conduct. I think such restrictions are counterproductive, creating cultures of silence (if a woman discloses that she has been raped, she can be penalized for engaging in sex). But there are also some reasonable requirements, such as affirmative consent, that are not necessarily the law of the land.

Moreover, the criminal justice system takes a long time, and victims need swift justice in order to deal with the trauma and go forward as students.

Finally, if a perpetrator is convicted in the criminal justice system, that record is ruinous for future life and employment. Campus convictions come in degrees, and many involve mandatory counseling and other lesser penalties. For this reason, having the criminal justice system as the only option, would deter reporting and bringing charges, since victims often hesitate before ruining the perpetrator's life, and yet they seek some measure of recognition. They want the wrong done to them to be acknowledged—both that it happened and that it was wrong—and they want accountability for the perpetrator; but typically they are not seeking maximal revenge. Nor do they want lengthy involvement with the formal criminal justice system.

These are reasons why campus tribunals are not replaceable by the criminal justice system. However, it must also be said that these tribunals often do their job poorly. Faculty and administrators who serve on them are rarely well trained, and they do not always understand the quasi-legal issues with clarity. Procedures are often poorly defined, and the accused, who typically lack legal representation, are at a disadvantage.

Procedural Issues for Tribunals

How, then, can these tribunals be made to work better?

In this section I'll refer to several key stages in the debate. *Stage One* was the "Dear Colleague" letter issued by the Obama administration, laying out standards to which all universities must conform to receive federal money.[4] *Stage Two* involved a series of objections to these standards, some issued by Betsy DeVos once she became secretary of education,[5] but similar objections were raised earlier by legal professionals—most famously by a group of twenty-eight Harvard Law School professors, drawn from both the left and the right, in a letter published initially in the *Boston Globe* but widely reprinted.[6] Next, in *Stage Three*, came the new Department of Education draft rule, which, like all administrative rules was subject to "notice and comment,"[7] and received over 124,000 comments.[8] Finally, in *Stage Four* (May 2020), the Department of Education issued its Final Rule, which is now legally binding on all colleges and universities that receive federal money.[9] I'll proceed issue by issue.

First, all involved need to get clear about the best *burden of proof.* This issue has been one of the largest political disputes. Three standards are currently in use in our legal system. The most stringent, used throughout the United States in the criminal justice system, is proof *beyond a reasonable doubt.* Many countries do not use this standard for criminal trials, but our tradition has judged that convicting an innocent person is more heinous and more to be avoided than letting a guilty person go free. Together with this exacting standard, our criminal justice system gives the accused a constitutional right to the "effective" and cost-free assistance of legal counsel, although great disparities still exist between public defenders provided free of charge and the sort of lawyer that a more affluent defendant typically would engage—not always because of quality, but because public defenders are overworked and usually don't have enough time to devote to each client. But at least there is cost-free representation. Furthermore, our Constitution's "confrontation clause" gives accused parties the right to confront witnesses testifying to their guilt. Over time other rights have been inferred from constitutional guarantees, the most famous being the Miranda warnings that must be read to defendants on arrest, warning them of their right to counsel and their right to remain silent. So our system is protective of defendants in multiple ways.

In civil trials, the standard, instead, is "preponderance of the evidence," which means anything over 50 percent. Obviously this is a much weaker standard. Nor are free lawyers always provided in civil cases (some states do, most don't). Still, the civil litigation system has firm procedural structures that safeguard the parties—especially a lengthy period of "discovery," which gives both sides a chance to examine the other side's evidence. Without such structural safeguards, and without legal counsel assisting the parties, many people feel that the "preponderance" standard is likely to lead to error.

A third intermediate standard is "clear and convincing evidence," which is used in ways specified by the relevant state laws, often in areas such as paternity and child custody. This standard is typically thought to mean that it is about 75 percent likely that the person did what is alleged.

Before the "Dear Colleague" letter issued by the Obama administration,[10] most universities used "clear and convincing evidence" as the standard in sexual assault tribunals. The Obama administration insisted, instead, on the civil "preponderance of the evidence" standard. The Harvard Law School faculty letter, and DeVos in her own remarks, held that this standard was not protective enough of the accused. So far, it seems that nobody favors the "reasonable doubt" standard, which would be very difficult to apply in the informal and evidentially challenged situation of a tribunal. So the choice is between the other two standards, and in the end the Department of Education's Final Rule gives every college that choice.

It's important to be clear that a college tribunal will not take away a defendant's liberty. That dire consequence is our legal system's primary reason for choosing reasonable doubt. Courts, however, have repeatedly held that educational opportunities are economic or property interests, not matters of freedom. So it seems that there is nothing at all odd about using either the civil justice standard of *preponderance*, or the tougher standard of *clear and convincing evidence*. This is where the debate occurs.

In real life, both sides have merit. *Preponderance* defenders believe, rightly, that in the typical alcohol-fueled interaction any stronger standard will be very difficult to meet. However, it is also true that education, albeit a property interest, is one of special defining importance in our society. So it's important to be protective of the accused. And the civil standard is probably a bad idea in a setting that lacks the procedural safeguards that are usually present in civil trials. *Clear and convincing* makes more sense, I believe; but if a school should opt for preponderance—as I said, the Final Rule ultimately, and rather surprisingly, gives institutions a choice between these two—a careful tribunal would probably think in terms of a kind of *preponderance plus*, not necessarily convicting someone where the evidence suggests a mere 50.5 percent likelihood of guilt. The 50.5 approach would really not be protective enough of the accused. Many preponderance-based tribunals actually interpret the standards somewhat more strongly. Whatever the standard, members of tribunals need better training about the whole issue of evidence and the burden of proof.

A second issue of great importance is the *definition of sexual harassment*. The campus process typically runs together the two things our legal system has carefully kept apart—namely sexual assault or abuse, and (workplace) sexual harassment. There is no harm in this combination so long as sub-definitions are clearly drawn. Sexual assault is typically defined as a single act, not a pattern of actions: you only need to rape a woman once to be guilty of rape! Sexual harassment, by contrast, has two forms. If there is a quid pro quo, a single act suffices. But in "hostile environment" harassment, the plaintiff needs to show a pattern of actions that are sufficiently "serious" and "pervasive," as well as "unwelcome." One demeaning comment or gross overture will not suffice. This distinction seems correct.

In terms of this legal background, the Dear Colleague letter was far from adequate. It defined sexual harassment as "unwelcome conduct of a sexual nature," including "unwelcome sexual advances, requests for sexual favors, and other verbal, non-verbal, or physical conduct of a sexual nature." This meant in practice that one gross or demeaning comment, with no prior evidence of its unwelcomeness, would be actionable. The Department of Education's Final Rule, by contrast (*Stage Four*), hews closely to legal standards accepted elsewhere in our legal system. There are three categories of sexual harassment: (1) "any instance of *quid pro quo* harassment by a school's employee," (2) "any unwelcome conduct that a reasonable person would find so severe, pervasive, and objectively offensive that it denies a person equal educational access"; and (3) "any instance of sexual assault as defined in the Clery Act [a federal statute dealing with campus security], dating violence, domestic violence, or stalking, as defined in the Violence Against Women Act." In other words, a single unannounced act can still be sexual assault or a quid pro quo, but verbal harassment must form a pattern that meets the Supreme Court standard of pervasiveness and severity, as determined from the point of view of a reasonable observer. The Final Rule protects someone who makes a deeply offensive remark without advance notice of its unwelcomeness and who does not persist.

On most grounds the Department of Education's Final Rule is an advance over the Obama administration's rule, and also over the Department of Education's first rule (*Stage Three*), under DeVos, which did not include dating violence, domestic violence, or stalking. The Final Rule is perhaps too narrow in its requirement that the accuser show that the harassment is not just severe, pervasive, and objectively offensive, but that it also has a deleterious effect on the person's equal educational access. Campuses are academic organizations, but they are also social organizations. Social harassment does not always affect someone's ability to study, and why should that need to be shown? Why isn't the poisoning of the person's campus social life sufficient? There are other issues that have been raised, but on balance the "notice and comment" process seems to have worked pretty well.

I shall not go into the details of the various discussions of the questioning and confrontation process in the old and new rules. What I want to focus on, instead, is what I consider to be one of the largest problems with campus tribunals, which has not been addressed by any of these rules: the lack of *access to free legal counsel for the accused*. Most institutions not only do not provide a lawyer for the accused party; they actively discourage the hiring of lawyers. Typically the accused is permitted to have one supporter or advisor, but when the accused asks if this person can be a lawyer, they are usually discouraged. This is wrong. "Advisors" are typically faculty or administrators who have no legal training and who cannot do an energetic job of defending their client's rights. And it is also wrong to require people to hire their own lawyers. Free legal assistance would go a long way to dispelling the worries of the twenty-eight Harvard Law School faculty members (*Stage Two*) about the system's unfairness. Columbia University does provide free legal counsel for the accused, and so, now, does Harvard Law School (though not the rest of Harvard). My own university has recently begun to implement a policy offering free legal counsel to both defendants and plaintiffs. I have not been able to find out how many other institutions do this. And some federal grant money is available to support accused students at state universities. But the linchpin of our justice system is legal representation. Perhaps this requirement could be waived for minor offenses for which the likely penalty is alcohol counseling, for example; but in cases where the accused faces expulsion it should be mandatory, no matter what it costs. Colleges and universities have many doctors, nurses, and psychologists on their payrolls. And they do have a staff of lawyers, only not for this purpose. They should enlarge their legal departments to include lawyers at the service of students, for just this sort of problem.

I've said that tribunals are often poorly trained. The best solution to this problem, since membership of tribunals rotates, is *mandatory sexual assault and sexual harassment training for all faculty and administrators*. Such training is now required in most universities, as it is in most businesses. At the University of Chicago, each administrator and faculty member must complete the course online every year. It is not perfect, but it does supply a uniform level of awareness.

The Title IX Process

A welcome element of experienced professionalism is now supplied by the presence of Title IX offices on campuses. Typically they do face-to-face training as well as online training, though not as often. But they also play a crucial role through a strong norm of *mandatory reporting*, which is helping to close the information gap. If a student discloses sexual harassment or assault to any faculty member or administrator, that person is required immediately to inform the Title IX coordinator, giving the complainant's name. The coordinator will then contact the complainant, typically promising her complete confidentiality and anonymity if she requests it. The complainant usually also has decisional autonomy: nothing will be done, and the alleged perpetrator will not be contacted, unless the complainant gives a go-ahead. Meanwhile the coordinator can advise the complainant about how the process works.

Mandatory reporting is controversial. Many have feared that it will discourage disclosures: the minute you open up to someone you trust, the information also goes to someone else you don't know. But on the whole mandatory reporting seems wise. The Title IX staff, in my experience, behave with restraint and professionalism, protecting confidentiality. Once faculty and administrators have experience with the coordinators, my experience is that they do come to trust them. And faculty (and others) are relieved of a huge burden of dealing with the whole of a traumatized person's subsequent life and choices. Faculty usually are not equipped to shoulder this burden, however well-intentioned they are.

The letter by the twenty-eight Harvard Law School professors objected to too much centralized power being vested in the Title IX office, in the scheme at first proposed by Harvard Law School in its attempt to institutionalize the Obama administration standards. The main problem they identified was that the Title IX office did both investigation and adjudication. Their letter was surely correct to say that this setup is very unfair and unwise. Harvard Law School quickly heeded their criticism, separating the two functions. The primary function of the Title IX office should be— and by now for the most part is—investigative and advisory. The tribunals themselves typically consist of faculty, and sometimes administrators, and are constituted according to procedures subject to faculty autonomy and faculty governance. They have many defects, but they are not an alien bureaucracy invading the campus, as the Harvard letter had feared.

We have all learned a great deal from these somewhat painful debates. And progress has been made. Although in some ways DeVos has been a polarizing figure, the Final Rule adopted by the Department of Education under her aegis, thanks to the notice-and-comment process, is debatable but still arguably fair. It seems distinctly superior both to the draft rule and to the standards articulated by the Obama administration. We now need to address the gaps in the process that remain, particularly in the area of legal representation.

PART III

RECALCITRANT CITADELS: THE JUDICIARY, ARTS, SPORTS

Abuses of Power and
Lack of Accountability

At last: Women's complaints of sexual assault and sexual harassment are serious business. Not everywhere and not with everyone—consider the failure to carry out a full investigation of allegations about Brett Kavanaugh during his Senate confirmation hearing, just as in the Clarence Thomas hearings in 1991. But the #MeToo movement has made great strides, shaping a public awareness of the ubiquity of these particular harms to women and the toll they take.

As we've seen, this movement is by no means the creation of celebrity whistleblowers. Ordinary women and their lawyers have been raising their voices for decades, and their efforts have made great progress in shaping a legal culture in which women's allegations can be taken seriously, even if women do not always prevail. The multiplication of voices has begun to create a culture of confidence: if these courageous women are not afraid to come forward, many women have reasoned, then I, too, should be willing to speak out. The whole idea of #MeToo is one of solidarity in a demand for accountability. The hashtag #MeToo gives support to women: you don't have to stand out there alone; you stand with all of us, and we stand with one another in demanding justice.

The culture of #MeToo has been a tonic for our entire society, waking up anyone who will listen. It also brings some problems with it. All too often clear adjudication of women's accusations proves impossible because the alleged wrongs are long in the past. Often the statute of limitations prevents legal action; even where it doesn't, the lapse of years means a dearth of evidence. Usually there is no rape kit, and witnesses, if any, are often gone or have forgotten. This is bad news for the woman who makes the complaint, since it prevents her from pursuing justice. But it is also bad news for the accused, since the informality of these accusations means that there is no due process and, often, no thorough investigation. Even though the woman does not find justice, the man also can lose a great deal—a career, a livelihood, peace of mind—with no recourse. Law, with its safeguards, is replaced by a culture of public shaming that people concerned with justice have endeavored for centuries to replace with the rule of law. Punishment by shame has its defenders today, but it has defects that I'll address more fully in my Conclusion. Law is impartial, as a culture based on shame is not. And we should where possible rely on law to deter bad behavior, not on informal censure.

However, #MeToo also gives a powerful nudge to lawmakers and to the public in general: this behavior is bad, and it should incur some sort of sanction, whether criminal or civil. It also sends a message to institutions: make clear rules, if you haven't done so already, defining acceptable and unacceptable behavior, and enforce them fairly and without exception. By now we know that in well-defined workplaces such as law firms, businesses, and universities, clear institutional rules about sexual harassment and sexual assault have great deterrent and reformative power. In the 1970s, sexual harassment was ubiquitous in all these contexts, and even men who would shrink from such conduct themselves did not have sufficient conviction of its wrongfulness to forbid it to others. Victims had nowhere to turn, and even their just grievance was often seen as mere shrinking-violet weakness. Often, too, even well-intentioned men thought that at least some of this conduct was acceptable: consensual sexual relationships between supervisors and supervisees seemed to many to be "natural" expressions of erotic desire, not damaging abuses of power.

Today, by contrast, clear rules typically define what kinds of relationships are and are not permitted in the workplace, so no fuzzy halo of eros can delude men into continuing what used to be "business as usual." People in general like to conform their behavior to laws and rules—some because they think it is right, others because they fear the consequences.

Rules also educate the next generation. Today, after a generation of life with sexual harassment laws, malefactors in these more clearly rule-governed workplaces tend to be people who have atypical issues with boundaries: psychopaths, substance abusers, and so forth. In general there is a lot of accountability in the rule-governed workplace, and the #MeToo outpouring has given further support to a workplace culture that supports those rules. Even people who wield enormous power—like McDonald's CEO Stephen Easterbrook, fired for a consensual affair with an employee in violation of company policy—are being held to account if they violate clear rules stated publicly for all.[1] While Easterbrook's exit package of around $42 million somewhat undercut this victory for rule-governed justice, and certainly highlighted the pay gap within large corporations, his case shows striking impartiality about the application of workplace rules.

Other domains, however, still resist accountability. In these domains malefactors are neither deterred nor held to account. Law has not yet assumed its deterrent role, inspiring fear, and perhaps that fact makes law fail, as well, to reform more deeply the behavior of people who participate in these spheres. The people I shall study suffer from what we might call inflamed pride, believing that the rules that apply to others do not apply to them. Pride encourages bad behavior. But the lack of institutional clarity encourages pride. Because institutions are weak, the men we'll consider believe with good reason that even if there are rules that in theory apply to them, the rules will not be enforced in their case. These domains of well-protected pride are typically areas in which a few people of unusual talent make a lot of money or wield a lot of power over other people. Because they are hard to replace they are insulated. The CEO has a lofty position but can be easily replaced. The politician has replacements clamoring at the door. Not so the gifted star athlete, the rare artistic performer, or, for institutional reasons, the influential federal judge. Part III focuses on these three citadels of pride, asking what makes them so resistant to accountability and how reform might be achieved.

The three areas are different, but one reform is crucial for all: clear well-defined public rules and established procedures of enforcement.

Together with these reforms goes a culture of whistleblowing, with explicit policies protecting whistleblowers from retaliation. Given our history of lax or non-existent enforcement in these areas, however, the public must also get involved. We are all consumers, with considerable influence over the success of entertainment media, whether in arts or in sports. When bad behavior becomes a liability in the search for profit, the pride-greed nexus can be broken. That means that even when men don't want to reform, consumer behavior can push them in that direction.

In two of my three cases, such remedies should eventually be sufficient. But in one case, college sports, the structure of influences and incentives is so diseased that I believe Division I college football and basketball will have to be totally dismantled—although basketball has already made great strides in the direction of replacing college sports with a minor league system. My contention will be controversial, but here I follow the eloquent arguments of lawyer (and University of Chicago Law School graduate) Adam Silver, commissioner of the NBA, one of the most influential and respected figures in sports.

Men, too, have been victims of sexual assault and harassment by powerful men. And sexual abuse is at times one expression of a broader abuse of power by men who consider themselves above the law. Women have long argued that sexual abuse is primarily about power and its abuse, only secondarily about sex. I agree. The real issues are pride and objectification, not giving others full respect as equal human beings. This failing is culturally linked to the male sex because men dominate in pervasive structures of power, but there is no reason to think it will victimize only the male sex. People in a lower position in the power hierarchy are vulnerable to abuse, and when the powerful male has a same-sex orientation that abuse may be sexualized.

To repeat: this book is, in a sense, about women, but it is really about hierarchies of power and the abuses they engender in people who are raised to think that they are above the law and that other people aren't fully real.

CHAPTER 6

Pride and Privilege

THE FEDERAL JUDICIARY

Complete the following sentence: "Being a judge means . . ."
Judge Alex Kozinski: "never having to say you're sorry."

—Audience question posed to various participants
at Federalist Society event, November 14, 2015

Federal judges have great power over virtually every area of American life. Once appointed and confirmed, they hold their positions for life; they are removed only rarely and with great difficulty. Sometimes they are kept in line by their own ambition: particularly if they aspire to a seat on the Supreme Court, they will be watchful, and susceptible to pressures from political forces and from the public. If that ambition is either absent or derailed (by advancing age, by a reputation for controversial opinions, or just by a lack of fit with the politics of the day), they may come to feel that they can do and say whatever they please.

That was the point of Judge Alex Kozinski's joke at the Federalist Society forum—for it was a joke, although, like so many of his jokes, it revealed a lot about the man. If you're a federal judge, he was saying, your behavior has to be really super-egregious for it to be worth anyone's while to hold you to account. Kozinski's career illustrates the truth in that joke. For many years he got away with truly flagrant bad behavior, thumbing his nose at norms of proper conduct—both sexualized conduct toward female clerks and general harsh and bullying conduct toward all clerks. And even though he was ultimately forced into retirement, he walked away with his full pension and still pursues a lucrative legal practice. He has never acknowledged the harms his behavior inflicted over the years.

I'll focus here on the federal appellate judiciary. State judges have such varying rules of employment that it's hard to generalize about them; some are appointed to life terms, some for a more limited term; many are elected, and a large proportion can at least be recalled by popular vote. Federal judges, by contrast, are always appointed by the president. Some (e.g., judges of the U.S. Tax Court, the U.S. Court of Federal Claims, and other "Article I judges") are specialized and not especially political; ditto "Article IV" judges of territorial courts. The most powerful judges in the federal system are called "Article III judges," after the constitutional provision that describes them; all are appointed by the president and require Senate confirmation. There are three tiers: district judges (673 today), appellate judges (each attached to a circuit; 179 today), and justices of the U.S. Supreme Court (9).

A federal district judgeship is an important job, and yet the job is rather inconspicuous and not an occasion for public status or pride. Supreme Court judges are so few and so constantly in the public eye that it is hard to form generalizations about them or from their behavior to that of other judges. For one thing, their workload is very small compared to that of appellate judges. For another, if they should misbehave, public pressure outside the judiciary itself can be brought to bear—as happened with the resignation of Justice Abe Fortas in 1969, under threat of impeachment for various types of financial corruption.

Appellate judges constitute, so to speak, the sweet spot for misconduct. The appointment is a rare honor, thus an occasion for pride. It comes with enormous influence: most cases never go beyond the appellate tier to the Supreme Court, given how rarely the Supreme Court accepts cases. So most of the way we live under law, in most areas governed by federal law, is crafted at the appellate level. And yet this influence is almost always exercised in obscurity, away from the public eye; so the force of public pressure is rarely brought to bear, even when malefaction becomes known.

Federal Judges and Their Power

Federal appellate judges are virtually always lawyers with law degrees from a distinguished law school. Usually they have practiced law for at least a time. Sometimes they have been academics, although these days publication on any controversial issue is a liability, giving material for opponents to use. Their entire career and life prior to their nomination by the president is very carefully vetted by the president's advisors— although not nearly to the extent that a potential Supreme Court nominee is vetted. Red flags about Alex Kozinski surfaced during his vetting, causing his confirmation hearing to be reopened, but did not ultimately suffice to derail his nomination (although they probably did ensure that he would never get a Supreme Court nod). The confirmation process for appellate judges used to be fairly straightforward, but has become increasingly politicized with time. By now, the whole process is so arduous and time-consuming that people don't want to redo it often.

Once confirmed, the judge holds that position for life "during good behavior," a qualification that means little, given the difficulty of impeaching a judge. Over time seniority typically increases influence; thus, those who have a political or financial stake in the opinions of the judge would almost always prefer that person to remain, quite apart from the difficulty of removal and the further difficulty of confirming someone new. This makes the judge unlike most CEOs, who can be here one day, gone the next. Investors want the company to do well, and they know that the company transcends any individual; appellate judges, by contrast, are often valued for their individual contributions. Life tenure increases the political stakes for the appointing party or faction; once they get a suitable judge seated they don't want to yield, and will seek to rebut any allegations, whether during the confirmation process or later. At times, judges who are not doing their job, for whatever reason, can be quietly persuaded to retire, especially since after serving for ten years they get their full salary for life (at the highest level reached), provided the total of their age and their years of service is at least eighty.[1] This

otherwise excellent arrangement has created a loophole for judicial misconduct, a lucrative exit option for a judge facing charges.

Academics, too, are protected, and the institution of tenure, in the
United States,[2] makes it difficult to get rid of any individual professor.
However, even the most senior academic is subject to annual review of
both publication and teaching, and deans have a host of strategies to
lure the underperforming into retirement. Moreover, they are peers of
all other faculty at their rank, and nobody is indispensable. Nor do they
represent powerful political or financial interests, at least not directly,
and they are appointed and tenured through a process of peer review that
is at least supposed to insulate the appointment from political pressures.
Furthermore, every day they are exposed to peer critique from their colleagues and from the community of scholars, which makes it harder, at
least, to get a swelled head. By contrast, judicial appellate circuits don't
typically meet together to exchange criticism; often the judges sit in different cities. The Seventh Circuit, sitting in Chicago, and containing
a significant proportion of academics (still teaching regularly, in some
cases), has developed habits of collegiality and critical exchange that are
good models (generally unrealized[3]) for the federal judiciary as a whole.

Appellate judges also have a constant succession of superbly talented
underlings: judicial clerks. Federal appellate judges typically have two
clerks per year. The job of judicial clerk (or "chambers judicial clerk"
as distinct from staff clerks) is all about helping the judge. Clerking is
supposed to teach a young lawyer useful skills, and a federal appellate clerkship is certainly reputation-enhancing, whether it leads on
to a career-making Supreme Court clerkship or to other types of legal
employment. (Clerkships are attractive to hiring committees at large
law firms.) But it is a rare judge who focuses on helping clerks develop
their talents. Some do, and they should be commended. And some judges
really don't want clerks to do work that they think they ought to do
themselves, such as drafting opinions. But today it is a fact that clerks
write virtually all draft opinions for most appellate judges and almost all
Supreme Court justices. They don't simply plug in citations, they write
the argument—typically after some conversation with the judge, and

aimed at expressing the judge's view, not their own view—but the writing is usually theirs. Thousands of bright law students apply for these jobs every year. What could contribute more to judges' sense of superiority and immunity than to know that the best and brightest of current law school graduates are working night and day (often the hours are very long), and queuing up eagerly for the next round, to do work that you do not wish to do, although you could and probably should?

Here is a large difference from the academy. Academics have graduate students, but those students are supposed to be developing the capacity to do their own independent work, and the supervisor is supposed to focus on mentoring them and, later, helping them get jobs. Occasionally, academics may be in a position to hire a research assistant, and that paid researcher would indeed work for the professor, but that role, billed by the hour, is understood to be totally distinct from the role of pursuing a PhD, even if sometimes the same person might play both roles, particularly for temporary summer money. Most PhD students never serve as RAs, and many RAs are not PhD students. PhD students never work very long at an RA job, because they are receiving funding for pursuing their own work and are usually prohibited from taking much other employment. Academics may have research memos from RAs that help them draft their chapters. But if they really use an entire draft of an RA's memo they are expected to make that RA a co-author. Judicial clerks never get co-author credit, and yet they are usually, in fact, the sole authors, with the judge a helpful advisor.

The power differential between judges and clerks is vast. The judge has enormous power over the course of the clerk's entire subsequent career. Even if law clerks go on to pursue a career in the legal academy, rather than in legal practice, and are being evaluated to some extent on the basis of their own publications, the law school hiring committee would be sure to phone, for a reference, the judge for whom each person clerked. A bad reference would be damaging. Some judges, moreover, have more power than others: those with a national reputation, or those known as "feeder judges," appellate judges who are trusted by one or more Supreme Court justice and therefore more able than others to land coveted Supreme

Court clerkships for their own clerks. As Alex Kozinski himself wrote, "Judge and law clerk are in fact tethered together by an invisible cord for the rest of their mutual careers."[4] This romantic statement, however, implies mutuality and reciprocity. In the judge-clerk relationship there is in fact no reciprocity, since the judge is utterly free to speak about the clerk, but the clerk is bound for life by a stringent code of confidentiality. Here is another large difference from the academy, where current and former PhD candidates have no duty of confidentiality, and where dependence on a supervisor is short-lived: afterward, the supervisor is usually not even permitted to act as a reference for tenure or promotion.

"Although the Code of Conduct does not define confidential information, the term generally includes any information you receive through your clerkship that is not part of the public record." So states the official code of ethics for federal judicial clerks.[5] Clerks are forbidden to disclose any such information, whether to the public or to "family, friends, and former colleagues," and whether in a signed or in an anonymous communication, unless the judge for whom they clerked explicitly authorizes the disclosure. "This obligation *continues* after your court service concludes." Clerks who have later leaked gossipy information about a judge's chambers have been publicly castigated, so the looseness of the code's language has been understood to forbid virtually all reporting on the character and comportment of a judge. Whereas the clerk can be held to account in future references for the smallest lapse, a judge's lapses, it would appear, must be shrouded in total darkness. Being a judge really does seem to mean never having to say you're sorry. As we'll see, the loose language has now been reinterpreted. For a long time, however, it gave Kozinski an immunity that he wore with glee.

Inadequate Rules of Conduct

Confusion about rules was not limited to the code for judicial clerks. The codes governing judges were also grossly inadequate. As discussed in Chapter 5, large workplaces today in business and the academy have developed clear public rules governing sexual conduct. They not only forbid sexual assault and sexual harassment; they also define certain types of sexual relationships as inappropriate—typically all relationships with a supervisor-supervisee structure. Some codes say only that such relationships are unwise. Far better are rules that simply don't permit them. This clarity may rule out many innocuous relationships, but really, relationships with a clear power differential are rarely innocuous. They involve covert pressure—whether to enter or not to terminate the relationship. They also raise issues of favoritism and fairness that affect other employees. Clear rules against such relationships protect workplace fairness and avoid endless bickering about welcomeness and unwelcomeness in the aftermath of a broken relationship.

As to the legitimate concern about forbidding many good relationships: people of good will can usually find a way to accommodate their conduct to fit the rules. For CEOs, such accommodation is probably impossible, since they are the "supervisor" of all employees. But usually there can be a change of supervisors, and procedures ensuring that the more senior party does not participate in decisions about the more junior party's future. Good arrangements require transparency. (Unfortunately many workplace relationships are adulterous, and the related secrecy is a major source of rule violation.)

As Chapter 5 argued, workplace harassment is not "natural." It is a cultural product, and this means that it can be deterred by clear rules. Sexual harassment has proven to be a highly deterrable offense. People fear career sanctions, and most of them also want to do the right thing. Some combination of these motives produces pretty good results in cases where the rules are clear and public.

No such clarity existed in the federal judiciary until very recently. Federal judges are accountable to the "Code of Conduct for United States Judges" (which I'll call "Code for Judges") and also to the "Rules for Judicial Conduct and Judicial Disability Proceedings" (JCJD), the latter being a mechanism for filing complaints against a judge and also for complaining that a judge is unable to discharge his or her duties. Prior to March 2019, neither of these codes mentioned workplace sexual harassment. The Code for Judges instructed judges to "act at all times in a manner that promotes public confidence in the integrity and impartiality of the judiciary" and to avoid "all impropriety and appearance of impropriety." It did not enumerate the acts that could violate these provisions. Both the JCJD and a related Code for Employees did list examples, but those did not include sexual misconduct; the focus was entirely on nepotism and unjust enrichment.[6]

Thus it was left to individual judges to ask themselves whether sexual overtures, showing pornography to clerks, making sexual remarks, sending erotic emails, or bullying clerks in other ways constituted impropriety. Although by the 1990s one might have hoped that most judges would reason that such behavior was indeed improper, and surely many did, the laxness of the rules gave encouragement to bad behavior. It was all too easy to think, "I can get away with this"—as was very much the case in the career of one judge who did get away with a lot of bad behavior over the years, only to face, very late in his career, a punishment that remains, today, light and incomplete.

A Mephistophelean Career

Born in Bucharest, Romania, in 1950 to a Jewish family, Alex Kozinski came to the United States at the age of only twelve.[7] He still speaks with a trace of a foreign accent, and seems to enjoy this as an element of his flamboyant persona. After getting a BA in economics and a JD, both at UCLA, he clerked for both Anthony Kennedy (when Kennedy was a judge on the Ninth Circuit Court of Appeals) in 1975–76 and then on the Supreme Court, for Chief Justice Warren Burger in 1976–77. After a couple of years in private practice, he went to work in the Reagan administration in the Office of Legal Counsel, and, in 1981–82, as special counsel to the U.S. Merit Systems Protection Board—during which appointment he helped staff rewrite the firing of a mining whistleblower so that it would pass legal scrutiny[8]—an incident that surfaced later, during his confirmation hearing for the Ninth Circuit. He served as a judge on the U.S.

Claims Court from 1982 to 1985.[9] At that point President Reagan nominated Kozinski to fill a new seat on the Ninth Circuit Court of Appeals, where he served from 1985 to 2017, including a seven-year period as chief judge. At the time of his confirmation he was one of the youngest appellate judges in the United States, a rising star.

Kozinski ascended rapidly to the judicial heights, becoming one of the nation's most famous and admired appellate judges, a "feeder judge" for the Supreme Court, a maker or breaker of young careers. Kozinski dazzled many by his intellect, although—unlike his maverick libertarian counterpart Judge Richard Posner of the Seventh Circuit—Kozinski wrote no books and few articles, and his reputation for brilliance has never really been tested by the give-and-take of rigorous academic argument. (Judges have it easy that way, and all too often acquire an unearned confidence in their intellectual superiority.) Kozinski has also dazzled many by his charm. Clever, witty, outrageous, and frequently obscene, he has a way of turning all eyes in his direction. Running through the jovial banter, however, is a streak of cruelty. Meeting him for the first time in spring 2014, at a lecture of mine at UCLA (with his reputation preceding him),[10] I thought he was rather like what Goethe created in the character of Mephistopheles in *Faust*: a dangerous figure, a spirit of denial ("I am the spirit who always negates"), but at the same time a witty subversive spirit with a delight in outrageousness that draws some people even while it repels others. (And of course Mephistopheles often both attracts and repels the same people—including, clearly, Goethe himself.) Above all, Mephistopheles is a spirit whose boundless self-involvement leaves no place for compassion or gentleness.

Early in Kozinski's career, his bad conduct as a boss was already widely known. At the time of his confirmation to the Ninth Circuit, he was initially approved rapidly by the Senate Judiciary Committee, but the hearing was then reopened—a very unusual event—in response both to revelation of the whistleblower issue and to affidavits from former OSC employees, who said Kozinski was "harsh, cruel, demeaning, sadistic, disingenuous and without compassion."[11] This is extraordinarily strong language to use of any boss, but it was not a wake-up call for Kozinski, who, by a flood of accounts, continued to behave like that throughout his judicial career, unleashed by his subsequent narrow confirmation from the constraint of accountability to any employees (such as those at OSC) who were not wholly dependent upon him for their future, as judicial clerks typically are. It's important to bear in mind that Kozinski was an equal-opportunity abuser, in a sense—even though, given his virtual obsession with matters sexual, his cruelty took, very often, an anti-woman turn.

Kozinski's obsession with himself as a sexual being was evident early in his career. Weirdly for an aspiring leader of the law (well, he was only eighteen), he became a contestant on the TV show *The Dating Game*, competing against David Lander, the actor who played Squiggy on *Laverne & Shirley*, in a segment that originally aired on Thanksgiving Day 1968. (The segment is preserved and can be viewed on YouTube: https://www.youtube.com/watch?v=OdjCdbGucCU). Kozinski, "Bachelor Number Two," defeats Squiggy by flaunting his foreign accent (it sounds like a Dracula imitation, except that it's real) and using poetic phrases ("flower of my heart") that sound like they come from an old vampire movie. Having won the date with Rita, he goes over and kisses her very aggressively on the mouth, grabbing the back of her neck in a pretty ominous fashion. Maybe it was supposed to be romantic, of a piece with his corny rhetoric. Today it just seems creepy, and an omen.

As time went on, Kozinski kept seizing opportunities to proclaim his sexual superiority, albeit in a less Transylvanian and more jocular style, with a sui generis type of narcissistic self-deprecation. A "humorous" blog called *Underneath Their Robes*, which retails gossip about the federal judiciary, runs an ongoing feature called "Hotties of the Federal Judiciary."[12] Judges who turn up there are typically quite embarrassed, though no doubt some are also secretly flattered. Self-nomination would be unthinkable for, let's say, all but one—who wrote to the blog's letters column in June 2004, nominating himself for the contest to select male "superhotties." It's a long letter, with a long list of quasi-jocular qualifications, so a brief extract must suffice:

Dear A3G [the abbreviation for "Article III Groupie," the editor's pseudonym]:

I must say that I'm severely disappointed in the slate of candidates you have fielded for your Judicial Hottie contest. While I think the list of female candidates is excellent, the list of male candidates is, frankly, lacking. And what it's lacking is me.

Sure, John Roberts and Jeff Sutton are young and extremely handsome, but so what? I have it on very good authority that discerning females and gay men find graying, pudgy, middle-aged men with an accent close to Gov. Schwarzenegger's almost totally irresistible.

So I nominate myself . . . Here are the arguments in support of my nomination.

*I am the only Article III judge to have appeared on the Dating Game— and I was on twice. I even won once, and I have the tape to prove it.

*I had my own photo-spread in George Magazine, with lots of sexy pictures of me jumping. This was a few years back, but I've only gotten cuter with age.[13]

And so it continues, for two full pages. Of course it is funny—sort of. And it is intended as a joke—sort of. But there is something off about going to such public lengths to proclaim one's sexual superiority, even in jest, and that "offness" is characteristic of the sort of person described by the OSC employees, for whom nobody else is fully real. A person of extreme pride in Dante's exact sense.

The sexualization of everything continued. Here is how a former clerk (for a different judge), the writer Dahlia Lithwick, describes her first meeting with Kozinski in 1996 at an orientation for new clerks:

One of my co-clerks and I were introduced to the already legendary, lifetime-tenured young judge at a reception, and we talked for a while. I cannot recall what we talked about. I remember only feeling quite small and very dirty. Without my prompting, my former co-clerk described this interaction in an email to me this week: "He completely ignored me and appeared to be undressing you with his eyes," he wrote. "I had never seen anyone ogle another person like that and still have not seen anything like it. Was so uncomfortable to watch, and I wasn't even the object of the stare."[14]

A few weeks later, Lithwick phoned Kozinski's chambers to speak to one of his clerks about a social plan. Kozinski himself answered. He asked where Lithwick was. She said in her hotel room. He then said, "What are you wearing?" She reported this to her judge, who was "horrified"—but took no action.

Multiply this incident a hundred times, add some unwanted touchings (including breast-groping and forcible kissing); a chambers suffused with gratuitous sexual joking and frequent requests to look at pornography; add the "Easy Rider gag list," an email list sent to clerks, former clerks, and others, containing jokes that Kozinski liked, a large proportion sexual and quite a number cruel; and add to all that frequent outbursts asserting his total control of every aspect of his clerks' lives—and you have the flagrant but never-acted-on backstory of Kozinski's judicial career. His misbehavior was truly notorious. Some law schools and many more individual professors refused to recommend women to his chambers. But his power continued unchecked, and he had a steady stream of victims. It's an understatement to say that both seriousness and pervasiveness, the two indicia of a hostile environment, were amply demonstrated.

Kozinski was justly admired as a judge. His national reputation for brilliance was not unearned though it was helped along by his flamboyance, which made the well-known legal website *Above the Law* pay a lot of attention to him, even going along with some of his misogynistic humor. (Kathryn Rubino, the editor who succeeded David Lat, later deplored the blog's "tendencies toward idolization," noting, "Time has shown that there was a lot of darkness under the 'playful' personality Kozinski used."[15]) On the whole, he can be categorized as a libertarian. He consistently defended a broad view of expressive and artistic liberty, sometimes stirring up controversy (as with his defense, in dissent, of the speech rights of anti-abortion activists, and as, in another dissent, his attempt to narrow the definition of "true threats" for which a person could be held legally liable), but sometimes pleasing artists by defending artistic liberty against a broad understanding of intellectual property rights, in cases involving parody and satire. He influentially argued that commercial speech should be given the same protection as political speech, and wrote an article to that effect.[16] (This much-cited article is one main source of his reputation as pro-business.)

In criminal cases he sometimes stood up for the underdog: he found, for example, that the indiscriminate practice of shackling pretrial prisoners is a constitutional violation. On the death penalty he issued an odd and equivocal dissenting opinion, saying that the use of a cocktail of lethal chemicals was simply an attempt to mask the brutality of the death penalty, and that if we are to use the death penalty we ought to show clearly, as by use of a firing squad, the cruelty inherent in the practice. It is not clear in which direction he really was urging the law to go. Here and elsewhere, he enjoyed the role of unpredictable maverick.

It is therefore not surprising that a bright young clerk such as Brett Kavanaugh would admire Kozinski and seek to remain loyal to him, even have sympathy with him in his disgrace. It is, however, totally incredible that Kavanaugh had never heard of any of Kozinski's misbehavior to women—as Kavanaugh stated under oath in his Supreme Court confirmation hearing. Kavanaugh could have said many things, including "We were all powerless and under his control," and/or "I believe that my duty of confidentiality bars me from speaking further about his conduct." The fact that Kavanaugh did not make one of these plausible replies but chose the path of "see no evil" is regrettable, and it undermines his credibility with respect to everything else he said.[17]

There were warnings that Kozinski might, after all, not be above the rules. In 2008, the *Los Angeles Times* revealed that a personal file server that Kozinski believed to be private was, in fact, accessible to the public if a person knew where to search.[18] The folder, titled "stuff," contained sexually explicit images, including one of cows with women's faces, and another of a half-naked man "cavorting with a sexually aroused farm animal."[19] Kozinski promptly demanded an investigation of himself, and according to procedure, the job was performed by a different circuit. The Third Circuit report accepted Kozinski's disclaimer that he believed he had blocked all public access to the site, and acknowledged his apology, but nonetheless admonished him for his carelessness, noting that his conduct did not meet the high standard demanded of judges. Although Kozinski was not further disciplined, the episode was widely publicized and brought him considerable public shame. Still, it could have seemed a sign of his power that the Third Circuit stopped at a mild admonition; so it seems that Kozinski was not warned.

Another warning sign might have been the fact that Kozinski himself, as chief judge, was called on to investigate complaints against Montana federal District Court judge Richard Cebull, who had sent hundreds of racist and misogynistic emails (one of which "joked" that Barack Obama was the product of sex between his mother and a dog). Here complaining witnesses did step forward, producing evidence. The five-judge panel headed by Kozinski disciplined Cebull but did not remove him; at Kozinski's urging, most of the proceedings were kept confidential.[20] But here Kozinski controlled the outcome; thus, Kozinski was not warned. And indeed he had reason to feel safe. After all, everyone knew what Kozinski was doing and nobody did anything about it. He was a somebody, whereas Cebull was a nobody. In particular no clerk came forward to complain, although so many had cause for complaint. What greater sign could there be than that of his total control of his clerks, past and present?

On December 8, 2017, the floodgates opened. Six women, all former clerks or externs, came forward by name to the *Washington Post* with stories of Kozinski's harassment, followed by nine more a few days later.[21] The group was led by Heidi Bond, a former Kozinski clerk and now a writer of historical romances under the pseudonym Courtney Milan. Ironically it was by driving women such as Milan and Lithwick

away from careers in law that Kozinski manufactured his own down-
fall. Many other women came forward anonymously. Bond (Milan)
wrote extensively about both her own experience and that of others, giving detailed examples of the pornography he forced clerks to examine,
his explicit and suggestive sexual conversations, and the now-infamous
jokes on the "gag list" emails.[22] Other notable articles were those by Lithwick and Katherine Ku.[23] All told the same story of unwanted sexualization of everything, forced sexual conversation, occasional groping, and
humiliation through making women look at and discuss pornography—
all in the context of a broader program of total control and domination,
in which a clerk's duty of nondisclosure was warped into a duty of total
loyalty to Kozinski himself. (To Bond: "I control what you read, what
you write, what you eat. You don't sleep if I say so. You don't shit unless
I say so. Do you understand?")[24]

Kozinski initially contested the veracity of the women's stories through
his lawyer—ironically the famous feminist law professor Susan Estrich,
one of the architects of rape law reform. But the way he did it was to
express regret that his "unusual sense of humor" had been misunderstood. He also expressed defiance, telling the *Los Angeles Times*, after
the first set of accusations was published, "If that is all they are able to
dredge up after 35 years, I am not too worried." After the second set
of accusations, further anonymous accusations and detailed writing by
Bond and Lithwick, however, matters quickly took a different course.
Judge Sidney Thomas, chief judge of the Ninth Circuit, called for an
investigation into Kozinski's conduct and asked Chief Justice Roberts to
assign the investigation, as is usual, to the judicial council of another circuit.[25] The chief justice agreed, choosing the Second Circuit on December 15, 2017.[26] Before the inquiry could begin, however, on December
18, Kozinski announced his retirement effective immediately; since the
judicial council no longer had jurisdiction over him, the complaint was
dismissed, though its gravity was noted.

By retiring quickly, Kozinski kept his full pension, including full salary for life. He also probably deterred others from coming forward, since
they could have little to gain once official investigations were closed. He

also avoided being disbarred. Just one day after announcing his retirement, on December 19, Kozinski reactivated his California bar status.
(Someone who voluntarily becomes "inactive" can reactivate at any
time so long as dues are paid.) The "good character" requirement for
bar membership has always been a weak one, but here, because of the
technical ease of reactivation, there was apparently no deliberation at all
prior to reactivation, nor has Kozinski faced formal disciplinary action
since—although we cannot be sure because California's Rules of the
State Bar make all proceedings related to an attorney's moral character
confidential. He enjoys a lucrative legal practice.

By July 2018, Kozinski was back in the public spotlight, granting interviews and publishing a tribute to Supreme Court Justice Anthony Kennedy
on the occasion of his retirement. One of his early accusers, law professor
Emily Murphy (on the faculty at the University of California, Hastings
College of Law), said "I worry that it signals to women that our profession
doesn't actually care about harassment. And it substantiates a concern
that several of us had after he resigned—that in the absence of an investigation or formal process, it would be easier to downplay his conduct and
rehabilitate him from something we never got to the bottom of."[27]

The Kozinski case shows us several things about the federal judiciary
that should make us very uneasy. First, his case is an outlier in terms of
the sheer number of harassed clerks (and remember that male clerks also
suffered from bullying and from an enforced atmosphere of misogyny
that many surely deplored). So the case shows, basically, that even an
egregious abuser can survive for twenty years if he is bright, flamboyant, well-connected, and shameless. It also shows structural weaknesses:
nothing in the institution's codes of conduct came to the women's aid,
and the duty of confidentiality, as then interpreted, worked against them.
It also shows the ease with which an accused judge can duck formal
proceedings by choosing retirement—at which point similar structural
weaknesses in bar rules ensure him an ongoing livelihood (in addition to
full retirement benefits).

The case invites us to imagine that many malefactors less shameless and more selective in their abuse may be lurking in the shadows,

unpunished and undeterred. Indeed we know this anyway, because of the very short list of federal judges who have faced formal complaints that even a very diligent inquiry unearths: no other appellate judge, and only five district court judges—all of whom escaped sanctions by choosing to retire.[28]

Justice Roberts Calls for Reform

In the wake of the Kozinski resignation, Chief Justice John Roberts called for reform and took action. In his 2017 year-end report (only two days after Kozinski announced his resignation), Roberts announced that the "judiciary will begin 2018 by undertaking a careful evaluation of whether its standards of conduct and its procedures for investigating and correcting inappropriate behavior are adequate to ensure an exemplary workplace for every judge and every court employee."[29] He established a bipartisan commission to study the relevant codes and to recommend changes. The group reported back six months later, recommending numerous reforms. On March 12, 2019, some of their recommendations were adopted in the relevant codes.

The working group found that the federal judiciary has a harassment problem.[30] The group did not limit its analysis to sexual harassment, but that was its primary emphasis throughout. It pointed out features of the judicial workplace that encourage underreporting, especially the asymmetry of power between judges and clerks and the lifelong dependence of the latter on the former. Another factor is the short tenure of clerkships: the group reasoned that longer job tenure often makes employees more comfortable in submitting complaints. It recommended changes in three areas: (1) substantive standards, (2) complaint procedures, and (3) ex ante education to prevent harassment. In the first area, it made explicit a judge's duty not to "make, nor in any way tolerate, conduct and statements that constitute harassment or other forms of bullying, including on the basis of race, color, religion, sex, national origin, age, disability, sexual orientation, and gender identity."

Judges also have an affirmative duty to combat harassment in the judicial workplace, especially if it stems from other judges on the court. The group emphasized that while the relationship between judges and clerks is strong, stamping out harassment would only strengthen those relationships. On procedure, the group recommended making it clear that confidentiality requirements do not apply "to reporting or disclosing judicial misconduct." It also recognized the need for more informal grievance procedures in addition to formal ones, including teams of employees who can advise other employees on how to handle specific problems they have, and methods to track, mitigate, and prevent instances of harassment. Finally the group recommended mandatory workplace standards training similar to those in existence in many other workplaces, including "bystander intervention training." Given the special role played by chief judges in setting the tone for the workplace, they also recommended special training for chief judges.

These recommendations have been implemented, including the important conduct exception to the duty of confidentiality. One important further change is the statement that a failure to report another judge's misconduct is itself judicial misconduct. It's amazing, and a clear sign of judicial pride, that it has taken so long to move the federal judiciary into the modern workplace world, and Chief Justice Roberts is to be applauded for having insisted on reform—although it should not have taken a major embarrassment to make these obvious changes.

The Reinhardt Scandal

Sexual abuse knows no politics. On March 29, 2018, Judge Stephen Reinhardt of the Ninth Circuit Court of Appeals, a beloved "liberal lion," died of a heart attack. A little less than two years after his death, his ugly career as a sexual harasser and all-purpose misogynist emerged into public view, when a former clerk, Olivia Warren, testified before the Subcommittee on Courts, Intellectual Property, and the Internet of the House Judiciary Committee, which was holding hearings on protecting federal judiciary employees from sexual harassment and work-place misconduct. Warren's testimony about her experience of sexual harassment is on record in a report from that committee.[31] Because Reinhardt died during Warren's clerkship year, her attempt to file a for-mal complaint with the Office of Judicial Integrity went nowhere, and her formal complaint to Harvard Law School, her alma mater, to take up the matter didn't achieve any result either, so far as she was aware. Her story, like Kozinski's, opened up a can of worms as confirmations piled up, and seventy of Reinhardt's former clerks signed an open letter asking for further reforms.[32] It's clear that Reinhardt, like Kozinski, had a long history of making ugly and demeaning sexualized comments to and about women.

The details are depressingly similar, though in detail rather different. Although, as Tolstoy says, each unhappy family is unhappy in its own way, rehearsing all the details of Reinhardt's special type of harassment would shed no further light on our topic. Basically, he constantly made sexualized comments about women's bodies, particularly when hiring new clerks, rating them by their photos, often denigrating those he found unattractive. Since Warren was among those, she was subjected to a con-stant diet of insults directed at both her and her husband, who must, Reinhardt said, be either a wimp or gay to stay with her and who surely would be unable to perform sexually. He defended Judge Kozinski, Har-vey Weinstein, and other men accused of sexual misconduct. He attacked feminists using pejorative terms for lesbians. And so on.

In her testimony, Warren expressed skepticism that the reforms insti-tuted by Chief Justice Roberts would solve the problem of harassment in the federal judiciary: she thought there was too little protection for whistleblower confidentiality. She also thought that elite law schools too rarely warn young potential clerks about abuses of power. After her testimony, a large group of law student organizations at Yale, Harvard, and Stanford law schools proposed some additional reforms, urging the centralization of complaints in the Office of Judicial Integrity (where Warren had attempted to complain to no avail).[33] Although a centralized approach might perform better than the current piecemeal approach, this remedy is too weak, I believe, for the deep problems endemic to the entire institution of the clerkship.

The Post-Reform Judiciary

Pride is sticky. The human and structural features that have for a long time made the judiciary virtually above the law remain in place, so the question is whether the welcome reforms will have the desired effect. Social change is surely important: the #MeToo movement, combined with Kozinski's fall, should at least put future Kozinskis on notice that they can't assume they will never have to say they are sorry. The publicity accorded Judge Reinhardt's misdeeds should further reinforce that message. There is reason to hope that a new generation of judges will be educated differently and, insofar as they are not educated, will at least be deterred.

The stickiest point remains the intimate nature of the judge-clerk relationship. In a law firm, typically no young associate works all the time for the same partner. Rotation and shared accountability promote transparency. In the academy, the PhD supervisor has great asymmetrical power—for about three years. But then as time goes on post-PhD, the young scholar publishes her own work and thus becomes ever more independent of the mentor's favor. This is never the case for the former clerk who goes on to firm work. (Lawyers in firms have by and large not revealed their experience with Kozinski.[34]) In addition, many academic departments have opened up the supervision process by having dissertation committees of three or more members who are to some extent equals in authority and who all meet regularly with the candidate. Accountability is spread around, making it more likely that complaints will be heard.

To me, as an outsider who often recommends law students for clerkships, this seems like a good direction for the job of judicial clerk to take. A rotation among three judges over the course of the year or, alternately, a three-judge committee agreeing to divide the services of all their clerks in some mutually agreeable way, would greatly improve transparency and pierce the veil of secrecy. But I am realistic: nobody will go for this solution. There is such a romanticization of the judge-clerk relationship, and such an investment in the dubious idea that it has life-long educational benefits, that such a radical reform will not fly. The most in that direction that could be feasible would be to have the chief judge appoint to each clerk one or two "secondary judges" in addition to the primary (hiring) judge, who would have a secondary function supervising the clerk's work and thus would be potential referees in the future. Or, a less labor-intensive alternative, the chief judge could appoint one or two judges each year to play the role of "clerkship advisors," people to whom clerks are specifically directed to turn with labor-related issues. All of these changes are more feasible in circuits like the Seventh, which is geographically concentrated. Each circuit probably needs to approach the issue in a way that suits its own size, geography, and history.

Whatever the merit and fate of these suggestions, judges should not congratulate themselves on solving the sexual harassment problem. Despite laudable reform efforts, the basic structures are still in place that make judicial pride lead to abuse.

On December 9, 2019, Alex Kozinski returned to the circuit he had dishonored, making an oral argument before the circuit in a copyright case.[35]

CHAPTER 7

Narcissism and Impunity

THE PERFORMING ARTS

A young violin student is asked: If you could save just one person, who would it be—the conductor, or the violinist's own mother. "If you pick your mother," says the conductor, "you will walk out this door and never see me again. If you pick me, you will close the door, step into this house, and be with me forever."

—Violinist Albin Ifsich, of a long-ago

encounter with conductor James Levine[1]

Harvey Weinstein, Bill Cosby, James Levine, Plácido Domingo: What do these figures have in common? All wielded great power in the world of the performing arts. All used that power to abuse women (or, in Levine's case, teenage men). All are now disgraced—each through an outpouring of victim narratives whose cumulative weight has convinced management to terminate their contracts (or, in Weinstein's case, to back away from his failing production company). Lest we feel reassured that justice and the voices of the vulnerable have triumphed, however, we observe one further commonality: all are at the end of their careers anyway. Weinstein, though only sixty-eight, is ill and can barely walk; Cosby, eighty-three, is blind and sick, his TV career long behind him; Levine, seventy-seven, had reached a point of being virtually unable to conduct on account of Parkinson's disease, before management at the Metropolitan Opera decided to believe the rumors about him that had been ubiquitous since the early

1980s. Domingo is the most complex: eighty, physically vigorous, and singing well at an age that continues to astound audiences and critics, he still strikes the public (and employers) as vulnerable just because we all know his singing career must end soon, even if we don't know precisely when. But at the same time, significantly, being the most vigorous he is also the least disgraced, still able to get a thirty-minute standing ovation in Europe, despite the termination of all his U.S. contracts.[2] In each case, credible reports about these men's sexual predation circulated for years—in Cosby's case backed up by civil lawsuits and an infamous deposition. And yet society somehow ignored the voices of victims—until the perpetrators were old, sick, unable to dazzle us, and, significantly, unable to make money for others through their huge talents. Their current disgrace therefore gives no reason for optimism: it does not show that people with their type of power are no longer above the law. They were considered expendable because they were expendable already. Younger figures too have fallen, but none, so far as I can think, with the star status and field-defining power of these four. Can't we do better, insulating people in the arts against the abuse of big stars before they are about to fall?

All my case studies, like the case of Alex Kozinski, discussed in Chapter 6, will document a particular type of deformed pride—the pride of people who think that their ability to dazzle others puts them above society's rules and even laws. Unlike Kozinski, however, these distinguished artists show us something profoundly sad about human beings: that deep and subtle insight, and the ability to illuminate our lives in areas of the most profound human importance, can coexist with a warped, narcissistic, and utterly compassionless character. If Alex Kozinski dropped off the face of the earth, we would probably not feel that our world was lacking in any profound insight that he supplied. James Levine and Plácido Domingo, by contrast, contribute such beauty and illumination to our world that we must also reckon with the legacy of their work, once we acknowledge their diseased treatment of others.

Pride and Artistic Talent

Performing arts are seductive; passion is central to their content and mode of influence. Because passions are everywhere in theater, opera, and even symphonic music, it is easy for corrupt uses of these passions to creep in. "You're too stiff. Show me that you really feel the part. Let it all out." And because the performing arts use the body to express passion, the body is hard to leave out of the whole employment relationship.

In arts teaching, coaching, and, often, directing, bodily touching— usually off-limits in law firms and academic classrooms—is ubiquitous, necessary, and usually good. Singing teachers, for example, often have to put their hands on the student's back, chest, and jaw. Dance teachers always touch legs, arms, backs. Moreover, the intimacy of what is explored in performing art means that there are very proper uses of *solitude à deux* for teacher and pupil. If all singing lessons were in a group setting, much less would be learned, and this is also the case for instrumental music.

Acting typically combines various types of boundary-crossing. Scenes are often rehearsed by just two people before they are presented to the group. Scenes may, and often do, include various forms of touching, as suggested by the script. And later on the director or coach may step in, perhaps playing bits of the scene with one or the other actor, or goading them both to more authentic expression. And there is also emotional boundary-crossing: you often have to act erotic love, or sexual attraction, or other complicated passions.

Add to this a standard way of teaching acting since the early days of the Group Theater in the United States, channeling Konstantin Stanislavski (highly selectively). Namely, the way of achieving authenticity as an actor is to use various pieces of emotional memory from your own life, so that you are showing what, at that moment, you are yourself really feeling on the basis of such memories. This means that a teacher will feel entitled to try to summon up real emotions of various kinds in the performer, on the hypothesis (often false) that such emotions, once they have been displayed toward the teacher in a class, will be available for use henceforth where appropriate in a scene.

I vividly recall being humiliated in front of my NYU class by a very famous acting teacher (whose origins were in the Group Theatre). I got angry, and (encouraged by the overall atmosphere he created in the classroom) I slapped him in the face. He heralded my reaction as a breakthrough in my development as an actress. Unsurprisingly, this authentic expression of emotion was not deposited in my expressive repertoire. I know of no case in which this particular teacher used erotic seduction to "achieve" a similar "breakthrough," but the theory, at any rate, supported such teaching. And if the teacher didn't try to seduce you, your fellow actor usually would. Since we all believed that acting was a piece of your reality, we were encouraged to believe that the only way to play an erotic scene was to develop erotic feelings for your scene-mate. In those days (the late 1960s), many also thought that drug use was a passport to greater authenticity, and I have been an interested observer of whose careers in my cohort lasted and whose didn't: typically the heaviest drug users are unknown today.

There were dissenters. Another equally famous acting teacher at NYU was shocked at the excesses of soi-disant realism in our work. In one scene of jealousy, my scene partner internalized the mindset of the domestic abuser so well that he twisted and badly bruised my arm. I thought then that this was cool, a mark of our authenticity. Seeing my bruises, this teacher reproved us in the sternest possible terms. Some lines must never be crossed, he said. His own method of freeing our bodies, far more congenial to me, and I think far more compatible with ethical norms, was to have us rehearse a scene from Shakespeare, for example, while galloping around the room like horses. We were so focused on strenuous activity that we could not freeze up, and our voices rang out in a new way. But to the Group Theatre guy this was heresy and falseness. The Group Theatre attitude and similar attitudes greatly increase actors' vulnerability to abuse even today.

This attitude, or myth, is much less present in the world of classical music, but insofar as opera is merging into or at least requiring acting, in this era of HD productions, sometimes the myths of the acting profession creep in.

Abusers are often shielded not only by this "myth of authenticity," but by another myth, which pervades all the performing arts, and indeed all the other arts as well. This is an age-old myth, at least as old as Romanticism. The myth is that the constraint of usual social norms and rules is bad for artists. They have to be permitted to be transgressive, to break the rules, or else their creativity will be stifled. Genius is beyond good and evil. This myth is basically false: there are many artists who are perfectly capable of maintaining a boundary between their inner freedom in the realm of creation and the way they live outside it. However, the myth is so pervasive that for many it can become a self-fulfilling prophecy. An artist who sincerely believes that breaking society's rules is necessary for success, by long habit actually becomes unable to create without transgressing. It's revealing that the myth is overwhelmingly about male creativity, used by males for males. And it's revealing, too, that the myth mainly concerns sexual rules. I can't think of an artist I've known who believed that being creative licensed him to commit theft or burglary. It's just a handy way, for a small number of talented men, to arrive at a conclusion so often coveted by male pride: I am above sexual laws, and other people aren't fully real.

Victims are often confused by this myth. Art and artists are dazzling. People are easily lured by charisma, as in the familiar phenomenon of the "groupie." (The *Underneath Their Robes* blog character who writes as "Article III Groupie" plays on the similarity between artistic and judicial glamor.) Sometimes artists even create a cult around themselves, seducing an entire group, as repeatedly happened with James Levine. Powerful men often get willing volunteers for sex, but they also, all too often, feel entitled to take the sex they want, whether fully voluntary or not.

As for the rest of the world: we, too—spectators and fans—are bewitched, dazzled, and confused by the glamor of the powerful, and often by the real illumination they give us. We love being swept away by the power of the passions and erotic feelings they summon up, and to that extent we are reluctant to criticize their conduct, or we think of it as "natural."

There's another factor: if the arts we love are to thrive, they need star power. Star power generates both ticket sales and donations. Even if we dislike star power and star influence, but just want the art we love to persist and do well, we can ill afford to get rid of the star, however badly behaved. And some people may not care so much about the health of the art, but more about making money on their investments. Hence the fact that some stars whose gifts make money for others are held to account only when they are too old and ill to make money for others any longer.

Workplaces without Borders

We've already seen that what is helpful, where sexual harassment and sexual assault are concerned, is a well-defined workplace, where it's clear who is a member and who is not. Such workplaces (universities, most corporate environments, law firms, etc.) can establish clear rules that educate, deter bad behavior ex ante, and set standards of fairness for ex post sanctions. One key concept of sexual harassment law, the "hostile work environment," is designed for such workplaces, and the other key concept, the "quid pro quo," is easiest to apply there, where rules for promotion and dismissal are well understood and there's at least some shared understanding of who deserves what. Of course there is turnover: new students, for example, enter a university each year and old ones leave. At any given time, however, it is clear who is a student and who is not, and therefore who is governed by the rules concerning students and who is not. (Or it should be clear: irremediable muddiness about this issue is one of the several fatal flaws in Division I college sports, as we'll see in my next chapter.) The same holds for other roles in such institutions.

In the performing arts, it is not like this at all, with a few exceptions. Clear exceptions are players in symphony orchestras, who typically stay in one workplace for a long time, who even may eventually have tenure, and whose employment follows clear rules stated in their union contract. Singers in opera choruses are similar exceptions. Even where orchestras and choruses use extra part-time members, the terms of that use are usually spelled out in the contract. Dancers who are employed long-term in a single dance company are also exceptions. But most employment in theater, film, television performance, dance, and solo music (vocal and instrumental soloists, small ensembles) is temporary, and even if the performers are union members there's a limit to the protections that unions can offer. Actors are hired for a single engagement, which may be longer or shorter, but is rarely extremely long. Even stars in long-running hit TV shows usually renegotiate their contract each year. Dancers in a hit Broadway show that runs, say, ten years are usually not hired for the entire run of the show, since their skills may deteriorate. Yes, orchestras and choruses sometimes have to re-audition, but that process is spelled out in the contract, and this is rarely the case in live theater or television. In any case few shows run for very long.

Actors, however established, always have to audition and have every reason to be insecure. As Heidi Klum often said on *Project Runway*: "One day you're in, the next day you're out." Short of world-famous stardom, even fame is never solid (and is always beset by aging, a stigmatized identity). Actors must depend on connections, usually mediated by agents who help them secure the next audition, whether in theater, television, or film. Auditions are not rule-governed, and are notoriously unpredictable. (Contrast, again, symphony orchestras, where rules for auditions are described in the union contract, and where gender- and race-blind auditioning, behind a curtain—at least until the final round, when the player must play with the orchestra—has created a revolution in the cast of characters of U.S. orchestras, especially by contrast to those in Europe today, where there's no such practice.) The same is basically true of solo musicians and singers, whether in cabaret or opera. Basically, you are always selling yourself to someone, and your good fortune only lasts so long. In Europe, national repertory companies sometimes offer tenured employment, but even in those U.S. repertory companies that have "regulars," those people cannot be assured of employment year to year. In short, while you are engaged in one job, you must always have your mind on two or three others. And even if the current job involves no abusers, you still have to fear the predation of those who control the next opportunity.

In short, the whole art world, in each of these arts, is, for the most part, one big borderless workplace. This means that certain people with great power and wealth can influence everyone's chances, more or less. Even if you are not currently employed by Harvey Weinstein or seeking employment within his production company, in a very real sense you always are seeking employment and you don't know when you will need the good favor of a person of such wealth, power, and ubiquitous influence. Even if you are not employed in one of the orchestras that James Levine used to conduct, he was such a towering figure that he influenced the perception of the talents of musicians not directly hired by him, particularly because he regularly taught in programs that trained much younger musicians and charted their path upward. Even if you are not performing alongside Plácido Domingo now, you might perform with him next year; even if you have no current connection with the Los Angeles Opera, where he was general director until 2019, you don't want to rule out the possibility of ever being hired there in the future. In the academy, figures of towering influence can also block the path of someone who wants to move to that person's university or some other place where that person has outsize influence. But academic stars don't have a wide sway over all hiring, which is typically done by a vote of the entire department, and it is perfectly possible to get secure and, eventually, tenured employment that is not vulnerable to that individual. In the performing arts, you are always auditioning, always vulnerable.

Big stars in this way insulate themselves against whistleblowing. They don't need a judicial clerk's requirement of confidentiality. The neediness of the performer is their insulation.

Two further art world mechanisms protect stars. One is the box office value of their sheer star power. Even if at one time they might have been replaceable by others, once they are already stars they appear irreplaceable—until they are old, infirm, or ill. People involved with a production fear alienating the luminary, since they see their livelihood as dependent on the star. And in artistic realms less dependent than others on ticket sales and more dependent on donors, the big star is often key to the generous involvement of the donor community. Big opera companies, for example, get considerably more of their annual income from donations than from ticket sales.[3] The donor community in classical music and opera (and very likely in Broadway theater as well) is likely to be relatively old, white, artistically and socially conservative, and unevenly educated in music, in the sense that the (rare) well-educated donor will assess a conductor or performer's artistic achievement on the basis of her own faculties, whereas the more typical donor will go by name recognition and prestige.

Many things, in short, conspire to protect the famous once they are famous, but the biggest problem is the sheer unreliability of employment itself. Traditional sexual harassment law is virtually impossible to apply, when the star is harassing a variety of temporary or merely possible employees. A career as a performer entails permanent vulnerability, both financial and physical.

Arts and Their Differences

Different arts construct different types and degrees of vulnerability. One variable is the role of innate talent, which appears to be extremely strong in classical music, far less strong in acting. If you are singled out as musically gifted by the natural lottery, it's difficult, at least, for a powerful foe to block those gifts from showing themselves, though it is still possible to make the gifted person's life a misery by harassment. Another huge factor is specialized training. It simply is not possible to have a career in classical music or ballet, or most types of modern dance, without many years of extremely arduous study and disciplined practice. Usually this training starts in childhood, although classical singers often begin later, since the maturation of the voice, especially the male voice, takes time. Some first-rank opera singers had no specialized training until they were in college[4]—although typically their lives were already formed by music in some other way (playing piano, singing in a church choir, etc.). Many other classical singers were already singers but had never even attended an opera—until some teacher pointed the way. Most classical and jazz instrumentalists similarly begin training early, and here late discoveries are almost nonexistent.

Because of oversupply, talent and training are not enough. They do, however, narrow the group of possible hires and make it virtually impossible to slip in an incompetent favorite. And those who don't want the constant insecurity of freelance employment can opt for something more solid: a chair in a symphony orchestra (with blind auditioning), if one's talent is sufficient, or, for the singer, a position in an opera company's chorus.[5] Another option is to have a solid job as a church or synagogue musician and supplement that with freelance jobs. Many other musicians teach music, or hold some other type of day job, and play or sing on the side.

If there is oversupply even in classical music, it's painfully obvious that actors in theater, film, and television face a very high ratio of decently qualified applicants to positions. Acting does have some natural requirements of voice, body, and imagination, but they are hugely fluid, and the requirements of a given role can be multiply realized. If you audition for a symphony orchestra, you'd better be able to play the notes that are set in front of you. Roles in theater and TV are usually more open, admitting a wide range of vocal and physical realizations. In film and TV, moreover, technology can greatly compensate for performers' deficiencies (making them look taller, more vivid, and so forth, and taking away the need to remember all the lines for a long role). Nor is training clearly a requirement. Some actors learn a lot through training in acting, voice, and movement, but some do better without it. It's probably safe to say that for every role for which auditions are held, there are over a thousand people who could play that role decently. And open auditions (known as "cattle calls") may in fact be attended by as many as a thousand. Luck plays a part, self-marketing and connections play a part, and, sure, skill plays a part. But the skill factor plays a much smaller role than in classical music.

Pop music is somewhat mysterious to me, but I think it is more similar to acting than to classical music. Some stars have superb natural vocal or instrumental gifts, and skills developed by long practice and training. Lady Gaga has talent and training every bit as striking as most talents in classical music, and we can say the same of instrumental geniuses such as Keith Richards and Eric Clapton. Often, however, the performer is basically an actor and self-marketer, made more presentable by technology. The number of aspirants is huge, the number who succeed tiny, and much of the difference is made by luck and connections.

Because there may be a huge pool of qualified applicants for every role, the hirer, whether director or producer, has enormous power in singling out this person or that. There's no such thing as a symphony orchestra's blind audition in acting, and how could there be? So connections to the powerful person can play a large role in making or breaking a career. This really creates great room for corruption. A powerful hirer—say, a Harvey Weinstein—can truly make or break hundreds of careers. Add to that the porousness of the workplace, and you find that one corrupt powerful person can disrupt life for thousands, since more or less everyone who is not already his employee is a would-be or potential employee.

The corruption is often reciprocal: the insecurity of employment makes at least some people volunteer to be used by a Harvey Weinstein. The applicant may think, that's the only way I can stand out from the crowd, and give myself an edge. That fact contributes to the tendency of a Weinstein to go on abusing: they are all "asking for it," the powerful person may wrongly think. And it certainly contributes to the unwillingness of many others who think the same way to take women's charges of abuse seriously. Often, too, the threat of reprisals by the Weinstein figure can lead weak and insecure people to give in to his demands even when they are unwelcome. You may draw the line at sleeping your way to a role but still unhappily agree to sleep with such a person in face of a threat of blacklisting. Although such a case fits the classic *Meritor v. Vinson* model of sexual harassment,[6] it is not always perceived as illegal sexual harassment.

The short-term nature of acting employment magnifies these problems, since even if you are happily employed now, you know you won't be tomorrow. So, a Weinstein still has great power over you.

Usually the powerful person who is in a position to exploit is a director or producer or conductor, or, in Weinstein's case, the head of a production company. Sometimes, however, it is another actor. Most actors are insecure about future employment throughout their careers. But, as I've said, there are a few who attain real power and security—either by being acknowledged as stars whose presence can make the success of a movie or by playing a long-running nationally visible role in a successful TV show. Bill Cosby's power was of that sort, and it was power over not only aspiring actors but others who worked in the media world and other related enterprises. (Andrea Constand, his leading accuser, met him through their shared connection with Temple University.) He was shielded not only by his power over insecure women but also by his power over investors and sponsors, who made money through his fame. Sometimes these types of power combine: James Levine and Plácido Domingo had power over potential or actual employees, but that power was buttressed and protected against whistleblowing by the money their talents made for others.

Although my focus is on the performing arts, it's worth noting that painting and fine art generally are perhaps the most insecure of all, since the ratio of talent to decent purchasing prices is high, and the aspiring artist depends almost entirely on the whim of wealthy collectors, and on the power of hype and self-marketing, for the all-important "edge." Women complain less often of sexual harassment, however, than of exclusion and blatant discrimination. Opera, ballet, and theater have guaranteed places for women, and the symphony orchestra has the blind audition. There is no such thing in the fine arts. Even though museums these days put on an increasing number of special exhibits of the work of woman artists, woman artists themselves view this as a cheap gesture by contrast with what is still lacking: the acquisition of works by woman artists for museums' permanent collections.

Profiles in Corruption

I focus now on just one area of the world of the performing arts—classical music—and on four cases that show us different trajectories of abuse and possible accountability: conductors James Levine and Charles Dutoit, singer-conductor-manager Plácido Domingo, and singer/voice teacher David Daniels.

These are extraordinary classical musicians. All stand credibly accused of serial sexual harassment or assault. All have been either partially or totally disgraced. All had largely unheeded reputations for sexual exploitation going back many years. All have been brought low only at the end of their careers, when they were no longer dazzling audiences or generating income for others or were thought, at any rate, to be at the end of their careers. And remember: because of the role of innate talent, the world of classical music is probably less corrupt than the world of theater and film.

David Daniels

Born in 1966, Daniels was for many years the leading operatic countertenor in the United States and was prominent in Europe as well. A countertenor, sometimes called "male alto," is a male who is able to sing in a register more typical of female mezzo-sopranos.[7] As baroque music increased in popularity in U.S. opera houses from the 1980s on—thanks in large part to the popularity of English singer Alfred Deller (1912–1979), the first acclaimed countertenor of recent years, who tirelessly promoted baroque music—a need arose for singers who could sing roles originally written by Handel and other composers for *castrati*, castrated male singers who were once enormously fashionable, and whose voices combined the high notes and flexibility associated with female singers with a power usually achieved only by male voices.[8] Once the voice was established and popular, living composers began to write roles for it.[9]

Good countertenors are extremely rare. Countertenors who also have sensitive artistry and acting ability are super-rare, perhaps two or three in each generation. That rarity forms the background to Daniels's disgraceful career.

Daniels initially trained as a tenor, without much success. As a graduate student at the music school of the University of Michigan, he reinvented himself as a countertenor, and his career took off. For many years he was in demand all over the world, justly celebrated for the agility and expressiveness of his voice and also for his dashing dramatic portrayals, such as the title role in Handel's *Giulio Cesare*.[10] In 2013 the opera *Oscar*, an account of Oscar Wilde's later life, written for Daniels by composer Theodore Morrison, and one of the most eagerly awaited new works in recent years, had its world premiere at the Santa Fe Opera.[11]

Daniels is openly gay and has become something of a gay icon in the gay-friendly opera world; in 2014 he married conductor Scott Walters (b. 1981) in a ceremony performed by Justice Ruth Bader Ginsburg.

By 2015 there was noticeable roughness and an occasional decline in agility in Daniels's performances. By that time, too, other countertenors were taking his place. Anthony Roth Costanza (b. 1982) sang the title role in Philip Glass's *Aknaten* at the Metropolitan Opera in 2019–20. For reasons probably related to his vocal decline, in 2015 Daniels accepted a teaching appointment at his alma mater, the University of Michigan School of Music, Theatre & Dance. In the fall of 2018 he was awarded tenure, and was earning an annual salary of close to $200,000. Although all subsequent events are difficult to pin down due to the curtain of secrecy drawn by UM around the complaints against Daniels and its own investigation, it would appear that the award of tenure postdates the first wave of complaints.

In 2018, Daniels was charged in a lawsuit against UM by former UM graduate student Andrew Lipian, who alleges that Daniels harassed and assaulted him between 2016 and 2018 during private voice lessons and on other occasions—including sending him a video of Daniels masturbating, and once slipping him an Ambien pretending it was Tylenol, after which Daniels allegedly undressed and sexually assaulted him. Lipian says that UM knew of the harassment but did nothing about it. This suit involves the oddity that UM at one point tried to get evidence that Lipian is gay in order to rebut Lipian's claims that the sexual contact was unwelcome. While it is true that Lipian himself mentioned in his filing that he was straight and married, this is surely not relevant to the claim of unwelcomeness; it seems inexcusable of UM to foster a stereotype of gay men as sexually omnivorous, as Lipian's lawyer has pointed out.[12] Lipian appears to have a strong case as to the institution's prior knowledge. His legal filing states that prior to joining UM "Daniels already had a reputation for being sexually aggressive, continually talking about sex and making sexual overtures," and that one professor has testified that when faculty in his department learned that Daniels was being hired, they discussed a potential problem and concluded, "Someone's got to tell him to keep his hands off the . . . students."[13] Soon after Lipian filed his lawsuit in 2018, San Francisco Opera removed Daniels from a new production of Handel's *Orlando*.

Meanwhile, an internal UM investigation into Daniels's conduct has interviewed fifty people and has uncovered at least twenty first-hand claims of misconduct by Daniels. These range from sexually suggestive conversation to soliciting sex from two students for pay over the hookup phone app Grindr, a felony in Michigan. Daniels also allegedly proposed paying to watch a UM student and an alumnus have sex at the Graduate Ann Arbor hotel. (The student backed out at the last minute.)[14] Although it seems likely that the full results of the investigation will never be made public, a search of the faculty page of the UM School of Music, Theatre & Dance in late December 2019 shows that Daniels has disappeared entirely.[15]

There was worse to come. In January 2019 both Daniels and his husband were indicted on a felony charge of sexual assault in Texas for an incident in 2010, in which a young baritone singer named Samuel Schultz, then a student at Rice University, alleges that Daniels and Walters drugged and raped him after a closing-night party at the Houston Grand Opera. (Schultz actually came forward before Lipian did, but it took time to get a grand jury indictment.) Schultz—who knows that he is risking a promising career with a lineup of engagements by coming forward—says that fear of retaliation prevented him from speaking out sooner.[16] He claims that he was flattered when the two invited him to a continuation of the after-party back at their apartment; he was then offered a drink, blacked out, and woke up the next afternoon alone, naked, "scared, confused, and bleeding," with no memory of what had happened. When Daniels and Walters returned, Daniels allegedly told Schultz not to worry about "the bareback thing, I'm totally negative." Schultz immediately told two people who have corroborated his story. He also immediately called a health center, which could not give him an appointment for two weeks, so there is no forensic evidence. Daniels and Walters have denied the allegations, claiming the sex was consensual. Schultz, meanwhile, says that the trauma and the fear of seeing the two men again almost made him abandon his singing career. "But I refuse to stop. If I stop singing, they hold all the power. They raped me. They will not take away my voice."[17]

On March 28, 2020, Daniels was terminated at the University of Michigan, the first time in more than sixty years that the university's board of regents had voted to terminate a tenured faculty member, according to board chair Ron Weiser, who said that Daniels was given no severance pay. The board gives no specifics, referring only to the "safety and well-being of our students . . . jeopardized" by Daniels.[18]

It's hard to believe that Daniels and Walters will be convicted on the criminal charge, given the length of time and the he-said/they-said nature of the case. However, the groundswell of information at Michigan seems sufficient to establish, even without a criminal conviction, that Daniels was a serial sexual harasser who should not have been appointed in the first place without an extensive inquiry, and probably not at all, and whose termination is a good thing. The university's unfortunate policy of secrecy will probably prevent us from knowing all that we would like to know.

Daniels had a reputation for sexual aggressiveness for years, and yet nothing was done about it—until he entered a university, with its clear rules and complaint procedures. His star power, his rare talent, and the scarcity of other gifted countertenors obviously made people close their eyes, his charisma initially lured his young victims, and fear of reprisal then made them reluctant to come forward. His case, like my other three, show the baneful effect of the cult of star power, but also the possibility for institutions to proclaim new norms of decency, as the San Francisco Opera eloquently did in this case, describing its sexual harassment policy in great detail.[19] Would they have taken this courageous stance, however, if he had not been past his prime as a singer?

Charles Dutoit

Born in 1936, Swiss conductor Dutoit has conducted to great acclaim all over the world. He has been music director of the Orchestre Symphonique de Montréal, the Royal Philharmonic in London, and the Orchestre National de France, and has held prestigious posts with orchestras in Japan, the United States, Russia, and other nations. His list of awards occupies pages. His distinctive achievement lies, above all, in his subtle understanding of French orchestral works, which many conductors trained to give German works pride of place do not program often and do not interpret with the greatest refinement. Many people have felt that it is a revelation to hear composers such as Ravel and Debussy conducted by Dutoit, and he has been immensely in demand as guest conductor for that reason.

For many years—complaints date back to at least 1985—Dutoit had a reputation for harassing female musicians and other orchestra employees. It's pretty much the same story: people warned women not to be alone with him (see my next section), but nobody thought to discipline him for his conduct or not to engage him in the first place.

As with Alex Kozinski, the floodgates opened in 2017, when a group of accusers came forward. First four, then six more, then others.[20] Most of the claims allege forcible groping. Singer Paula Rasmussen says that he "shoved my hand down his pants and shoved his tongue down my throat" at the Los Angeles Opera in 1991. Internationally acclaimed soprano Sylvia McNair says that when she was starting her career, in 1985, Dutoit "pressed his knee way up between my legs and pressed himself all over me" and "tried to have his way" with her in a hotel elevator, after a rehearsal in Minnesota.[21] All the other stories are depressingly similar—except that an anonymous accuser charges Dutoit with rape.[22]

No criminal charges have been filed—in most cases the incidents are too long ago, and the accusers were not ready to go to the authorities at the time. Dutoit has denied all the charges. However, both the Boston Symphony Orchestra and the Philadelphia Orchestra have conducted internal investigations and have found the accusations credible.[23] Dutoit's engagements with a number of orchestras, including Philadelphia, were terminated, and he withdrew from engagements with the Chicago Symphony, the New York Philharmonic, and the Cleveland Orchestra. Once again, his age makes these decisions virtually cost-free for the orchestras and certainly not courageous.

It is depressing to think of the world in which young musicians made their way twenty or so years ago, and indeed until 2017. Some did, in fact, complain; others somehow let things be known informally. But from 1985 until 2017—when Dutoit was eighty-three, likely bound for retirement—a code of silence and of fear protected him. This was not off-color joking that could be attributed (at first at least) to growing up in another era. The behavior that has been alleged was criminal, and he would have known that. But he also knew—like Kozinski, like Daniels—that his charisma and talent prevented vulnerable young artists from speaking out, and ensured that management would have done nothing if they had. Sylvia McNair probably would have ruined her wonderful career had she come forward, and she would not have achieved anything for other women.

I include Dutoit in part because, though outstanding, he is not a world-famous figure like Levine and Domingo, who might be thought to be unique in their power over artists' careers. The Dutoit story suggests that it is not only the world-famous who are insulated by their power as conductors. Thus it is all too likely that other powerful abusers, still in their prime, are still abusing other young artists.

James Levine

James Levine (b. 1943) conducted the orchestra of the Metropolitan Opera in New York for over forty years (1976–2017). He has also conducted the Ravinia Festival near Chicago and the Boston Symphony Orchestra (music director 2001–2011). He also founded the Met's Lindemann Young Artist Development Program. In summers he often taught at the Meadow Brook School of Music in Michigan and also taught young musicians at the Ravinia Festival. Afflicted with Parkinson's disease since 1994 (although he denied it for many years), Levine has become increasingly disabled and has needed extended leaves of absence. Just before his fall he required a motorized wheelchair and a special conducting platform, and even then his beat could be difficult to follow.

Levine is one of the greatest musicians of our time. As a conductor he molded the Met's orchestra into one of the world's premiere orchestras, through leadership, charisma, and a sui generis power of eliciting devoted teamwork. His interpretations show not simply technical command but also deep emotional insight. It is a cruel paradox that this man who preyed on the young, depriving them of later love and joy in the name of total control, is one of our time's superlative interpreters of both Mozart, for whom human love and freedom win out every time over religion and authority, and Wagner, whose *Ring* suggests that the world can be redeemed from the cruelty of greed only by personal love. When you saw Levine conduct,[24] he seemed like a Mozartean human being: full of fun, cherubic, exuding joy in his musicians and the music they made together. He was, alas, very different: or rather, he was both what he appeared, and also something very different.

Rumors about Levine exploiting young men circulated already in the late 1970s. I first heard them in around 1980 from a member of the Met orchestra. In the wake of the cascade of revelations beginning in 2017, we know the truth: for decades, Levine created a cult of himself that included as a key article permission for sexual abuse. The long and detailed account in the *Boston Globe*'s 2018 article "In the Maestro's Thrall," by Malcolm Gay and Kay Lazar,[25] supported by frank on-the-record interviews with many former Levine groupies, makes it clear that this cult was a kind of religion of art, with Levine as the high priest. (The authors do not make an explicit comparison to the Catholic Church's pedophilia crimes—which the *Boston Globe* also had a heroic role in exposing—but the comparison is inevitable for the reader.) During his summer programs, Levine would gather a group of devotees, who were to be united by utter loyalty and submission to his genius and utter devotion to the value of music. The question in my epigraph—would the young man choose to save Levine or his own mother—tests the former. To test the latter, Levine would ask whether the young musician would save the last remaining manuscript of Beethoven's Ninth, or a baby.[26] There was only one right answer.

Students were lured by encouragement; then their defenses were broken down by ruthless criticism and humiliation. Almost immediately, sex became a prominent topic. During private lessons, Levine questioned students about their masturbation habits. For those who stayed in the little group—some report being scared off at that point—Levine progressed to mutual masturbation and oral sex, sometimes between the pupil and himself, and sometimes as a group exercise with everyone blindfolded and people pairing off in twos. Levine defended the mingling of sex and music as part of his "holistic conception" of art. Learning to experience sexual arousal was supposed to both teach self-control and get rid of inhibition. "Basically, the theory was if you were less inhibited sexually, you'd be a better musician," said one former student. The ultimate aim, Levine told his students, was to create a perfect, "celestial," orchestra. Students in the little group were supposed to have no outside sexual or love relationships; even love of one's own family was frowned on as a distraction.

Isolated by the secrecy of the relationship and by the homophobia of the times, by shame and by fear, students now report that they felt they could not speak to their parents or friends. "I was by myself in the world," says ex-student James Lestock. This secrecy continued until, in December 2017, a key month in so many of our stories, a group of former students went to the press. When three had come forward—bass player Chris Brown, cellist Lestock , and violinist Ashok Pai—the Metropolitan Opera suspended Levine on December 3, appointing an outside law firm to investigate the charges.[27] The Ravinia Festival and the Boston Symphony canceled his engagements promptly, the BSO saying that Levine would never again "be employed or contracted by the BSO at any time in the future."[28] A fourth accuser, violinist Albin Ifsich, came forward. Five more came forward during the Met's investigation and are included in the Met's response to Levine's defamation suit.[29] In March 2018, its investigation concluded, the Met terminated its relationship with Levine, citing "sexually abusive and harassing behavior."[30] In response to Levine's suit for breach of contract and defamation, a New York State Supreme Court judge dismissed most of Levine's claims, though the court did rule that one statement made in March was defamatory. The lawsuit was finally settled in August 2019.[31]

Although Peter Gelb and the rest of the Metropolitan Opera management reacted with apparent surprise to the 2017 allegations, they also admitted that an anonymous letter in 1979 had warned of Levine's conduct (which was in any case notorious). Closer to the time in question, Ashok Pai had already pursued a criminal charge against Levine in October 2016, charging him with sexually abusing him for years, but the Met's management, contacted by the Lake Forest (Illinois) police, did nothing after Levine denied the charges, which were eventually dropped because Pai was sixteen when the abuse allegedly began. Although today in Illinois the statutory age of consent is eighteen when the older party is in a supervisory relationship with the complainant, that was not the case when the first abuse allegedly occurred: sixteen was the age for all.

The people who have come forward—now including five new accusers, for a total of nine—were all around the age of consent when Levine abused them, but most states now require a higher age where there is supervisory authority. So, but for inadequacies in earlier laws and statute of limitations issues, Levine could be criminally charged. What is totally clear in any case is that Levine grossly abused his authority and that the men in question, as they all say today, felt they could not say no. And they were damaged. Brown and Ifsich have had successful careers in classical music; Pai and Lestock have left music. All are scarred. "I don't know why it was so traumatic," Brown, now sixty-six, said to a reporter, tears in his eyes. "I don't know why I got so depressed. But it has to be because of what happened. And I care deeply for those who were also abused, all the people who were in that situation."[32] Lestock, similarly, describes carrying the pain of abuse for years. Both say they were moved to come forward to help others. "The truth can be very useful," said Lestock. "The truth creates good."[33]

It's an incredibly sad and terrible saga. Brilliant art was for years linked to heinous abuse of power, and indeed of art itself. We probably will never know how many more were abused. Now that Levine has fallen there is no incentive for others to come forward. Clearly he should have been investigated much earlier and much more aggressively. The Met's inquiry cleared the Met management of any cover-up, but many opportunities to do a thorough investigation had been batted away: Ashok Pai's claims in 2016; an occasion on which Levine scoffed at talk of wrongdoing in an interview with the New York Times; and speculation in Germany a decade later, which led to another Times interview in which Levine said, "I've never been able to speak in public generalities about my private life."[34] It seems hard for a concerned member of the opera-going public not to conclude that the Met acted only when a swell of #MeToo publicity and the prompt action of other orchestras forced its hand—and when Levine was more of a liability than an asset. They protected Levine and refused to investigate him when he was a crucial element in their artistic and financial success. They protected Levine's victims only when he was too old and sick to make money and create art for them—and probably too old and sick to abuse anyone anymore. And in September 2020, the Met disclosed that it had paid Levine $3.5 million in a settlement.[35] In the context of the cancellation of the 2020–21 season and great financial hardship for many, this news has, rightly, given rise to criticism.

Plácido Domingo

Spanish singer Plácido Domingo (b. 1941) is one of the greatest opera singers in the history of the genre. A tenor for decades (and the only living member of the famous "Three Tenors"), he has recently taken on baritone roles, prolonging his career. Today, at eighty, he sings magnificently (with some off days) and still wows audiences. Attractive and with a rare ability to project joy and love of life, he is one of the few tenors whose acting matches his singing. His charisma was evident since the very start of his career. (I know: I was lucky enough to be at his unexpected Metropolitan Opera debut in 1968, when he went on, unannounced, for another ailing singer. With tickets given by parents of a friend, we were transfixed.)

Domingo is a real artist, known for interpretive insight as well as vocal power. He also has rare emotional expressiveness, and people are lured to opera because he is there. And as artistic director and sometimes conductor at Los Angeles Opera, he has energized that company and given great encouragement to performers of many kinds. In short, he is a genius and a force for good. Since opera is losing ground with the public and needs all the help it can get, it is understandable, though reprehensible, that the evident facts about Domingo's sexual harassment have been silenced for years.

A flood of accusations in summer and fall of 2019, however, have led to termination of Domingo's American contracts, except at LA Opera, where, like Kozinski, he preempted action by resigning. Domingo no doubt has many women volunteering to sleep with him, despite his long-term marriage. Not content with that, however, he has repeatedly pursued nonconsenting women with coercive groping and harassing phone calls. His pattern is different from that of Dutoit: he seems sometimes to seek a relationship, not a one-time encounter; he becomes very fixated on certain individuals, usually singers, phoning them at home late at night; and he can be notoriously tenacious in his pursuit. And he has not been accused of rape. Such is his power in the industry that most of his more than twenty accusers came forward anonymously, albeit with detailed times, places, and details. Mezzo-soprano Patricia Wulf and soprano Angela Turner Wilson have given detailed named accounts.[36] Many report being terrified about his likely impact on their careers. They also report a loss of confidence, a doubt in their own talent. "It was like watching someone be psychologically killed," a colleague of one accuser said. "She got smaller and smaller as a person."[37]

At first, Domingo did not apologize in any way. He denied the accusations, saying his behavior has always been respectful and gentlemanly, and adding that "rules and standards" are "very different than they were in the past."[38] The accusers reject Domingo's denials, saying that he could not, for example, have thought it gentlemanly to squeeze someone's breast so painfully.[39]

As is the case with all of our malefactors, Domingo's behavior was notorious for years. Women were warned never to be alone with him backstage. Rather than just do their work, they had to spend time thinking up avoidance stratagems. He would grab them, grope them, squeeze their breasts, force kisses on them. Two say that after months of harassment and forcible groping they slept with him just to end the saga. (In one case it did, in the other it didn't.) Nobody was there to help them. An earlier complainant at Tanglewood, intern Fiona Allen, was not really taken seriously, but told simply not to be alone with him. It was all an "open secret."

Domingo is a truly great artist, and also a big star whose presence in a production guarantees an audience, lifting other careers along with his own. People are entranced by his art; many people who work with him like him. (Even his accusers find him a generous person.) Unlike our other three, he has people coming to his defense: tenor Andrea Bocelli decried the absence of a full investigation.[40] And I have discussed the case with a leading female diva whom I know, and who has worked extensively with him over the years. I have not tried to put her on the spot by asking for the use of her name, but let me insist that there are few people in any profession whom I find more insightful and decent. She is adamant that Domingo is an energetic womanizer but has never used force or threatened anyone with retaliation. Of course it's hard for anyone to know a negative, but my informant has been around him for decades and no doubt heard all the reports that circulated over the years. A first conclusion, in trying to sort this out, might be that Domingo has repeatedly persisted beyond the point when he should have accepted a refusal, and that he was insensitive to the implicit pressure of career consequences created by his sheer star power and omnipresence in the industry, and the huge investment of many others in his presence. He thus committed sexual harassment as most workplaces define it. But his conduct still seems less predatory than that of Levine and not physically brutal in the manner of Daniels and Dutoit.

Two inquiries have now confirmed something like this picture. The first was conducted by AGMA, the American Guild of Musical Artists. Their report concludes that Domingo "had, in fact, engaged in inappropriate activity, ranging from flirtation to sexual advances, in and outside of the workplace. Many of the witnesses expressed fear of retaliation in the industry as their reason for not coming forward sooner."[41] The report mentions unwanted touching and persistent requests for meetings that struck some witnesses as like "stalking." Notice, however, that he is not accused of using physical force—beyond unwanted touching—or making a threat to retaliate against the woman. Instead we find a diffuse fear of retaliation, which, as I noted, would be plausible enough given how much money opera houses have invested in Domingo's presence. He certainly should have been sensitive to that fear, and he was not. But did he act to inspire it? There is no support for that in the report.[42]

It looks, then, as if there is evidence that the companies in question tolerated a "hostile environment," and that this is more like that type of sexual harassment, rather than the "quid pro quo" type, or criminal sexual abuse. In a hostile environment case, the pervasiveness of the harassment is crucial, and even more crucial is the failure of the companies to listen to women's complaints. The companies surely seem culpable, for not having sexual harassment–compliant mechanisms, known to all parties and adequately structured, in the first place or for having them and failing to implement them in a constructive way. Whether his behavior was as "pervasive" as that of Kozinski and Reinhardt remains in doubt, given the evidence to date. For one thing, except in LA he did not have the kind of overall power that Kozinski and Reinhardt had in their chambers; his power derived from the desire of companies to please him, in order to augment their artistic and financial status.

The second inquiry was conducted by the LA Opera, who hired the law firm Gibson, Dunn, and Crutcher LLP to conduct it. Domingo cooperated in the inquiry. A summary of its findings has been released.[43] The report finds the accusers credible: Domingo made them uncomfortable by his advances. They found his denials "sincere," but "found some of them to be less credible or lacking in awareness." As a result of extensive interviews, Gibson, Dunn found "no evidence that Mr. Domingo ever engaged in a quid pro quo or retaliated against any woman by not casting or otherwise hiring her at LA Opera." They then went on to urge that LA Opera more proactively address such problems in the future by creating a more formal process for investigating and resolving sexual harassment complaints, and by instituting specialized sexual harassment training for both managers and contractors.

On February 24, 2020 (just before the AGMA findings were made public), Domingo apologized profusely:

> I have taken time over the last several months to reflect on the allegations that various colleagues of mine have made against me. I respect that these women finally felt comfortable enough to speak out, and I want them to know that I am truly sorry for the hurt that I caused them. I accept full responsibility for my actions, and I have grown from this experience.[44]

Three days later, however (and two weeks before the release of the LA Opera report), he issued a statement qualifying his apology:

> My apology was sincere and heartfelt, to any colleague who I have made to feel uncomfortable, or hurt in any manner, by anything I have said or done. As I have said it repeatedly, it was never my intention to hurt or offend anyone.
>
> But I know what I have not done and I'll deny it again. I have never behaved aggressively toward anyone, and I have never done anything to obstruct or hurt anyone's career in any way. On the contrary, I have devoted much of my half century in the world of opera supporting the industry and promoting the career of countless singers.[45]

The general reaction to this second statement was that he had simply unapologized. A *New York Times* headline read, "Plácido Domingo Walks Back Apology on Harassment Claims."[46] This reaction seems to me unfair. He still apologizes for the pain and discomfort he caused. He qualifies that apology by denying career retaliation, and by denying the use of force (what he apparently meant by "behaved aggressively"). And the Gibson, Dunn report that came out two weeks later appears to agree with Domingo's second statement.

Domingo still seems pretty clueless about the impact of his sheer power on those he pursued, in the totality of the circumstances. And he has a pretty narrow view of what "aggressiveness" consists in, apparently excluding a good deal of touching and even groping. However, once again, the Gibson, Dunn report does put him in a different category from the sinister actions of Levine, Dutoit, and Daniels; and his second statement simply asserts that difference. Perhaps he was urged by his friends and supporters to make this further statement.

Fame brings power, and power brings with it extra responsibilities; Domingo is certainly guilty of heedlessness and irresponsibility. But let's be precise: to call his behavior "predatory," as the *Washington Post* did, is probably excessive and inaccurate,[47] and it is possible that his second statement was made in response to that damaging article.

Solutions?

Are there solutions here for star-power corruption? Solutions not just for aging stars like our four, brought to justice long after much of their abuse—and star power—is past, but solutions promising to nip the abuse in the bud while the star is still a star?

#MeToo. All four of these cases, like that of Kozinski, go back decades. But accountability set in only in 2017–19. It's impossible to avoid the conclusion that the new atmosphere of respect for complaining voices created by the #MeToo movement helped these complainants come forward at last. If our society continues to listen respectfully to victims' voices, we may hope that many future abuses will be nipped in the bud. But then victims have a duty to come forward. Even if we now should excuse the Sylvia McNairs of the world, who pursued their careers without speaking out, when speaking out would have achieved nothing and would probably have derailed their budding careers, we now live in a different world and should demand more of the abused.

Criminal law. The Daniels case shows us that when the criminal law is allegedly broken even the powerful can be indicted, even while still actively performing—although, at fifty-three, Daniels's performance future was already short, given the nature of his voice and the reliance of baroque countertenor music on great agility. Perhaps going forward other criminal indictments will be lodged during the star's prime—although star power and artist vulnerability militate against it. Furthermore, many of these cases fit the paradigm of sexual harassment more than that of sexual assault—only there is no closed workplace to charge with tolerating abuse, as the "hostile work environment" tort requires.

University rules. The Daniels case also shows us that when the star joins a more normal, bounded workplace accountability is heightened. The University of Michigan was key in both assisting his extradition to Texas on the criminal charge and investigating student complaints at Michigan itself—resulting in his eventual termination.

Unions. Ideally, unions have both the responsibility of protecting their members and some power to ensure a suitable contract setting up guidelines and procedures. The most important unions in the performing arts are the Actors' Equity Association (actors in live theater), the Screen Actors Guild (SAG), the American Federation of Television and Radio Artists (AFTRA), the American Federation of Musicians of the United States and Canada (AFM), the American Guild of Musical Artists (AGMA, representing performers in opera, chorus, dance, and figure skating, as well as various backstage personnel), and the American Guild of Variety Artists (AGVA, representing artists in cabaret, comedy, revues, circus work, and nightclubs). All these unions belong to the AFL-CIO, which has a strong anti-discrimination and anti-harassment policy, which binds all member organizations and entities with whom they make contracts. The policy states that the union in question does not discriminate against or allow harassment of any employee based on the employee's race, ethnicity, religion, color, sex, age, national origin, sexual orientation, disability, gender identity or expression, ancestry, pregnancy, or any other basis prohibited by law, or based on the employee's protected activity under the anti-discrimination statutes (that is, opposition to prohibited discrimination or participation in the statutory complaint process).[48]

The policy offers a useful account of what behavior constitutes sexual harassment, following the general outlines of Title VII. It also gives examples of sexual harassment, including sexually oriented jokes and gestures, quid-pro-quo arrangements, and the display or distribution of pornography. And it spells out procedures used to investigate claims. These are internal to each member union. A first step is for the complainant to contact both the employer and a union representative. Both informal dispute resolution and a more formal process are described.

Member unions typically supplement these policies with their own more specific guidelines. AGMA, for example, in addition to a formal policy similar to that of the AFL-CIO, gives specific helpful advice to its members, even creating an online portal where a complainant may file a complaint, and promising confidentiality.

Such union policies, which standardly become part of any contract in the relevant area, offer good deterrents and good remedial procedures in any area where there is a bounded workplace. Even a formal audition process would be covered under the policy. Any harassed employee who was under contract and represented by any of these unions when the harassment occurred could in theory complain through such procedures. The women harassed by Dutoit and Domingo were on the job and could have lodged complaints with both management and their union representatives. (Note, however, that Dutoit typically singled out guest soloists for abuse, not people with whom he had an ongoing daily work relationship, which possibly explains the absence of union-related complaints.) And companies that have adopted policies of their own mirroring union policies can and do use them to terminate artists, as San

Francisco Opera did with David Daniels. However, Domingo was also the management at LA Opera, and all the women who made complaints about his behavior reported fear that their stories would not be taken seriously (despite ubiquitous awareness of the two men's conduct).

Good policies need to include procedures for independent investigations like the one invited by the LA Opera in Domingo's case. Unions are helpful, good contracts are helpful—but insufficient, when star power is in question. The fact that Dutoit was toppled relatively easily—well, not until the age of eighty-three—shows that he is perceived as less powerful, less irreplaceable, than Domingo. As for Levine's victims, they were not connected to any professional contract (rather, to a summer program for talented youth) and were not yet protected by any union.

It is not surprising that Samuel Schultz was elected as an AGMA officer. Maybe he can prevent for others the type of star abuse he says he suffered from Daniels and Walters.

Stars are powerful, but they are also vulnerable. They can be preyed upon by extortionate false accusations. For this reason any good policy needs to have some type of due process and an opportunity for the accused to respond. The LA Opera inquiry seems to have been exemplary in that regard, and perhaps that very strategy—retaining an independent law firm to conduct the inquiry—should be the norm going forward. Most of the legal work for symphonies and opera companies is already done pro bono by large law firms. They could add this crucial function to their contribution.[49]

Watching and warning. All four men had such widespread reputations for abuse that in three of the four cases (I haven't found anyone who claims to have tried to keep young men out of Levine's clutches!), many people worked behind the scenes to protect vulnerable employees from the maestro's likely behavior. When Daniels went to Michigan, the music school was informally told that they had better keep students away from him. And as we see, when one did complain, the complaint was dealt with respectfully and promptly.

When Dutoit went to conduct the Philadelphia Orchestra, according to the orchestra's president, rumors of inappropriate behavior were widespread, so leadership "made it clear to everyone who worked on staff with the Philadelphia Orchestra to be careful and bring to us any examples of any behavior that was inappropriate. No one did while I was there."[50] (Pianist Jenny Chai, however, claims that she was sexually assaulted by Dutoit during that period.) And Fiona Allen, an administrator who formerly interned with Tanglewood when Dutoit was a guest conductor and was harassed by Dutoit after delivering a document to his dressing room, reported after being warned, too late, never to see him alone, "They had a system in place. And the system was called: Don't go in there by yourself. Like, we've had complaints, therefore the way we get around that is that we send people in, in pairs. Not: We don't employ that person anymore."[51] It seems hardly necessary to report that such "watchfulness," even if it did impede the harasser from acting (and we don't know that it did), itself constitutes a hostile work environment: you can't do your work without taking elaborate precautions against abuse.

In the case of Domingo, the strategies grew ever more elaborate over the years. A production coordinator who worked with Domingo at both the LA Opera and the Houston Grand Opera told the Associated Press that she made it a point never to put Domingo in rehearsal rooms alone with young female singers, and also that she "tried" to assign him male dressers. "I never would have sent any woman of any sort into his dressing room," she concluded. She also invited Domingo's wife Marta to attend company parties, "because if Marta was around, he behaves."[52] But management stratagems were usually not sufficient: women had to find their own avoidance mechanisms—turning their head at the last minute to avoid an unwelcome wet kiss, locking their dressing room doors and not going out until a dresser said that the coast was clear. Once again: this seems to amount to a "hostile work environment." Women stated, further, that they did not go to management with complaints (even where Domingo was not the management) because they feared both disbelief and retaliation (presumably from management heavily invested in Domingo, not from Domingo himself).

Vigilance, while it may work for a time, is no substitute for a decent workplace environment. The LA Opera report on Domingo by Gibson, Dunn is correct in insisting that the institution must have clearer policies about acceptable behavior and mandatory training of management and staff.

Donor pressure. A useful avenue for enforcement of norms is the pressure of donors to arts organizations, both publicly and behind the scenes, and both individually and through the board of directors. A large proportion of income in classical music is from donors, so they wield great power and should use it in cases such as these where complainants are powerless. Will this happen? Fame sells tickets and brings in donor money. The cost-benefit analysis about a figure such as Domingo must include the deep feelings of injured artists and of progressive members of the opera-going public, but also the opinions of other donors who have very different views about these matters, formed in an earlier era. As I've noted several times, cost-benefit analysis is likely to tilt against Domingo precisely because he is eighty, as it has already turned firmly against Levine, a similar marquee name, simply because he is too old and sick. That's not enough: donors need to empower women to complain by letting it be known that bad behavior will not be tolerated by the donors themselves. The way forward is for an enlightened CEO to empower donors who understand the issues abused women have been raising: Lyric Opera of Chicago has just elevated University of Chicago Law School faculty member Sylvia Neil, a lecturer in law and an expert in women's rights, to chair its board in future years.

Consumer pressure. The world of classical music is somewhat less sensitive to consumer pressure than the world of pop music or film, because it depends less on ticket sales. But of course ticket sales are an essential and highly coveted part of all the arts. Consumer protests and avoidances, whether organized or individual, clearly have the potential to ruin a show. The termination of Kevin Spacey's contracts probably owes more to thinking about viewers than to independent moral judgment. Here as in sports, we can and should all use the power we have.

Disgraced Stars and Their Work

All of these stars have been disgraced. Three, it seems, should remain disgraced. I think Domingo's case is different. He has apologized for what the reports find him really guilty of, though it is less clear that he fully understands how his sheer greatness itself creates pressure and intimidation. However, if this new understanding and this genuine respect for women proves more than a self-defensive posture, and shows itself over time in his conduct, I would certainly urge a public reconciliation—in that case alone among my four—especially in light of the way he has genuinely helped and respected women, and so many young artists, over the years. It is credible that attitudes of another era and the mores of a different country colored his behavior, even though the apparent inability to listen characteristic of star power also influenced him more than it should have. Well, let's wait and see.

Dante's poem showed only a small number of proud people in Purgatory, because to get there you need, first, to own up to and ask mercy for your bad acts. But Purgatory is long and hard, and the proud who get there need to show that they are working on their character traits in all sincerity. For the proud, this means above all listening to others as equals and showing them respect.

And what of the work of the unrepentant? I have so many recordings. What should I, what should radio stations, what should other consumers, do? I've investigated a bit and found that the standard recording contract in classical music gives musicians a one-time up-front fee, not a residual, so by buying their work nobody is paying them money. And the value of the art is what it is. I see no reason, then, not to listen to their, at least Levine's, work—I can do without Dutoit and Daniels—and even to be moved by it and wonder at it, pondering all the while the dark interconnections of the human heart, love and laughter with sinister cruelty.

CHAPTER 8

Masculinity and Corruption

THE SICK WORLD OF COLLEGE SPORTS

You look at it and there's so much good and so much outright terrible.

—Coach Bruce Arians about the 2019 record

of Tampa Bay quarterback Jameis Winston

Coach Arians was talking about Winston's work as an athlete, in a season in which Winston set an NFL all-time record by throwing thirty touchdown passes *and* thirty interceptions. Anyone who has watched Winston sees what Arians sees: such strength, such elegance and beauty in his long passes (two consecutive games that year with over 450 yards)—but such a mess too, such a lack of precision, combined with possibly incurable overconfidence. (Winston responded to the Arians comment by saying, "You look at my numbers, I'm ballin.' "[1]) To give you an idea of that interception number: it is six more than the total number of interceptions thrown in that same season by Tom Brady, Aaron Rodgers, Carson Wentz, and Russell Wilson.

Arians's remark might serve, as well, as a description of Winston's career as a human being to date: so much promise, so much real achievement, and yet so much undisciplined arrogance, so much lazy defiant flouting of society's laws—against theft, against nonconsensual sexual activity. (Don't worry: I know the two types of flaws do not always go together. Winston's "classmate," 2015 number-two draft pick Marcus Mariota, by all accounts an exemplary human being, has had an equally uneven pro career, though in his case injuries seem a big part of the picture.)

Arians's remark might serve, too, as a description of the world of college sports from which Winston emerged in 2015 as his draft year's brightest star—the world that cultivated his extraordinary athletic talent and exploited it for gain, but failed to give him a college education; a world that covered up for him when he raped a woman and shoplifted soda from Burger King and crab legs from Publix; a world that encouraged the arrogant above-the-law attitude that he flaunted until very recently—and, frequently called upon as a motivational speaker, taught the young men who look up to him.

Any human being can change and grow. There's hope that Winston will fulfill his athletic promise and that, whether he does or not, he will become a wiser, more respectful human being. There are signs that this is in fact happening, perhaps as a result of adversity and the introspection it often brings with it. I love watching him, so I would like this all to happen. But I'll argue that there is no hope for the world of college sports, meaning Division I football and basketball.

Professional sports have their problems of sexual harassment and domestic abuse, but these problems can be solved in much the way that the arts can solve their problems: vigilance, tough unions, careful oversight by management, and respectful attention to voices of complaint. In the world of Division I college sports, by contrast, there are such deep systemic problems in the whole setup—collective action problems and problems of external corporate influence—that the sexual and academic corruption that besets this entire world cannot be fixed. The NCAA has tried for years, to no avail, and that is not because good people have not given their lives to the cause. The problem is structured so as to be unfixable. The good and the outright terrible cannot be separated. We should therefore heed the wise call of NBA commissioner Adam Silver and get rid of the entire system, replacing it by a system of minor leagues (as in Europe and as in U.S. baseball), but combining them with "learning academies" for the players. Meanwhile, colleges and universities can continue with Division III sports, a system not without deep problems but, in principle, fixable.

Or so I shall argue, no doubt enraging many.

Sports and Masculinity

Competitive sports are without doubt the major source of entertainment in the United States, whether we count by spectator numbers or by earnings. They share accountability problems with the performing arts, but they also raise distinctive issues of their own. More than any other piece of our popular culture, sports serve as sources of role models for the young. Most young people have never heard of a single federal judge, so the corruption of an Alex Kozinski, while very bad, does not shape their ideas of masculinity. And even though some performers in film and popular music have large youth audiences, these stars do not have the pedagogical role in our society that sports stars do. When we see young people adoring pop stars—as in the past they adored Keith Richards or Michael Jackson, and as today they adore lawbreaker R. Kelly—we usually don't immediately worry that those young people will model their own behavior, or their ideas of what a real man is, on these figures: they are understood to be eccentric, albeit wonderful in some sui generis way. R. Kelly allegedly committed serious crimes against women, but it would be surprising if ten-year-olds were led to imitate his behavior.[2]

Sports figures, by contrast, are models for the average ten-year-old: models of manly and womanly excellence, of discipline, strength, speed, endurance. And since our nation never totally separates greatness from financial success, they are also models of how you use your body to turn yourself into a multimillionaire.

When I was a ten-year-old, baseball was the major source of heroes for boys, and there was no corresponding sports source of heroines. (Baseball stars were hardly uniformly exemplary, but ten-year-olds knew about the goodness of the good characters—Jackie Robinson, Willie Mays, Hank

Aaron—and they were unaware of Mickey Mantle's alcoholism or Ted Williams's crude attitudes toward women.) Now there are many sports sources of both heroes and heroines, but by far the most influential are the sports that have the largest share of our nation's attention, and today this means football and basketball. Baseball has slipped to third place in terms of the percentage of people who say it's their favorite sport, and even though it is still ahead of basketball in total TV viewers (both being far behind football), baseball just doesn't excite the young.

The heroes that today's male ten-year-olds emulate come above all from the world of football and basketball, and often these young men are influenced by their own participation in the cultures of masculinity in those sports.[3] This means that their heroes are men who were created as the men they are by the college sports system and the high school feeder system before it. So we're not simply talking now about a workplace and its problems. We're talking about the formation of generations of men.

Books could be, and many have been, written about the different ways masculinity is envisaged in different sports, and I won't add to this literature, except to say that in both basketball and baseball a wide diversity of skills need to be cultivated, including speed, deftness, and remarkable coordination. In both games attempts to reduce the sport to one or two things (height in basketball, pitching speed and home-run clout in baseball) have repeatedly been undone by the varied evolution of the game itself—by the deftness of a Steph Curry, who eclipsed all hype for seven-footers by his "small ball"; by LeBron James's insistence on feeding the ball to his teammates rather than doing a solo act; by pitchers like Justin Verlander and C. C. Sabathia (in his later years) who succeed by craft and guile rather than overwhelming speed, or like Mariano Rivera, whose pinpoint control and year-in-year-out consistency, while throwing just one pitch with endless variations, were his greatness; by hitters like Phil Rizzuto in the past and Jose Altuve in the present who defy the odds of height (5'5" and 5'6", respectively) with speed, craft, and grit; by sluggers like the great Willie Mays who insisted on also becoming great fielders and runners, helping their teams in ways that go way beyond individual stats.

When ten-year-olds emulate players in those sports or perhaps, today, soccer stars, there are a lot of attractive aspects of masculinity on offer. Former Oakland pitcher Vida Blue, born in 1949, says that when he was growing up, Willie Mays was "the epitome of what a young African American wanted to be."[4] What a great model: not just across-the-board skills (running, throwing, catching, hitting), but also passionate team-work, a joyful and non-angry temperament, skill at defusing conflict, no smoking or drinking—and, crucially, respectful treatment of women.

Football is at least a little bit different. It appears, at least, that brute strength and the ability to smash someone are paramount, and that giv-ing some other player's head a lethal blow is a virtue. I would never deny that there are great feats of grace, speed, agility, and teamwork in foot-ball. And grit of an admirable kind can be seen in the sheer determina-tion with which a superb runner like Seattle's Marshawn Lynch keeps going despite all bodies in his way. Even tackling is really an art, and you never do succeed by simple weight and crushing force. Nonetheless, if we ask what is above all communicated to the young, football sends a some-what unattractive message: force and domination is what it is all about.

On February 22, 2017, Jameis Winston made a guest appearance at a St. Petersburg, Florida, elementary school—the type of thing athletes do to show that they are good people and to help public relations for the sport. During the motivational talk, he said,

> All my boys stand up, all my ladies you can sit down.
>
> But all my boys, stand up. We strong, right? We strong! We strong, right? All my boys, tell me one time: I can do anything I put my mind to. A lot of boys aren't supposed to be soft-spoken. You know what I'm saying? One day y'all are going to have a very deep voice like this (in deep voice). One day, you'll have a very, very deep voice.
>
> . . . But the ladies—they're supposed to be silent, polite, gentle. My men, my men supposed to be strong.[5]

School officials and parents were very upset, and on February 23 Winston apologized for his "poor word choice."[6] Winston, a hero for

thousands of young men, is a product (though not a graduate) of Florida
State University.

Accountability in Professional Sports

Professional sports are similar to the (other) performing arts and can be
dealt with in similar ways: through collective bargaining, consumer pressure, and, an added factor, pressure by the companies that sponsor sports
matches, which can in turn be pressured by their consumers. The sports
world is more like a "normal" closed workplace than most of the arts,
in that players have relatively long-term contracts with a single team;
so it would appear that there is little danger of a Harvey Weinstein–like
presence influencing hiring throughout the entirety of a sport. (Perhaps,
too, the extreme homophobia of the male sports world and the absence
of women as players and as top-rank executives has to a great extent
prevented the sexual harassment of male players or would-be players by
management and its representatives.)

The world of professional sports in the United States is hardly a perfect
world. Both leagues and players associations have been lamentably slow
to take sexual assault, sexual harassment, and domestic violence seriously. Any honest narrative of professional sports life in my high school
years would show a virtual epidemic of sexual promiscuity (and drug
abuse); and yet Jim Bouton's forthright baseball book *Ball Four*[7] got bad
press, at first, not for baseball but for Bouton, because the sport didn't
like people telling the truth about its putative heroes. Baseball commissioner Bowie Kuhn called the book "detrimental to baseball" and tried to
get Bouton to sign a statement saying it was all fictional.[8]

Did the womanizing Bouton describes (and that honest biographies
of the great players of the past routinely describe) include sexual harassment? It's pretty obvious that the atmosphere of the locker room was
not respectful to women, and that if a woman had worked in that world
the notion of a hostile work environment would have had many appli-
cations. The reason we can't quite say that the clubhouses were hostile

work environments is simply that women suffered such total discrimination that they were not in that workplace at all. Women were sometimes ticket sellers or front office employees. But they simply were not allowed to enter the clubhouse even as journalists, far less as coaches, assistant coaches, or part of the management team. And of course it goes without saying that women were not players. Much heavy weather was made of the alleged impossibility of women entering a place where they might see an unclothed athlete.

So, all the womanizing was done outside of the workplace, though barely outside, often in the team-assigned hotels and motels. It was therefore thought to be no part of the sports world: it was the private life of the players, which the workplace had decided to protect as private, as they also protected domestic abuse, when it came to their attention.

No doubt sometimes there was sexual assault in these encounters, and often, too, domestic violence and spousal rape by players against their partners. But both management and players associations either ignored such behavior or kept it from the public. They not only didn't make and enforce rules against these abuses, they positively covered them up. Even so, however, the abused women generally were local women independent from the team, so it was not as if management encouraged players to view their fellow students as potential targets, or tacitly promised to cover up sexual abuse of such fellow students, members of the same allegedly academic institution. This is what the college system does all the time.

Today, women are increasingly present in the clubhouse as sports journalists. Many also work at a reasonably high level in management. At the NBA league office, 40 percent of the workforce is female.[9] Women have begun to be hired as assistant coaches: there are thirteen, current or retired, in the NBA; the NFL currently has four (two on the Tampa Bay Buccaneers, since Bruce Arians is a strong supporter of hiring women as coaches and hired the very first when he coached the Arizona Cardinals); in baseball, the San Francisco Giants hired the first full-time major league coach in January 2020.[10] The NBA has had six female referees, four currently active; baseball now has two female umpires, both still working in the minor leagues, and the NFL has one female referee. In

May 2019, Adam Silver announced a goal for the NBA: going forward new hires as coaches and referees ought to be around 50 percent female.[11]

At the same time that women are increasingly present in the male professional sports world, professional sports leagues in the United States have also faced up to the need for clear rules and policies about both sexual assault and domestic violence. Rules of conduct about both workplace encounters and the "private life" of the players have been announced as part of the contract. Major players in all the major sports have been suspended under these policies, though not with much consistency.

A catalyst in the transition to accountability was a 2014 incident in which NFL player Ray Rice, then of the Baltimore Ravens, was seen on video camera footage punching his fiancée in an elevator and knocking her out. He was arrested and indicted, his contract was terminated, and he was indefinitely suspended.[12] Although the suspension was overturned on appeal, Rice has not worked in the NFL since. The incident made the sports world aware of intense public opinion surrounding domestic abuse. Understanding that women are also sports consumers, and consumers of the products who sponsor sports, sports leagues moved toward explicit policies and greater accountability. As a result, many other players in all major sports have faced discipline. Now what is needed are consistent proactive policies fostering deterrence and education and backing up deterrence with a consistent effective system of sanctions.

Baseball has been especially proactive. In August 2015, Major League Baseball and the Major League Baseball Players Association agreed to a comprehensive policy on domestic violence, sexual assault, and child abuse, spelling out consequences for violations but also focusing on ex ante training and education.[13] Big-name players whose teams need them for victory have served long suspensions: Addison Russell of the Chicago Cubs, a valuable part of their 2016 World Series victory, later served a forty-game suspension for domestic violence, to which he admitted, and he credits the mandatory therapy for new understanding.[14] (The Cubs found him not so valuable on his return; they demoted him to the minor leagues and then let him go.) Domingo German, probably the New York Yankees' best pitcher in 2019, was suspended for eighty-one games in the middle of a pennant race, something that certainly hurt the team.[15] So baseball has shown a willingness to make really tough decisions.

Basketball, similarly, has a joint policy negotiated by the players association and the NBA and has not been hesitant to hand out suspensions of prominent players (usually shorter than in baseball), including Darren Collison and Ron Artest of the Sacramento Kings. (Artest's suspension and anger management therapy apparently turned his behavior around: he later won the NBA's citizenship award, and in 2011 he changed his name legally to Metta World Peace.) Part of the latest NBA policy is an agreement with the players union that the league has the power to investigate domestic violence and to punish players regardless of whether criminal charges have been resolved. The policy also emphasizes education and prevention through counseling, rookie training, and a confidential 24–7 hotline available to all NBA players, partners, and family members.[16]

Football, by contrast, has no shared agreement.[17] The league has a vague wishy-washy statement, but it is not even mentioned in the collective bargaining agreement with the players association. The association has a Commission on Violence Prevention, but it apparently does nothing: journalist Deborah Epstein resigned from the commission in June 2018, saying, "I simply cannot continue to be part of a body that exists in name only."[18] Suspensions sometimes are handed out (Winston served one, as we'll see), but often the league is inactive and the job of discipline is thrown mainly onto the teams, who mete out penalties erratically and on a case-by-case basis.[19]

The National Hockey League has no policy, just a case-by-case procedure.[20]

It's clear that all sports need to do better: a policy is only as good as its implementation, though baseball and basketball seem to be doing a pretty decent job. Both unions and management in all sports need to be pressured by both fans and sponsors (and by fans through the beer companies and other sponsors). But basically the situation is as it is in the arts, with the added advantage of relatively closed workplaces.[21]

Now to college sports. To see the American situation in context, let's bear in mind that in Europe there are no university sports teams in the U.S. sense. Students get together for informal fun, but universities do not sponsor teams that compete nationwide and command a wide television audience, meanwhile training players for a career in professional sports. Instead, the leagues themselves sponsor lower-level teams that perform this training function. Typically players who show early promise would go into one of those lower-tier teams rather than going to university.[22]

So too in U.S. baseball. Lower-tier minor league teams, most of them attached to and partially supported by major league teams, are as old as the leagues themselves. There are also unaffiliated minor league teams, but this has always been a tenuous proposition financially. The Negro Leagues did pretty well when they were the only place to see such great players as Satchel Paige and Cool Papa Bell. When the major leagues eventually, and for the most part grudgingly, opened their doors to African American athletes, the Negro Leagues rapidly went out of business, since they no longer made money for their largely white owners.

Today, in what I'll call the minor league system (encompassing all sports in Europe and baseball in the United States), virtually no young player goes directly to the majors. Players sign a contract with the organization and then are placed in a lower tier that suits their age and developmental stage, whether AAA or AA or A.[23] In the United States, baseball does exist as a college sport, and a small, and growing, percentage of eventual major league players do go to college, sometimes on a baseball scholarship. Today, 4.3 percent of players have a college degree, though often this is accomplished by going to school part-time while playing. Curtis Granderson, for example, the son of two teachers, got a degree in business management from the University of Illinois at Chicago while playing, though he says it was very difficult to do.[24] But nobody thinks that going to college before playing pro baseball is the normal route of development, and it tends to delay a pro career rather than promote it. Even the academically solid Jackie Robinson left UCLA just shy of a degree (although his widow Rachel, alive today at ninety-seven, got a graduate degree and became a professor at Yale School of Nursing).

The minor league system has one glaring defect: players do not learn skills that will get them employment should their pro sports career prove brief or a failure. One of the most tragic aspects of Roger Kahn's marvelous book, *The Boys of Summer,* which follows the post-baseball lives of the players for the Brooklyn Dodgers of the early 1950s,[25] almost twenty years later, is how tenuous their post-baseball economic lives are. There are exceptions: Carl Erskine and Joe Black became executives (the latter a signal victory in the racial climate of the day). But more often they don't have a real career, they don't have meaningful pensions—and they didn't earn today's astronomical major league salaries, which allow investment and savings. Their sense of sadness and loss is related to their lack of a future commensurate with their past. (Kahn's title cites the Dylan Thomas line, "I see the boys of summer in their ruin," implying that no longer playing baseball means "ruin" of necessity, rather than because of the lack of effective skills training and a nonexistent pension system.) And what of the players who never made it to the majors? They are clearly far more bereft. Any decent system of professional sports ought to prepare players for earning in life after sports.

Where issues of sexual assault are concerned, however, the minor league system has a big advantage: it is for the most part one large closed workplace, where the major leagues can set up clear rules for all and they can be written into the contracts negotiated with the players associations. Most players will be governed by that system from the time that they begin their lives as salaried players. It's not too surprising, therefore, that baseball has taken a leading role in promoting clear standards for sexual abuse and domestic violence. The fact that the NBA has been similarly proactive reflects strong leadership but perhaps, also, the fact that its players increasingly enter the NBA directly after high school. We should keep our eyes on college baseball, however, since in the past twenty years the major league draft has focused increasingly on college players, because they turn out to have better records once they get into the team system than do high school draftees.[26] Of course, once drafted, they will still spend some years in the minor leagues. But the college system bears part of the cost of training them. So far as I can tell, this trend has not yet produced the kind of corporate buy-in or the kind of sexual corruption we see in football and to some degree basketball, no doubt because college baseball is not very popular and is rarely televised. Still, it is a trend to be watched, in case the corruption begins to spread there.

In non-baseball popular sports in the United States, by contrast, players arrive at a "normal" closed workplace (or set of closed workplaces, where the leagues are weak and leave discipline to teams) relatively late in their careers, after years of preparation in the college system and the high school system that feeds it (though the NBA is increasingly an exception to this). But the college system is corrupt and sets up its prize athletes to believe that they are above the law, while giving them access to vulnerable campus women whose complaints are all too often ignored.

In Division I (D-I) football and basketball, at least above other sports, a corrupt system has taken hold. There is certainly academic corruption in many D-I sports, and other college D-I sports have had their share of sex scandals,[27] but these two disproportionately engage in a corrupt mixing of academics with big-money corporate funding, and shape national images of masculinity more than the others. Let me be clear: I do not oppose real professionalism, together with a competitive market for talent and payment to individual athletes. Indeed, this is what the minor league system has long had, and it has virtues of transparency and regulability that I shall favor as the best alternative to the current structure. The problem with the current college system, as we shall see, is that corporate money operates in a concealed way, with a pretense that the corporate entities are integral parts of an academic endeavor, while they resist all control by academic officials. And of course pay does not go to individual athletes. They are hostages to the system, dominated and exploited, while at the same time their misdeeds are covered up.

It is not too soon to mention race. Football and basketball, far more than other sports, are dominated by African American talent. It is no accident that a system has emerged that exploits that talent for no pay, while showing gross neglect of athletes' intellectual education and a tendency to encourage them in just the sort of masculine misbehavior that figures in the most damaging racial stereotypes.

Division I College Sports: A Diseased Structure

The colleges and universities whose football and basketball teams belong to Division I must shoulder a large financial burden to have such teams. Football, in particular, is very expensive at this level. The college must have a stadium of professional caliber, first-rate training and workout facilities, and superlative equipment—not because athletes really need these glitzy facilities but because star recruits are lured by them and donors also expect them. The biggest college stadiums seat over 100,000. There are ten college stadiums that have larger seating capacity than the largest professional football stadium. Prospective players will consider only the best, and so already, including groundskeeping, maintenance, and so forth, we are looking at a major expense. Universities compete to lure recruits by building. A typical recent example is the beachfront stadium with stunning practice facilities at Northwestern University near Chicago, which cost $260 million to build, even without maintenance.[28] Right now it is said to be the most expensive football complex in the Big Ten, but that's the bare minimum to attain star status.

Then there's the coach. In almost every state, the most highly paid state employee is the football coach of the state university team.[29] A typical salary for a leading college coach is $5 to $9 million, not including contractually specified bonuses.[30] This also means that the football coach, at both public and private universities, is usually the most highly paid individual on campus: the most highly paid college presidents earn between $1 and $2 million per year.[31] (CEOs of university-affiliated hospitals often outearn the university's president and can at times rival the football coach, but just barely.) The rest of the team's coaching staff is commensurately expensive. Teams must also travel to away games, and any star athlete would spurn the drab insides of a bus: private jet transport is the norm. And so forth. Basketball is also expensive but much less expensive than football. Equipment needs are more modest, basketball facilities are modest in size and virtually interchangeable, and coaches' salaries are, if high, typically modest by comparison to those in football. Mike Krzyzewski ("Coach K") of Duke and John Calipari of Kentucky are in football coach range, but there's a rapid drop-off after that.

Colleges typically sell these expenses to students, parents, alumni, and donors by pointing to the expected revenue of having a successful Division I team. For most colleges who compete for star status, however, the promise of revenue is illusory. Of the 130 teams in D-I, at most 20 can hope to make a profit.[32] Profit comes largely from TV contracts, not ticket sales, and only the top twenty (and that's generous) are deemed TV-worthy. The common belief that a splashy team increases alumni donations in a way proportional to the expense of such a team has been carefully examined in William Bowen's two rigorous and searching books, and has been found to be erroneous.[33]

What this all means is that a very large number of universities are competing for a very small number of money-making slots. To get a winning team they must attract the most talented players. But high-end talent in football and basketball is in short supply. That's how the natural lottery works. The professional leagues are less troubled by this, since they have a monopoly of the available talent, and an organized system, through the draft, of allocating it in a way that pretty decently gives all teams a shot. Not so in the college game. Each year, 130 schools are recruiting, and in each year there will be perhaps 20 players of major talent, and who they are is already pretty clear from their high school record. Schools may believe that it is foolish to lavish so much money on practice facilities and a coach's salary, but that's how you recruit top talent. Any school that draws a rational line loses.

The situation has the structure of a classic collective action problem: taken singly, schools might prefer not to spend to the hilt on football and basketball, but taken as a mutually competing group they must spend more and more, in what the late Myles Brand, former NCAA commissioner, called an "arms race."[34]

That's one arms race, the race for recruitment, won largely by expensive buildings and facilities and a whole scouting/marketing team that begins researching talent several years before college application even starts, traveling to high schools all over the country. Once the player arrives, however, two new arms races begin. One is an arms race over academic standards. Since the NCAA has rules of eligibility that require a decent minimum academic average, the collective action problem gives rise to all sorts of schemes to evade these rules, including bogus courses, papers written for students by others, suppression of whistleblowing, anything but a determination to give the athlete a real education. We'll discuss some examples of this effort to game the system in talking about Florida State, but they crop up in many places. Indeed, schools who genuinely and honestly uphold academic standards are well known as exceptions to the rule, and you can count them on the fingers of one hand: probably Stanford, Northwestern, Notre Dame, a couple of others—and of course a school that is honest one year may succumb to temptation the next. After all, when the coach makes four times as much money as the university president, how long can academic values and academic leadership withstand the pressure of the arms race, with its promise of profit?

The arms race that concerns me here, however, is the arms race to protect athletes from criminal investigation and indictment, in order to maintain their athletic eligibility. Athletes commit many potentially criminal offenses, including illegal drug use and sales, shoplifting and other property crimes, and drunk driving. But since we're talking about young men whose whole formation since the age of ten has led them to think they are icons of exciting masculinity and above the laws that apply to lesser men, many commit sexual offenses: sexual assault, harassment, stalking. Since an entire institution's TV fortunes may depend on one or two talents, these talents will be zealously shielded in the face of charges of sexual offenses, including, often, by university alums who are the town's police, prosecutors, and judges.

In any collective action problem, the difficulty is systemic. Each party taken singly may judge that standards should be upheld—and yet, the logic of the structure dictates that the defector reaps the profits. Things are even worse, however, in college sports, since the people who really make the decisions are not the same people who judge that standards ought to be upheld. (For this reason I don't see it as a classic "prisoner's dilemma" problem, because there is a multiplicity of players who have very different goals, and only some of them actually think it would be good to stamp out academic and sexual corruption.) Coaches, as I've said, are in many respects more powerful than university presidents, and can get a president who crosses them fired.

And there is something more. In all the major sports schools entering this fray, there are corporate entities attached to the school that have a large financial stake in the local team's success. The nexus takes different forms. Sometimes there is a single sports apparel franchise that makes a deal with the school and reaps profits, and sometimes in addition (as with Nike and the University of Oregon) this corporation's CEO is also a hugely influential university backer and donor.[35] Sometimes a composite corporate entity is formed from wealthy alumni and sports apparel franchises, such as the Seminole Boosters at Florida State University. In any case these entities foot the bill for much of the huge expense of fielding a winning team, and consequently have decisive influence.

These corporate entities have no clear interest in upholding academic standards or the integrity of women's bodies. They want victory and the profit that comes with victory. Any policy that opposes victory is a policy they will likely try to subvert. These entities are much more powerful than university faculty and presidents. As for the law, we shall see the extent to which they are even able to effect a cover-up of illegal conduct.

Once again: these corporate entities emphatically do not create a culture of real sports professionalism. They operate in a semi-clandestine manner, pretending to be part of the academic enterprise, while they pursue their own ends. And they determinedly resist the model of real professionalization, in which there is a market for talent and individual players are paid in accordance with their market value. They pretend this is because the players are students, while they actively subvert real education in a multitude of ways. Far from regulating player conduct in the manner of a real professional league, they give tacit encouragement to academic corruption and sexual misbehavior, as if these permissions to misbehave were fitting substitutes for the salaries they are determined to withhold.

Football above the Law:
The Case of Florida State University

It's useful to have a clear paradigm of the diseased structure in front of us as we contemplate possible reforms. Much has been written about sexual assault, academic corruption, and college sports in the past twenty years, including three serious studies of particular universities: Joshua Hunt's *University of Nike: How Corporate Cash Bought American Higher Education*, focusing on the University of Oregon;[36] Paula Lavigne and Mark Schlabach's *Violated: Exposing Rape at Baylor University amid College Football's Sexual Assault Crisis*;[37] and Mike McIntire's *Champions Way*, an analysis focusing on Florida State. All three have merit, all largely agree, and all discuss the defects in the college football structure much as I am doing here; but I give McIntire the edge for meticulous reporting and documentation, as well as due attention to criticism he has received, so I have chosen to focus on that case, which has the additional merit of focusing attention on both academic and sexual corruption.[38] But Florida State is not at all an isolated case. I am presenting it here as a paradigm that brings out features of the whole college football structure. Data show that the problem of sexual assault is depressingly ubiquitous in Division I football, as are allegations of evasion and cover-up. Roughly 58 percent of D-I football programs (148 schools) had at least one reported incident of sexual misconduct since 1990, and 42 percent of all incidents were handled by a criminal justice system; 26 percent of incidents involved at least one student's arrest.[39]

Florida State not only has an outsize proportion of its budget devoted to football, it also has a semi-private corporate entity, the Seminole Boosters, that supports FSU teams and also hopes to reap a profit from their success.* As McIntire shows, there has long been a tax issue about these corporate entities: they have so far avoided being taxed as private businesses by maintaining that they are part of the university and that

---

* In this discussion, parenthetical citations are to McIntire's *Champions Way*.

their role is "related to the educational function" (78). The Boosters collect revenue from skybox rentals and other concessions at games, as well as from media and licensing rights related to FSU sports. In 2013 their assets totaled $264 million (189). They operate largely independently of the school, with their own board of directors. The university president is supposed to approve their spending, but in 2011 then president Eric Barron said he had never gotten expenditure reports from them (190). Other booster groups are even less accountable: the Crimson Tide Foundation at the University of Alabama, deemed a "blended component unit" of the university, has made no separate reports since 2004 (194). At FSU, the Boosters contribute to the president's salary and benefits, and find ways to bypass NCAA restrictions on paying coaches by directing cash through a separate foundation (195). Boosters engage in business deals affecting the university (for example a tax-subsidized real estate development) with no accountability (196).

FSU has long covered up for the illegal activities of its star players. In 2003 one player was tried for theft and illegal gambling but got off with probation after the coach testified on his behalf. In the same year, another player was tried for sexual assault and acquitted, in an atmosphere of wide-eyed deference to FSU athletics that permeated the courtroom (47). Another player, Michael Gibson, was convicted of an especially brutal rape, confessed, and apologized in court; Coach Bobby Bowden wrote a letter of support for Gibson in an attempt to mitigate his sentence. At this point the local chapter of the National Organization for Women (NOW) wrote to the university's president saying, "Until FSU starts taking seriously sexual violence against women by athletes, the school will continue to send the despicable message to hundreds of young men that rape is okay" (48). In short FSU was long a teacher of male pride and sexual objectification.

There was also a tradition of academic corruption. Numerous faculty spoke to McIntire about pressure to pass illiterate athletes. Eventually he chose to focus on a particularly egregious and sad narrative that was also serialized in the *New York Times*, concerning corruption in the school of hospitality management, where many athletes are encouraged to take classes, and it is understood that these courses have minimal requirements and all athletes pass. McIntyre followed the story of one graduate teaching assistant, Christie Suggs, an older woman with a twelve-year-old son, who turned whistleblower and refused to pass athletes who had not made the grade. Deprived of her teaching assistantship, Suggs was forced to drop out of the PhD program, had no luck finding other employment, and eventually committed suicide (201–3). So, that's one especially ugly tale of academic corruption to put alongside the others we now know of—in particular the scandal over "paper courses" at the University of North Carolina–Chapel Hill, designed particularly for student athletes, where professors wrote papers for students and the paper was the only course requirement.[40]

Our topic here, however, is sexual corruption. Interestingly, Jameis Winston says he was an A student in high school (56), and I've seen no evidence that he had academic difficulties at FSU. But from a very young age he had a sense of his own specialness and invincibility. A video that Winston made of his own bedroom at home in Alabama—a room he calls the "Boom Boom Room"—shows walls lined with trophies. "You know, I was a superstar when I was a little kid too," he remarks. He chose FSU, by his own account, because of the amount of money they offered him (57).[41] Although he is talented in both football and baseball, and played both at FSU for a while, he quickly focused on football, and quickly became a star, winning the coveted Heisman Trophy (the highest individual award in college football) already in his freshman year.

There were signs of trouble. A sexual encounter with a medical student ended up traumatizing her and leading her to seek counseling for a feeling that she was violated (58). Winston later admitted in a deposition that he had had more than fifty sexual partners during his first year at FSU and did not remember their names. He added that he and his roommate Chris Casher used to watch each other having sex; he said it was "kind of like real live porn." Casher added that they often tried to have sex with the same girls: "it's kind of a football player thing. We can kind of, like, run 'em, that is kind of how we do it" (59). FSU athletes, living in a world of pride and objectification, rapidly internalized the lesson that women are just things and not fully real.

Living in a private off-campus housing development mostly for athletes, Winston and Casher had no supervision. After they did $4,000 worth of damage to the apartment, the landlord tried to evict them, but before a felony charge could ruin their careers, the athletic department somehow paid the damages (61). Other legal difficulties for Winston were also minimized: an arrest for squirrel-shooting with an illegal BB gun, a complaint by Burger King that he was stealing soda. A 2014 complaint that he shoplifted crab legs from Publix did earn him a civil citation and twenty hours of community service, but since this was not a felony charge it did not compromise eligibility. And a 2014 incident in which he stood on a table in the FSU student union and shouted, "Fuck her right in the pussy"—which had become an internet meme—earned him a one-game suspension.

Now to Erica Kinsman. Because she never had her day in court, it is necessary to prosecute on her behalf, so to speak, marshaling the facts that emerge from legal documents. Kinsman, a nineteen-year-old FSU student, was drinking at Potbelly's one night in December 2012, when she met a tall attractive African American man who asked for her phone number. Her friends, awed, said it was Chris Casher, a varsity linebacker. He texted her to meet him, and she went with him and two other guys in a taxi. The cab driver said she seemed drunk. She has memory gaps, but the next thing she remembers is Casher's roommate (whom she did not know by name) forcing himself on her. She tried to resist, but he held her down and said it would be OK, just let him finish. Then the third man who had shared the taxi came into the room and, according to Kinsman's testimony, said, "Dude, she's telling you to stop." Casher then started videotaping the sex. The roommate, however, got up and carried her into the bathroom and laid her down on the floor, locking the door first. He then finished, pushing her face into the tile floor. Kinsman told numerous friends and her parents that she had been raped; she went to the hospital and did a rape kit, but could not decide what to do next, since she didn't have a name, even though the exam found bruising and testable semen on her underwear. Right at the beginning of the new semester in January, however, she saw her assailant in one of her classes, and she quickly got his name: Jameis Winston.

The subsequent tale, as told by McIntire and many media sources, is one of an investigation that was disgracefully shoddy. Security cameras in Potbelly's were never examined; the cab driver was not questioned— until Kinsman gave them Winston's name. However, even at that point they did not bring him in for questioning; instead they phoned him and asked to make an appointment for him to talk. (He did not return their call.) *Then* phone records show the police immediately phoning the athletic department's legal "fixer," as well as the Boosters, Coach Jimbo Fisher, and a high-powered criminal defense lawyer. After that, the case was shelved. The police did not ask for DNA evidence, although a rape kit existed; they did not interview witnesses. They just stopped pursuing the complaint. In December 2013, State's Attorney Willie Meggs announced that they were dropping the case, citing "major issues" with the woman's testimony. Meanwhile, Winston continued his winning ways: athletes charged with a felony cannot play until their case is resolved, but Winston was never charged. By this time key evidence had disappeared (the video on Casher's phone, the security camera footage from Potbelly's).

Things might have ended there had the *New York Times* not reported the flawed police investigation.[42] At that point the university opened an investigation and charged Casher with a student-code violation for taking the video, and held a hearing about the charge against Winston. Kinsman's lawyer said that the police investigator, Scott Angulo (who has done private security work for the Seminole Boosters) warned her that since Tallahassee was a big football town she would be "raked over the coals" if she pursued the case—and she was indeed harassed on social media.[43]

Kinsman left Tallahassee to finish college elsewhere. But she returned and gave a detailed narrative to the hearing board. Winston's defense was that she had given consent by "moaning." The hearing took place just before FSU was to play in the 2015 Rose Bowl, with Winston their

star. So the honor of the whole school seemed at stake. The official hearing cleared Winston. The presiding judge, retired Florida Supreme Court
justice B. Harding, wrote, "I do not find the credibility of one story sub-
stantially stronger than that of the other. Both have their own strengths
and weaknesses" (198). The delaying tactics worked: Winston played in
the Rose Bowl—although FSU lost to Oregon, 59–20.

Things did not end there. Kinsman, who now divulged her name publicly, filed a civil suit, charging a Title IX violation by FSU. FSU settled in
2016 for $950,000—just before depositions were to begin. The Boosters
apparently paid a lot of the legal fees and other money involved (200). By
this time, however, Winston, drafted number one in the 2015 draft, was
on his way to stardom in the NFL.

Winston has racked up numerous NFL rookie records and other more
impressive records: youngest player to pass for 4,000 yards, most consecutive 450+-yard passing games, most touchdown passes before his
twenty-fourth birthday. His record is, however, mixed, with an outcome
we'll examine later. As one commentator puts it, Winston is "both marvelous and maddening."[44]

Meanwhile, trajectory of his sexual behavior supports my contention
that the professional leagues handle sexual assault somewhat better than
the college scene. When Winston allegedly groped a female Uber driver
in Arizona in 2016—a type of entitled objectifying behavior that was
part of his FSU pattern—she sued his team, the Tampa Bay Buccaneers.[45]
An NFL investigation concluded that he had violated the league's personal conduct policy by "touching the driver in an inappropriate and
sexual manner without her consent." Winston, who at first denied the
allegation, issued a public apology, stating that he has "eliminated alcohol from my life." He was suspended for the first three games of the 2018
season.[46] He was also required to undergo therapeutic intervention—note
the apparently successful treatment for his alcohol problem—and was
threatened with a heavier penalty should he reoffend. Despite what I've
called the wishy-washy nature of NFL discipline, in this case it seems to
have worked, at least so far. Winston is ambitious, and probably respon-

sive to deterrence. And he knows that unlike FSU, the NFL can get along fine without him.

And yet: it was in 2017 that Winston made the egregious motivational speech to elementary school students that I quoted earlier. Here we see someone who has basically learned nothing. Even when his laudable goal was to motivate students to strive, the only way he found to express that idea was a set of sexist stereotypes. Male force, male strength, female silence and non-resistance. But then, why would Winston be deterred or educated, when a public university, using taxpayer dollars, paid out a million of those dollars in 2016 to settle a complaint involving him, and when, at every step of the road, powerful university officials and alumni connived to corrupt the justice system? Even the NFL has been too indulgent.

Winston certainly has the vice of pride to a high degree, and has learned bad habits of objectification and victimization. And yet, he is at the same time a victim of a corrupt system. He has been exploited throughout his life, used as a tool for the enrichment of others, and never permitted to get a decent education. Very likely, too, he is already on the road to a horrible later life of dementia from CTE (chronic traumatic encephalopathy).[47] We can blame him, but the primary blame surely attaches to the college football system. His life can be turned around. The college football system is unfixable.

The Winston case is particularly egregious, in part because Tallahassee is a relatively small community in which virtually everyone involved seems to be focused on football success. In each case it is important to investigate the local context and see how it makes things either better or worse. But FSU typifies the structural flaws of the college system. Baylor University, similarly, covered up a series of egregious assaults. Even the apparent paragon of morality, Clinton prosecutor and former judge Kenneth Starr, took part—and eventually lost his job, first as president, and then as chancellor.[48] (In January 2019 he signed on as part of Donald Trump's defense team in the impeachment trial,[49] perhaps a case of typecasting, given his prior record of expertise in the art of coverup.) Starr's role is interesting, because he is an able and at times a decent individual, but the case shows how the forces involved in the college sports structure can manipulate such a person, getting him to violate principles that he very likely holds, albeit lightly. Each of the investigative books I've mentioned names other incidents, both at the school concerned and at other schools.

Nor should we think that basketball is exempt from the baneful pattern. Between 2015 and 2019, the University of Louisville had a series of sex scandals, including soliciting prostitution to encourage basketball recruits to choose the university, which led to heavy penalties from the NCAA,[50] and the eventual termination of Coach Rick Pitino, who was also implicated in a murky wire fraud and money-laundering scheme involving Adidas and other athletic officials at other schools, which was uncovered by an FBI probe, and which prompted a major reform effort that we shall later consider.[51]

A particularly dispiriting case not yet made much of in the expanding literature on college sports corruption transpired at Notre Dame, a school that has had a good record of genuinely educating its athletes and molding their conduct. A faculty athletic committee is, or at least used to be, centrally involved in matters relating to athletes, and it takes very seriously the university's scholastic and ethical mission.[52] In earlier cases, Notre Dame dealt well with troubled athletes: in particular the case of gifted linebacker Manti Te'o, who was scammed by someone who established an online relationship with him posing as a girlfriend, and who then created a hoax that this "girlfriend" had died. In this case a promising career was helped by appropriate intervention, and Te'o continues to have a productive career in the NFL (he signed with the Chicago Bears in 2020).

More recently, however, the school has apparently become more involved with investing apparel companies and has been less careful about recruitment and mentoring.[53] The school recruited Prince Shembo, an athlete who already had a bad record: he had been suspended in his senior year of high school for throwing a desk at a teacher who had taken away his cell phone.[54] At Notre Dame in 2010, he was accused of raping Lizzy Seeburg, a student at Saint Mary's College, a liberal arts college for women near Notre Dame. Seeburg, traumatized by the rape and also by texts from Shembo's teammates and classmates warning her not to "mess with ND football,"[55] committed suicide ten days later. Her family insists that Notre Dame was lax and did not pursue the investigation, and indeed this seems correct: Notre Dame denied that any assault or harassment took place, failed to interview the accused until more than two weeks after the incident (which was five days after Seeburg had killed herself), and failed to hold any kind of disciplinary hearing until six months later. The university also subsequently claimed that her suicide was caused by preexisting mental illness, a claim her therapists reject.[56] Meanwhile Shembo was drafted by the Atlanta Hawks, but was waived after he was arrested for allegedly killing his girlfriend's dog by kicking it to death. The dog (a five-pound Yorkshire terrier named Dior) was found to have died of blunt force trauma, having a fractured rib, a fractured liver, abdominal hemorrhage, thoracic hemorrhage, head trauma, and a long list of further injuries.[57] Felony charges of aggravated cruelty to an animal were dropped after Shembo pled guilty to a misdemeanor and paid a $1,000 fine.[58] Shembo is not currently employed in professional football. This disgraceful episode shows that the structures of the system can distort behavior even at one of the most conscientious Division I schools.

Recently, the astonishing decision of Notre Dame to start fall classes full steam in August 2020 amid the pandemic, and require all faculty and students to report to campus, appears to show greed taking precedence over faculty and student safety. In order to get football revenue, they have to bring back the football team. But since the players are supposed to be "student-athletes," they cannot come back unless students and faculty come back. The inadequacy of safety precautions and the lack of options for faculty and students who do not feel safe returning, was dramatized in a set of letters in the *New York Times*.[59]

Young football players enter a college sports program already primed to offend. Their pride has been nourished by years of social conditioning that encourages them to think they are special, and the recruitment process exacerbates that pride. Other people aren't fully real to them, and women in particular are often unreal, just props for pride. As Winston's roommate Chris Casher said of shared sex (often videotaped) with women whose names they never knew, "It's kind of a football player thing."

Collateral Damage:
The College System Protecting Pedophilia

Sexual violence in the college sports system usually takes other students or (in the Notre Dame case) students in other local institutions as its victims. But there are also younger victims, since the college system has also shielded serial pedophiles. The case I'll discuss is famous, so I can be brief. It's the case of Jerry Sandusky, who was an assistant football coach at Penn State for almost twenty years, serving under legendary coach Joe Paterno.[60] The scandal unfolded starting in 2011, thus approximately seventeen years after Sandusky began abusing boys (while employed as coach) through the Second Mile program, a charity for troubled boys he helped to found. Danger signs were apparent already in 1998, when a parent complained of inappropriate conduct with her eleven-year-old son and the police investigated. Sandusky admitted it was wrong to shower with the boy and promised not to do it again. He retired from Penn State officially in 1999, but retained emeritus status and full access to all athletic facilities. Several subsequent incidents of witnessed sexual abuse, including anal sex, took place and were reported and complained about, but law enforcement did not investigate. Only in 2008 was Sandusky even removed from the athletic program's activities involving children.

Those who seek more details can easily find them. Even after a grand jury investigation began in 2011, stonewalling was the norm, and one judge turned out to be a volunteer at Sandusky's charity. Eventually all local common pleas court judges had to recuse themselves because of conflicts of interest involving Penn State athletics. (Penn State, like FSU, is a small community, where intense loyalty to the football team can easily trump ethics.) It emerged that Paterno was involved in the long cover-up, although his death at the age of eighty-five in January 2012 prevented any indictment. Sandusky was found guilty on forty-five counts of sexual abuse in June 2012. FBI director Louis Freeh announced, a month later, that Penn State showed "total and consistent disregard" for child sex abuse victims while covering up for a serial predator. Eventually, after that finding (but of course its response was woefully late, and typically so), the NCAA fined Penn State and banned the football team from post-season competition for four years. In addition, the school lost all wins from 1998–2011. Simultaneously the Big Ten Conference ruled that Penn State's share of revenues from any bowl games for the next four seasons would be donated to charities working to prevent child sexual abuse. Appeals and lawsuits against Penn State are ongoing (and can be tracked in the continually updated article "Penn State Scandal Fast Facts"[61]).

This profoundly shocking story should come as no surprise. It's just what a study of the college system would lead us to expect. Power and greed drive everything in college sports, and these troubled and economically deprived young men who were abused by Sandusky were even more powerless than a woman like Erica Kinsman, who came forward courageously. They too were treated as mere things.[62]

The Failure of Reform

For a long time, many people thought that the corrupt system could be reformed by tougher rules and better enforcement by the NCAA. I now consider two phases of the reform effort: the long tenure of Myles Brand as NCAA president, from 2002 until his death from pancreatic cancer in 2009; and the recent independent Commission on College Basketball, headed by Condoleezza Rice and usually known as the "Rice Commission."

Brand, a philosopher and longtime university administrator, came to the NCAA after long experience with the corrupt college system—first as president of the University of Oregon, where Nike had long called the shots on many university decisions, thanks to the outsize influence of alumnus and major donor Phil Knight, co-founder and longtime CEO of Nike (now chairman emeritus),[63] and then as president of Indiana University. At IU, Brand made the decision to fire popular men's basketball coach Bob Knight, after he crossed a line that Brand had drawn against violent and abusive conduct toward players and other students.

The ensuing uproar included widespread vandalism on campus, a march by a crowd of 2,000 to Brand's house, and the burning of Brand in effigy. Brand and his wife Peg Brand (now Weiser), a professor in the philosophy department, were forced to move out of their house for a time, and Peg was unable to teach her classes because of threats. So, Brand knew the system's flaws first-hand and was highly motivated to fix them. His National Press Club speech in 2001, "Academics First: Reforming Intercollegiate Athletics," had already laid out a set of well-thought-out ideas for reform, and shortly after that speech he left IU for the NCAA.[64] Unlike some administrators Brand wrote prolifically and defended his ideas carefully, so his legacy gives an attractive picture of a model of reform that has dominated the NCAA long after his death.

Brand was a lover of college sports, and he strongly believed that high-level college sports belong in colleges and universities as a key part of their educational mission. He also believed that ethical thinking is, or ought to be, a major part of college sports, and that issues of diversity and inclusion should also be made central. He emphasized the need to promote greater racial diversity in the hiring of coaches, and praised the role of Title IX in promoting women's equality in college sports. Unlike Bill Bowen, whose idea that sports are one part of a student's college life has led him to be strongly critical of the pre-professionalization of sports teams, which separates athletes from the rest of a university's students and denies non-pre-professional students opportunities to try out for teams, Brand accepted the pre-professionalization as part of a great university. He said it is similar to the programs many universities have that train professional musicians alongside other students. But he insisted that athletes should be held to the same academic standards as other students and should have the full range of academic opportunities that other students have. He characteristically spoke in generalities about these views, not fully acknowledging the extent to which D-I football and basketball had already taken on a life of their own in universities—funded by apparel companies and other outside sources—and, more generally, not fully acknowledging the deforming role of big money in these sports.

His analogy to music programs makes little sense in such cases: there just is no big corporate money coming in to fund conservatories, and no national TV networks offering lucrative payments to televise university orchestra and opera broadcasts. Since IU has long had one of the nation's best conservatories, and the best overall in opera and musical theater, he must have known the flaw in his analogy, and known, as well, the extremely demanding academic programs required of IU conservatory students. But he stuck to his analogy: pre-professional athletics does have a place in great universities. His overall contention, however—often repeated—was that tough rules need to be made and enforced regarding the academic work of athletes, and that college presidents, especially in D-I schools, must set the tone and take ultimate responsibility. (Again, he typically ignored the relative powerlessness of college presidents in the face of multimillion-dollar coaches and the huge money brought in by corporate entities.)

Oddly, given Brand's overall emphasis on women's equality in his speeches, he never once mentioned the problem of sexual violence.[65] He gave many examples of problematic behavior, including drinking, gambling, and physical violence; but he never once, in the many speeches I've read, mentioned sexual violence as a problem college sports must remedy. Under Brand the NCAA did stop holding championships on campuses whose mascots represent American Indians in a hostile or demeaning manner—except where, as with the FSU Seminoles, the native nation in question approved. But that sort of symbolic victory also shows the limits of the association's power: symbolic change costs corporate entities little or nothing. It is little more than a sop to ethics by people determined to pull a veil over sexual violence and endemic academic corruption.

Brand tried hard to toughen enforcement on the academic side. He also devised a clearer way of measuring graduation rates, helping the NCAA track what was happening. An idealist who truly loved college sports, he used the powers of his office to make it the best it could be. His office, however, had little power. Not surprisingly, given the degree of commercialization already present and the extent of corruption it had already spawned, his reform effort was too little too late.[66]

Brand's career shows how far a brilliant, honorable head of the NCAA could go in reestablishing integrity. It was not far. Reforms of Brand's sort in D-III still seem possible and desirable, and Bill Bowen's books, by focusing on D-III, set forth a practicable agenda. But everything about Brand's career suggests that D-I cannot be fixed through the NCAA.

In the wake of the wire fraud/money-laundering operation involving Adidas and numerous D-I basketball programs, concerned lovers of the sport saw that a crisis was at hand, and an independent commission was formed, headed by Condoleezza Rice. Its report, released in April 2018, is admirably frank: "The crisis in college basketball is first and foremost a problem of failed accountability and lax responsibility . . . The levels of corruption and deception are now at a point that they threaten the very survival of the college game as we know it."[67] The commission frankly asks whether the effort to fix things—which must of necessity be long and difficult—is worth making. It insists that it is. (And it's obvious that Rice, who loves sports, would not have agreed to spend her time this way had she thought the situation hopeless.) Its main argument is that a college degree is extremely valuable in our society, and athletics is, for many people, the only way of getting that degree. Focusing throughout on male college basketball, since the female game, where little money is involved, was thought not to be a major source of corruption,[68] the commission also points out that a very small percentage of college basketball players make it to the NBA (about 1.2 percent), while a full 59 percent of D-I players believe that they will play there. "A player chagrined to discover that he lacks an NBA future may grow into his collegiate experience and adopt a different plan for the future." So the collegiate model still has value, it insists. But it gravely states that this is the last chance to reform that model.

Importantly, the report puts the blame on all the places where it belongs, including pre-college programs: "It is time for coaches, athletic directors, University Presidents, Boards of Trustees, the NCAA leadership and staff, apparel companies, agents, pre-collegiate coaches—and yes—parents and athletes—to accept their culpability in getting us to where we are today."[69]

The report makes a number of recommendations to strengthen academic options as players test their career prospects: allowing players to register for the NBA draft without losing academic eligibility if they are not drafted; allowing players to transfer and still play if they enter a graduate program; allowing players to sign deals with professional agents—something currently forbidden by the NCAA, but something that gives young athletes a lot of feedback about their professional prospects. One of the most significant recommendations is that the NCAA immediately establish a fund (paid for by universities, it seems) to pay for degree completion for players who change course and leave an athletic program. "Colleges and universities must fulfill their commitments to student-athletes to provide not just a venue for athletic competition, but also an education." Finally the commission recommends ending the "one and done" system in which young basketball players are required by age rules to go to college for one year; let them enter the NBA directly at eighteen if they don't want to go to college.

All this is long overdue and mostly wise (although I fear that those eighteen-year-olds are cut adrift with no alternative career path). But what about corruption? Here the Commission talks tough, but the bottom line seems to be more of the same. The NCAA must have tougher penalties with "significant deterrent effect." There are new elements: the NCAA must establish an independent investigative arm to address "complex cases"; and it must expand individual accountability for college presidents, coaches, and other rule-violators. Surely, however, the independent investigators would face formidable obstacles in getting information about corruption: after all, it took a lengthy FBI probe to uncover the wire fraud problem.

The Rice Commission's report is admirably tough and conveys an appropriate sense of emergency. However, it seems condemned to failure. First and most glaring, there is no buy-in from football, where the bulk of the money, and the corruption, resides. Basketball can't reform the system on its own. I don't know what went on in the background—

Rice is very involved in football, so a shared set of proposals would have made great sense—but football's absence condemns the report to futility. It recommends fixes that will cost universities a lot of money; why should universities buy in when the most costly, and lucrative, sport is absent?

Second, the report has no way of altering the financial structure of the current system of corporate funding and the perverse incentives it creates. Financial penalties are there, but by far the largest income for schools is from TV contracts, and thus the threatened post-season ban represents a small part of the revenue, and for a tiny number of schools. Finally, the report is utterly silent about sexual assault as a problem that must be urgently addressed. Generalized language of "complex cases" is hardly enough to convince us that the new tough rules will really tackle this problem with the seriousness it deserves; nor do we have reason to think that NCAA investigators will succeed where police have failed or been deflected. As for deterrence, it's hard to say: what exactly would deter behavior of the type I've chronicled here, and what level of risk will programs be willing to run in order to continue their lucrative but corrupt ways?

Admittedly the report spells out the possible penalties in solemn detail: competitive penalties up to a five-year post-season ban, financial penalties including loss of all revenue-sharing in post-season play. But if the parties concerned count on being above the rules, how far will these deterrents really deter? These programs think that on the whole they are above the criminal and civil law: so why would they fear the typically toothless NCAA?

Scrapping the System: What Next?

Where can we go from here? For basketball, the answer is relatively straightforward, and Adam Silver has already stated it: move as rapidly as possible to what I have called a minor league system, replacing the current preprofessional college system (but leaving D-III in place). There are two reasons why the future is now, as far as basketball is concerned:

First, talent and physical ability mature relatively young in basketball, and there is agreement all around that players should be encouraged to enter the NBA at eighteen rather than to have a meaningless one year in college. In football, because body mass seems to take longer to develop, we don't see eighteen-year-olds choosing this path. The second, and crucial, issue is that basketball is international, drawing players from Europe, Australia, China, and other nations, who all do professional sports through a minor league system. So the NBA is already using pro teams in many other nations as de facto minor leagues (just as baseball has long scouted the professional teams of Japan and Korea for talent), and using those teams' own minor leagues as well. And the NBA contributes further: Jointly with FIBA (the International Basketball Federation) it runs Basketball Without Borders to develop elite players globally; the program has reached 3,200 participants from 132 countries. Cameroon native Joel Embiid of the Philadelphia 76ers is an alum of the program. In addition, the NBA runs its own NBA Global Academies, in Australia, China, Mexico, Senegal, and India, where NBA-trained coaches teach top prospects the fundamentals of the game "as well as how to take care of their mind and body and apply the values of the game to everything they do off court."[70]

Meanwhile in the United States, the NBA G League has long existed as a minor league system: first developed as such under David Stern, it has expanded considerably under Adam Silver.[71] This year it will add a new team in Mexico City.[72] The G League offers a new "professional track" for elite players following high school if those players are not yet ready for the NBA: the contract pays $125,000 for a five-month season, and it includes year-round education programs and a scholarship program for players who want to pursue college after their playing days end. These programs need considerable expansion, if they are to serve all the players who could profit from them. In particular, funding for the college scholarship part of the program is crucial if the program is to answer the worry raised in the Rice Commission report: a college degree is very valuable, and only a small proportion of those who try for an NBA career will ultimately have one. The NBA and its fans must urge sponsors (such as Gatorade, which gave the G League its name) to contribute to this goal. But so far all signs are good: the G League now attracts top recruits in the upfront market manner, by paying them more.[73] This year the top high school basketball recruit signed with the G League.[74]

This leaves another problem hanging: many players who would not get into a top college without the (corrupt and hopeless) college system now get accepted because of that system. What is to become of them under a new minor league system? This is actually two worries: about the elite players who do get a minor league contract, and about players who don't quite make it to that level but might have gotten a basketball scholarship to college. For the first group, we ought to say: if they are not college material they should not be there, but should pursue vocational education, preferably with financial support from the NBA. For the second group, we would still have D-III teams, which give plenty of scholarships for students who are truly equipped to be student athletes. The D-III system has real problems of lowered admission standards, as Bowen's books show in great detail. But those problems can be fixed in the ways he recommends, with the help of a newly focused NCAA, dealing with D-III alone, since D-I would no longer exist. (Bowen points out that a small group of elite schools—including, I'm happy to say, the University of Chicago—has already adopted much better admissions standards, depriving coaches of their power to make a list of guaranteed admits.)

So: the day is not far away, with energetic work by the NBA, when D-I college basketball will be a thing of the past, replaced by real professionalism, with market competition, upfront payment to individual athletes, and league regulation. Problems will remain, but they are the problems that baseball has had for its entire history: how to make money after or instead of an athletic career.

Could football move in this same direction? There are serious obstacles. Two are the lack of international feeder teams (apart from the Canadian Football League), since football is purely a North American sport; and the later maturation of football bodies, which would make an NFL minor league system relatively costly. But the greatest obstacle is an apparent total lack of will on the part of corporate investors and college officials. It's not that they don't recognize the corruption of the system, or the ways it saps the integrity of academic and social life. Rather, those who run the system (the corporate entities, and university officials as their dupes) don't care. I have to add that zealous fans who fill those expensive 100,000-seat stadiums also appear not to care, since the facts I have recorded are knowable by any who care to know them, and the toothlessness or even complicity of the NCAA is plain for all to see. (Recall that Myles and Peg Brand had their life threatened by fans, not corporate investors, when Brand fired Bobby Knight.) Apparently nobody even cares enough to appoint a Rice Commission for college football. But the fans should not be blamed too much: they can't fix the system, though many who love the game and love their universities probably want to. It is unfixable due to its collective action structure and, above all, the greed of those most involved in the quest for victory.

Recently, however, law has delivered what may be a death blow to what remains of the college system. In September 2019, the California State Legislature passed the Fair Pay to Play Act, signed by Governor Gavin Newsom, allowing college players to receive money for endorsements—thus defying the forces that have opposed this idea for years.[75] The NCAA has objected that college athletes are students, and that the law would ruin college sports. They also say it is unconstitutional, though the legal grounds of that claim are obscure. Other states are following suit. If the NCAA were to push back by declaring California schools ineligible to compete, such a strategy cannot last if indeed other states follow California.

The rottenness of the entire system is revealed ever more clearly by the desperate struggles of those who profit from it to stop young athletes from making their own money. (I believe that the ugly legacy of racism taints the football hierarchy's disdain for its own athletes, in this case as much as in the case of players kneeling for the anthem.) This decision does mean, it seems, the end of D-I and, really, the end of the pretense that these athletes, exploited as bodies for others' profit, are actually students getting an education.

Predictably, the NCAA has reacted with what seems a desperate attempt to preserve the fiction of amateurism and its own control over the lives of college athletes. A working group has prepared a report, issued in April 2020, that recommends loosening the rules to allow D-I athletes limited scope to receive money for endorsements and the use of their name, image, and likeness.[76] (The NCAA has also, belatedly, updated its sexual assault policy.[77]) They try to salvage the pretense that these players are students, not employees, especially by forbidding them to do endorsements using the school's logo or uniform. But all this means is that the students are still being denied a salary, and the fair market value of their talents, which is the real issue. Nobody will be fooled by this, not least the players. Nothing can salvage the system except genuine professionalism and an open market for talents, but nothing can create that within the fictional world of "student athletes." Nothing short of a real minor league system will deliver the virtues of genuine professionalism. The demise of the fiction of D-I amateurism may be close at hand: in December 2020 the U.S. Supreme Court agreed to decide, in 2021, whether the NCAA has violated federal antitrust law in limiting what college athletes may be paid, accepting a case previously considered by the Ninth Circuit, which found in favor of the athletes in May 2020.[78]

What next for football? Unlike basketball, the sport has not prepared for the demise of the college system. There are several possibilities for its future (discounting meaningful reform of the college system, which is not possible). One, and the best, is to move rapidly in the NBA direction, creating a meaningful minor league system with real money in it. This is expensive, and those used to making a profit from the talents of young athletes seem unlikely to go there anytime soon. A second would be to allow the athletes to be professionals under the aegis of the university but stop the pretense that they are students: they would be like hired entertainers. This seems to me the worst option (apart from the system now in place), since it retains many incentives for corruption, and seems unlikely to assist the athletes who will need alternative career options. And the third? As many parents know and as leading athletes in other sports have said, football is dangerous for young bodies and especially brains. When LeBron James says he will not allow his own children to play football, can its demise be far behind?[79] Well yes, of course it can, since many people love it. And it's hard not to see the fascination of its tactics, or its moments of beauty. Maybe it will ultimately survive as something more like the flag football that thousands of elementary and high schools already substitute for it. But then, it will still need to solve the corruption problem. I'm predicting that only a move to minor leagues could ever do that.

And: what next for Jameis Winston? On March 20, 2020, the Tampa Bay Bucs signed forty-two-year-old free agent Tom Brady to become their starting quarterback in place of twenty-six-year-old Winston. On March 21, Winston said goodbye to the team: "It's been a great five seasons as a Buccaneer," Winston wrote. "All love and respect. I look forward to seeing y'all again in February."[80] It was pure Winston, the overconfident boast that he would be playing in next year's Super Bowl (the only NFL game that is played in February). As the days rolled on with no starting quarterback offer in sight, and with other teams making different choices, Winston, adrift and apparently increasingly frustrated, demonstrated his amazing strength by posting a video of himself pushing an SUV—a 2020 Ford Expedition weighing nearly three tons—uphill from a dead stop for approximately thirty seconds. Then he jogs off as if he had done nothing at all.[81]

In early April, Winston was still adrift. Bucs coach Bruce Arians claimed that he was urging other teams to make Winston an offer, but his actual statements were pretty equivocal, alluding to Winston's hard work but also to his "regression" in the season's last two games. (This condescending point makes me sympathize with Winston, since several of his receivers were injured and did not play those two games.) Some teams avoided decision on Winston by saying that they needed to "sit down" with him because of the character issues in his past, but that is not possible during the COVID-19 crisis. (They can't use Zoom like the rest of us?) The striking thing about the way all this was playing out is that Winston has been my chosen illustration of the corruption of the college system, but now he seems like a choice illustration of something else: the longstanding racism of the NFL, where the quarterback position is concerned.[82] It cannot be emphasized too often that racial denigration of

Black athletes has long been linked to the perverse incentives in the college system that encourage exactly those diseased models of masculinity that the white-dominated football world then turns around and derides.

After the draft, at the end of April, Winston (newly married to his long-term fiancée) signed a one-year contract with the New Orleans Saints as one of two backup quarterbacks for the legendary Drew Brees. He spoke judiciously, expressing pleasure at the opportunity to learn from one of the masters of the game.[83] Now that Brees has shown himself clueless about racial inequality and has apologized three times for an insensitive remark,[84] we can hope that Winston may become the master's teacher as well as his student. For my part, I wish him well.

This chapter has ranged beyond sexual assault to argue for dismantling what is in effect a large corrupt enterprise, fueled by pride and greed, that has long corrupted academic, social, and sexual life. But as I've said all along: sexual abuse is a type of abuse of power, not a thing apart. It can be ended, ultimately, only by dismantling corrupt power structures—both by energetically enforcing laws and rules and by substituting new structures for the old. Reform has failed. Good models for the future exist. We urgently need to do things differently.

The Way Forward

ACCOUNTABILITY WITHOUT MALICE, GENEROSITY WITHOUT CAPITULATION

A "Peculiar and Powerful Interest"

On the day I first wrote this sentence, Harvey Weinstein was convicted of rape. No trial is perfect, and this one was no exception, but even though he is just one dominant man and the trial just one instance of taking women's voices seriously, it is still a sign of things to come, of a culture of equal respect and concern that we can create if we keep trying. A jury of seven men and five women found him guilty beyond a reasonable doubt, on the say-so of his accusers, with no additional physical or eye-witness evidence. The jury was also, clearly, precise, attentive, and non-ideological: on other charges they didn't feel that the evidence was sufficient for conviction. So the verdict does not show that men are an endangered species, it shows that one extremely proud man has begun to pay for a life of disrespect and egoism.

This book has been about sexual objectification and sexual abuse. But in a larger sense its theme has been the vice of pride—the habitual tendency to think oneself above others and to treat others as not really counting, denying them full autonomy and not really listening to their voices. I've said that the abuse of power takes many forms. The sexualized domination of men over women (and at times over other men and boys) is a specific form of pride-domination, different from racial pride-domination and the manifold other forms that pride takes in our vice-filled world. My project has been not to compare all the many forms of domination and to trace their differences, but to focus on one form in the recent history of one country, to ask what has been done about it already and what remains to be done.

Although racial domination is a terrible evil and a separate topic—interwoven with my topic, in that Black women have often been singled out for special sexualized domination and abuse—what Abraham Lincoln said about slavery we should say about the sexual objectification and abuse of women by men: it is the outgrowth of a "peculiar and powerful interest," cultivated over many centuries, and it cannot be eradicated except by the most determined and prolonged effort.

Much of this effort must be done in families and schools, encouraging both young women and men to value their own autonomy and integrity, to cherish the equality of each and every person, and to stand up to abuse; encouraging young men to respect and value women as equals, to understand that a man never has the right to have sex with any other person, female or male, except under conditions of explicit consent. But peer pressure is powerful, so families do not always prevail when they try to impart non-sexist values. We also need to try, insofar as we can, to make the larger culture reflect the values of equal respect and non-pride. But it's hard. I hope my diagnosis of both objectification and pride may help people in thinking about why change is so hard, and how to proceed further.

Here is where law enters in. Well-intentioned people don't have to fight exhausting individual struggles if the law adequately reflects values of equal respect and non-objectification, and if good laws are enforced. Law gives us all a bulwark in our individual efforts. To be sure it's a non-ideal and sometimes leaky bulwark, but it is amazing the difference that is made by the simple recognition that sexual harassment in the workplace is not just personal, not just unfortunate, but also illegal. That is why this book focuses both on character traits and on law. The two live in a symbiosis, good or bad. For a long time it has been mostly bad: inadequate laws have encouraged male privilege and discouraged women from valuing their own voices or standing up for their equality. Now, slowly, law is becoming less the problem and more a part of the solution. To all the people (lawyers, plaintiffs, judges, politicians) who have contributed to this progress over many years, we owe gratitude.

"With Firmness in the Right"

My law students often enter law school wanting to produce social change and a better world. They then find out that law is not all about making the world better, and that in some ways law has even impeded progress. But in the area of women's equality, as I have taught "Feminist Philosophy" to generations of law students, I have been able to point to the quite wonderful progress women in America have made through law and lawyering—because of their own energy and investment, and that of their clients, sometimes against great odds. I love showing *The Accused* to first-year law students to remind them of what rape law was like in the 1980s, and what unheralded lawyers and a working-class plaintiff did to make the world somewhat better for all women. It took, and takes, "firmness in the right" to make progress like that. It has to be replicated case by case, and state by state. Still, by now, we are somewhere rather than nowhere.

As Judge Diane Wood has reminded us (Chapter 5), sexual harassment laws are applied by judges, who do not always decide rightly, not fully understanding the severity of the harassment a woman has faced. Still, I think on balance the trend is definitely positive. And the very fact that Diane Wood became chief judge of the Seventh Circuit Court of Appeals, bringing her immense legal knowledge, her work ethic, but also her inside understanding of sexism and discrimination into the deliberations of that court (as Judge Ruth Bader Ginsburg more famously did on the U.S. Supreme Court), is itself a change that could not have been imagined when those women entered law school. Law students today (both female and male) can aspire to be not only counsel for litigants but also judges, and we have to hope (it's hardly a fait accompli) that in the long run both federal and state courts will become better at listening to the voices of victims of sexual abuse. The huge recent increase in the number of women in Congress also gives us hope that at the legislative level women's voices will increasingly be heard.

But the "peculiar and powerful interest" remains. Vices are stubborn, and people all too often weak.

When Lincoln spoke of the need for "firmness in the right," he could hardly have imagined how long and how hard the struggle for racial justice—culpably unfinished today, with tragic and terrible results—would prove to be. Reconstruction was full of admirable efforts and hopes, and even laws. But the backlash it inspired proved too powerful, and white privilege established itself again, and remained entrenched for a hundred years, so that Martin Luther King Jr. could open his great "dream" speech with "Five score years ago, . . ." alluding to the centenary of Lincoln's Emancipation Proclamation, reached during that "sweltering summer of the Negro's legitimate discontent." Today we are reckoning with the incompleteness of that superb effort, in the face of tenacious racism and structural inequality. King famously said, "The arc of the moral universe is long, but it bends toward justice." He understood how slow progress could be but retained hope, as I do, that the overall movement of history will be toward racial justice.

It is difficult to believe that the same kind of movement toward justice will not also prevail where women's equality is concerned. I don't believe women will be defeated by the backlash they are certainly facing. I see them assuming places of power in so many parts of American life. Women's educational attainments, now outdoing those of men at the post-secondary level, in every country of the world, seem to herald an irreversible trend in the direction of empowerment and full equality. However, we should not be casually optimistic: it would have been difficult in 1865 to imagine the ravages of the Ku Klux Klan and the seemingly interminable evils of the Jim Crow era. Racism and sexism both seem so irrational that it is hard for reasonable and moral people to credit their depth—including, often, in themselves. That's where Dante's *Purgatorio* is especially profound: as the protagonist of his poem, he starts out taking what he thinks is a detached tour of the vices, only to recognize himself almost everywhere he goes.

The future for women, we know, is likely to be difficult. The need to dominate is a deep need in human life, probably in all of us to some extent. And because for so long, custom, law, and culture have nourished the vice of pride in men, the struggle for equal respect must contend with durable structures of domination that are very hard to undo. They include the unequal division of household and care labor, the all-too-common male need to be supported (asymmetrically) in the travails of life by a self-effacing helpmeet, and the need to assert sexual prowess and sexual dominance even when no mutuality or sympathy has been offered—and, for some, especially when it has not been offered.

Since I find Harvey Weinstein disgusting and pathetic in equal measure, and can't even imagine his inner world, or what he gets out of his in some ways absurd exploits, it is all too easy to suppose that there are few like him, and that they will not replicate themselves in the next generation. We should all certainly strive to bring up children who embody an ideal of equal respect and reciprocity, and, if we're lucky enough to be teachers, to nourish and also exemplify those ideals in our work. But we can't simply assume that this ideal is bound to be realized in the next generation.

Hoping for the best but expecting the worst, we must cling all the more to law, an institution that would not be needed if there were not a lot of badness in the world. I have suggested many concrete directions we need to take to make law more adequate, in the areas of both sexual assault and sexual harassment. And for those areas that I've called "citadels of pride" because they resist the law, we need to pursue other types of structural changes, such as modifying the structure of clerkship supervision (Chapter 6), giving unions greater power to police sexual harassment and abuse in the arts (Chapter 7), and abolishing Division I college football and basketball in favor of a minor league system that could be policed by both law and collective bargaining (Chapter 8).

"With Malice Toward None"

It would be easy for women, newly (in part) empowered, to turn to retribution, and to see in retributive anger an ally in our struggle. And indeed we see a certain amount of retributive glorying: in the harsh denunciations that are an integral part of "callout" culture, in a certain apocalyptic tone that is struck all too often on social media and the internet, and, perhaps most dangerous, in the desire to punish powerful and allegedly errant men by public shaming rather than by due process (whether legal or social). Because women's strong voices have too rarely been heard in the public realm, it is easy to think two things that are false: first, that retributive anger is an essential tool of the feminist struggle; and, second, that whenever a woman speaks strongly, demanding justice, she is really expressing retributive anger, trying to inflict suffering on dominant men.

It is sometimes indeed very difficult to distinguish a strong demand for justice from retributive anger seeking primarily to inflict pain. (Justice does often inflict pain.) For example: in the first Democratic debate at which Michael Bloomberg was present, in February 2020, Elizabeth Warren confronted him, criticizing him for his remarks about women, and challenging him to release women who had sued his company from the nondisclosure agreements they had signed. Warren, to me, seemed strong but not angry, just determined and pressing her case in a lawyerly way. And yet in media afterward she was called angry, and often people expressed approval of that anger. It seems to me that Warren gave reasons for her demand, and that the demand was connected to forward-looking principles of non-discrimination that create a better world for all in the workplace. The charge of anger, even if alleged friends are making it, is often a way of infantilizing women's demands and suggesting that they do not have reasons and aren't trying to improve the future.

Many feminists believe that retributive anger is a powerful aid to the feminist struggle, even if, like Lisa Tessman, they also believe that it distorts the personality. I've argued, however, that there is no tragic tension here, since the retributive type of anger, the type aimed at inflicting retrospective pain, is no help in the feminist struggle. I'm with King: that sort of anger is "confused," and *not* "radical." It follows a blind strike-back impulse rather than asking what will help (as King put it) to "create a world where [women] and [men] can live together."

Denouncing bad policies and opposing people who hold them in their bid for high office is a part of creating a good future. But of course the personal element in an event such as a presidential campaign makes that legitimate and principled denunciation hard to disentangle from the mere desire to win by putting your opponent down. We all need to ponder that distinction, trying, always, for the future-directed type of anger that I call "Transition-Anger," an anger that says, "That's outrageous and bad: that must not happen again." It seems to me sad that the principled expression of outrage is heard as retributive anger, and sadder still that people admire and like that (imputed) emotion.

As for public punishment by shaming: social media have brought us back to the witch trials and the pillory, a culture in which it is possible to give people what sociologist Erving Goffman called a "spoiled identity" without any due process, and no possibility of reintegration. I've long criticized the use of public shaming in the criminal law—as when people convicted of a given offense are made to wear signs or placards on their car or their person or their property.[1] Critics of this type of punishment have made five strong arguments: (1) these punishments assail human dignity by branding a whole person as defective, not just a single act; (2) they depart from the ideal of the rule of law, asking the mob to administer the punishment; (3) throughout history they have proved unreliable, migrating from people who have really done something bad to people who are merely unpopular; (4) they often increase the total amount of violence in society, because they create despair, inciting a desperate type of retaliation; (5) by punishing many things that are not illegal, they contribute to "net-widening," increasing society's amount of social control.[2]

All these arguments seem to me to have merit. But in the version of punishment by shaming recently proposed by criminologists, the suggestion has at least this mitigating factor: the person has to be indicted, tried, and convicted first. Shaming enters in only at the penalty phase. Even so, these punishments are vulnerable to my five objections. But in internet culture—as with the use, in many places and times, of the stocks, the pillory, and punitive tattooing and branding—there is no trial first: the mob is district attorney, judge, jury, and punisher. The new ascendancy of mob anger and retributive shaming is a huge threat to the creation of a world of decency and mutual respect. It is sad that some feminists, who ought to see the ugliness of these strategies (linked historically to witch-blaming and other forms of misogyny), at times, these days, seem to glory in public shaming, both of males and of dissenting feminists.

"With 'Charity' Toward All"

In denouncing "malice" Lincoln was clearly denouncing a retributivism not aimed at the goal of "a just and lasting peace." But what did he mean by "charity"? In Lincoln's biblical language, "charity" is the translation for Latin *caritas* and Greek *agapê*, the great virtue praised by St. Paul in 1 Corinthians 13. It is now translated "love." But as King so often said when asked what he meant by "love," this sort of love is not erotic or romantic love. It does not even require that you like the people, so it isn't friendly love either. *Agapê* is inclusive and universal, directed at the core of worth or goodness in every person. It is closely linked to respect for human dignity, but it is warmer: it reaches out in sisterhood and brotherhood.

The virtue opposed to the vice of pride is not humility in Hume's sense of thinking yourself lower than others. It is closely connected to respect and involves the willingness to listen to the voices of others, rather than closing off those voices in lofty superiority. This virtue at its best contains King's type of inclusive love. It involves seeing in all people a core of dignity and worth, and, further, a potential for change and growth, however obscured and blighted by the history of that person's deeds. So it draws a very strong distinction between deeds and the underlying person. Deeds may be utterly denounced, but the person always retains potentiality and movement. That is why Dante's Hell is so horrifying: these are human beings stripped of potentiality, and therefore of hope. And when living people are consigned to hell, this is its own very pernicious form of objectification, robbing them of autonomy, subjectivity, and possibility.

At this time of justified denunciation and unremitting vigilance, feminists, I believe, should also, and above all, be people of love. Just as women demand that their voices be heard, so we must also resolve to hear one another in all our differences, and to hear the voices of men, both those who agree with us and those who do not, both those who have behaved well and those who have not, creating a dialogical culture that is also a culture of empathetic imagination. To listen and to hear, in a climate of respect for human potentiality. And because that potentiality is sometimes impossible to see, we should also be people of practical faith, and of a trust that is to some extent as yet unjustified and unjustifiable. Even where hope cannot be supported by reasons—and really, hope can never be fully supported by reasons—feminists should be people of hope: hope that the relationship between women and men, so long based upon domination, might enjoy what Lincoln called "a new birth of freedom," as mutuality and respect for autonomy gradually displace pride.

Only that new freedom, and that love, can really create a just and lasting peace.

ACKNOWLEDGMENTS

For many years I have regularly taught "Feminist Philosophy" at the University of Chicago Law School and Philosophy Department, so my first thanks are to my generations of students, female and male, both law students and graduate students, whose thoughtful and challenging questions have shaped my thinking. My colleagues have created an ideal environment for work, by being both supportive and relentlessly skeptical, generous with time and comments, but refusing to accept pieties and requiring confrontation with tough questions. Early in my days at Chicago, the distinguished criminal law theorist Stephen Schulhofer was an invaluable source of insight. I audited his "Criminal Law," and later co-taught with him a seminar called "Sexual Autonomy and Law." Catharine MacKinnon was a regular faculty visitor at Chicago, although she never accepted the permanent position we offered to her. An inspiring teacher and colleague, and a surprisingly optimistic presence, she always loved to bring women and men together around ideas of how things could get better, and she has always given her students, male as well as female, credit for new ways of seeing the world. I found her a terrific source of understanding, even though we often differed. Meanwhile two judges who have also been faculty colleagues shaped my thinking and taught me a great deal about the law in action: Judge Richard Posner, now retired from the Seventh Circuit Court of Appeals, and Diane Wood, until recently chief judge of that same court. To see them shaping the law and pointing out its defects brought reality to my sometimes abstract philosophical speculations. Saul Levmore, a great collaborator and friend, organized with me a conference about the use of the Internet for misogynistic purposes, which became the book *The Offensive Internet* (Cambridge: Harvard University Press, 2010). I'm grateful to him for that and for tough-minded comments on most of the chapters of the present book.

This book project began with an invitation to speak at the opening of the Yeoh Tiong Lay Centre for Politics, Philosophy, & Law at the Dickson Poon School of Law at King's College London, and with the specific request for a feminist topic, in order to show that the new center takes women's equality to be among its major concerns. I am extremely grateful to John Tasioulas for the invitation and for arranging a wonderful panel of feminist thinkers to discuss my lecture (an early version of Chapter 4 of the present book); their superb comments remain online, as also my attempts to reply to them. John remembers the occasion as one on which "political foes came together over your book," meaning not that we all agreed, but that we all listened to one another in the spirit that Dante calls humility. I hope that experience will be repeated many times in the future. Editorial work on that paper was expertly done by Emily Dupree later, as one of my research assistants, and the paper was published in a Festschrift for my dear friend Josh Cohen, the book *Ideas That Matter: Democracy, Justice, Rights*, ed. Debra Satz and Annabelle Lever (New York: Oxford University Press, 2019). Josh was important to Chapter 3 as well: he and Deb Chasman, editors of the *Boston Review*, published an edited version of my draft chapter in a special collection of essays on the topic of anger, both as a pamphlet and online in the *Review*. Their edits were so helpful that I took over most of them as I revised the manuscript.

Chapter 2 was delivered as a Philip Quinn Memorial Lecture at the University of Notre Dame's Philosophy Department. Phil had been a colleague of mine at Brown and remained an admired friend, a person who always sought to bring out the aspirational best in the Catholic institution to which he had chosen to move. So I chose my reflections on what

I believe one of the richest and best aspects of the Catholic philosophical tradition, Dante's account of Purgatory, to dignify the occasion. I am grateful to Paul Weithman for inviting me and for arranging for someone else to read the lecture in my absence, since the chosen date was the week preceding my daughter's death.

For help with Chapter 8 (on sports) I am especially grateful to NBA commissioner Adam Silver, an alumnus of our law school, who sent me a lot of background information and told me about his own ideas and plans; to Peg Brand Weiser, widow of NCAA head Myles Brand, for showing me a largely unpublished collection of Brand's speeches; to Notre Dame political science professor Eileen Hunt Botting for background information about athletics and academics at the University of Notre Dame; to Saul Levmore and Alan Nussbaum for comments on a draft; and to the entire law school faculty for challenging and helpful comments at a work-in-progress workshop, at a time in April 2020 when all actual sports had been suspended.

Gina Schouten of the Harvard Philosophy Department wrote up some wonderful comments to present at a workshop on Chapters 6 and 7 at Brown University, scheduled for March 18, 2020. Because of the COVID-19 pandemic, that workshop never took place, but I still have the comments and am so grateful to her.

During the summer of 2019 and throughout the year 2019–20, I was very lucky to have two superb research assistants who investigated sources in connection with the various issues discussed in Parts II and III of the book: Sarah Hough and Jared Mayer. I could not have finished the book without their help.

Throughout, I have immense gratitude to my agent, Sydelle Kramer, and especially to my splendid editor at Norton, Alane Mason, for encouragement, superb editing, and helpful, often tough, criticism.

My daughter Rachel died on December 3, 2019, of a drug-resistant infection following successful transplant surgery. During much of my work on Parts II and III of the book she was hospitalized, and during her final weeks of life, as it turned out, I was writing a draft of Chapter 6, about the federal judiciary. Rachel was a lawyer whose great passion was animal rights. You can learn about her career here: https://hd-ca.org/news/in-memoriam-rachel-nussbaum-wichert. My next book after this one, already in progress, will continue her commitments and thoughts. But this book was related to her also, since she had a passion to defend the dignity and the rights of all creatures, particularly the weakest. And she was always allergic to abuses of power and to narcissistic self-flaunting. All the time I spent writing about the judiciary and the behavior of Judge Alex Kozinski, sitting there in her hospital room, I was motivated to keep going by the thought that he is the antitype to all that Rachel was and fought for. Kozinski's atrocious behavior—in a weird way for which he deserves absolutely no credit, or really, anti-credit—helped me to endure the tragic death of my child and to find a way to mourn her. Her gentleness, decency, and profound integrity is a beacon for all of us who have to struggle with a world in which pride and abuses of power still win success. I therefore dedicate this book to her memory.

NOTES

PREFACE

1. As a feminist, I've long worked in developing countries, particularly India, where feminist activists often express surprise that anyone would turn to law to attain justice. I think that actually much good has been accomplished for women in India through law, through courageous legal activism, but the delays and corruptions of the daily administration of law, where it often takes nine years for a rape case to get to court, during which time essential evidence has mysteriously vanished, make many women on the ground skeptical.

2. An admirable recent treatment of the problem of care labor by a young feminist philosopher is Gina Schouten, *Liberalism, Neutrality, and the Gendered Division of Labor* (New York: Oxford University Press, 2019). On domestic violence, see Rachel Louise Snyder, *No Visible Bruises: What We Don't Know about Domestic Violence Can Kill Us* (New York: Bloomsbury, 2019). Although domestic violence obviously overlaps considerably with my topic, I do not really treat it here, and I am happy to be able to refer readers to this impressive book. Evidence is accumulating that domestic violence has skyrocketed during the COVID-19 pandemic; see B. Boserup, M. McKenney, and A. Elkbuli, "Alarming Trends in US Domestic Violence during the COVID-19 Pandemic," *American Journal of Emergency Medicine*, April 28, 2020, https://www.ajemjournal.com/article/S0735 -6757(20)30307-7/fulltext.

3. For my arguments against punishment by shaming, see Martha C. Nussbaum, *Hiding from Humanity: Disgust, Shame, and the Law* (Princeton, NJ: Princeton University Press, 2004); and the Conclusion to this book.

4. On shame's creation of a "spoiled identity," see Erving Goffman's classic *Stigma:*

Notes on the Management of Spoiled Identity (New York: Simon and Schuster, 1963).

5. Martha C. Nussbaum, "'Don't Smile So Much': Philosophy and Women in the 1970s," in *Singing in the Fire: Stories of Women in Philosophy*, ed. Linda Martín Alcoff, American 1st ed. (Lanham, MD: Rowman and Littlefield, 2003), 93–108.

6. Martha C. Nussbaum, "Why Some Men Are above the Law," *Huffington Post*, January 15, 2016, http://www.huffingtonpost.com/martha-c-nussbaum/why -some-men-are-above-the-law_b_8992754.html. I did not name Waite at that time, since I wanted to make a point that this is a general problem and did not want the debate to get deflected onto a gossipy track.

CHAPTER 1: OBJECTIFICATION

1. Here I define "autonomy" broadly and capaciously, not as entailing a denial that religious authority may also be an important source of choice. For the history of the latter, narrower, use, see Jerome Schneewind, *The Invention of Autonomy* (Cambridge: Cambridge University Press, 1997).

2. All quotes in this paragraph are from John Stuart Mill, *The Subjection of Women*, ed. Susan Moller Okin (1869; repr., Indianapolis, IN: Hackett, 1988), 15–16.

3. Mill introduced the first bill for women's suffrage in the British Parliament in 1866. When he married Harriet Taylor in 1851, he renounced all unequal rights that would have been his by marriage.

4. Vivian Gornick, *The Solitude of Self: Thinking about Elizabeth Cady Stanton* (New York: Farrar, Straus, and Giroux, 2005). I reviewed Gornick's book in "In a Lonely Place," *Nation*, February 27, 2006, 26–30.

5. The speech is not, however, sectarian; it represents a widely disseminated set of American ideas. Indeed, in its emphasis on personal choice and agency, it is in tension with at least some forms of Protestantism, but totally in line with shared American traditions.

6. For my own reconstruction of Williams's arguments, see Martha C. Nussbaum, *Liberty of Conscience: In Defense of America's Tradition of Religious Equality* (New York: Basic Books, 2008).

7. Elizabeth Cady Stanton, "The Destructive Male" (speech, Women's Suffrage Convention, Washington, DC, 1868), Great Speeches Collection, *The History Place*, https://www.historyplace.com/speeches/stanton.htm.

8. Elizabeth Cady Stanton to Susan B. Anthony, July 20, 1857, in *Elizabeth Cady Stanton as Revealed in Her Letters, Diary and Reminiscences*, ed. Theodore Stanton and Harriet Stanton Blatch, vol. 2 (New York: Harper, 1922), 29–70.

9. Kate Manne, *Down Girl: The Logic of Misogyny* (New York: Oxford University Press, 2018).

10. Martha C. Nussbaum, *The Monarchy of Fear: A Philosopher Looks at Our Political Crisis* (New York: Simon and Schuster, 2018), chap. 6.

11. See Catharine A. MacKinnon, *Feminism Unmodified: Discourses on Life and Law* (Cambridge, MA: Harvard University Press, 1987), 262n1.

12. Or, really, a sentient being, since humans often objectify nonhuman animals. But that is a subject for another time.

13. Martha C. Nussbaum, "Objectification," *Philosophy and Public Affairs* 24 (1995): 249–91, reprinted in Nussbaum, *Sex and Social Justice* (New York: Oxford University Press, 1999), 213–39.

14. Rae Langton, *Sexual Solipsism* (Oxford: Oxford University Press, 2008).

15. Langton also adds "reduction to appearance" and "reduction to body." I think the former is captured by the denials of autonomy and subjectivity. The latter appears problematic to me, since we are all bodies, and there is nothing wrong or low about that.

16. Sharon G. Smith et al., *The National Intimate Partner and Sexual Violence Survey (NISVS): 2010–2012 State Report* (Atlanta: National Center for Injury Prevention and Control, Centers for Disease Control and Prevention, 2017), www.cdc.gov/violenceprevention/pdf/NISVS-StateReportBook.pdf.

17. See Edward Laumann, *The Social Organization of Sexuality* (Chicago: University of Chicago Press, 1994); and Edward Laumann, Robert T. Michael, John H. Gagnon, and Gina Kolata, *Sex in America: A Definitive Survey* (New York: Warner, 1995).

18. Laumann et al., *Sex in America*, 223.

19. Laumann et al., *Sex in America*, 229.

20. Laumann et al., *Sex in America*, 229.

21. On causal connections between pornography and the "real world," see Anne Eaton, "A Sensible Antiporn Feminism," *Ethics* 117 (2007): 674–715, written before the internet made pornography ubiquitous. Some reasonable critics of MacKinnon's arguments about pornography pointed to the value of some pornography in empowering women, LGBTQ people, and others. But now, in quantitative terms, the internet is saturated with the sort of pornography that objectifies women, even if other types exist.

22. See Manne's *Down Girl* for discussion of this movement and some of its salient crimes.

CHAPTER 2: VICES OF DOMINATION

1. For Dante's influence in the United States, see Sinclair Lewis's *Babbitt* (1922), a Dante-inspired "sinscape" of the American Midwest, in which even characters who despise liberal arts education all know of Dante, and most are familiar with the general outline of his trilogy, no doubt assisted by the emphasis on Dante apropos of the six hundredth anniversary of the poet's death in 1921.

2. David Hume, *A Treatise of Human Nature*, ed. L. A. Selby-Bigge, 2nd ed., revised by P. H. Nidditch (1940; Oxford, Clarendon Press, 1978), 291. Within this discussion, all quotations from this work refer to the edition cited here.

3.   Donald Davidson, "Hume's Cognitive Theory of Pride," *Journal of Philosophy* 73 (1976): 744–57.

4.   Tanika Sarkar, "Conjugality and Hindu Nationalism: Resisting Colonial Reason and the Death of a Child-Wife," in *Hindu Wife, Hindu Nation: Community, Religion, and Cultural Nationalism* (New Delhi, India: Permanent Black, 2001), 191–225.

5.   But she does, in fact, say "*fammi vendetta*," so her demand for justice is confusingly mingled with retribution. Despite the fact that Greek and Roman philosophical views of punishment focused on deterrence and reform and eschewed the retributivism of traditional religion, Christian philosophical views are often harshly retributive.

6.   Robert Frank, *The Darwin Economy: Liberty, Competition and the Common Good* (Princeton, NJ: Princeton University Press, 2011).

7.   Quoted in Henry Abelove, "Freud, Male Homosexuality, and the Americans," in *The Lesbian and Gay Studies Reader*, ed. Henry Abelove, Michèle A. Barale, and David M. Halperin (New York: Routledge, 1993), 381–93, at 387; further source information given there.

8.   Quoted by Abelove from Jones's autobiography: Ernest Jones, *Free Associations: Memories of a Psycho-analyst.*

9.   Abelove, "Freud, Male Homosexuality, and the Americans." This paragraph, and the previous one, are similar to text in my paper "The Morning and the Evening Star: Religion, Money, and Love in Sinclair Lewis's *Babbitt* and *Elmer Gantry*" in *Power, Prose, and Purse: Law, Literature, and Economic Transformation*, ed. Alison L. LaCroix, Saul Levmore, and Martha C. Nussbaum (New York: Oxford University Press, 2019), 95–124.

10. I discuss this in *The Monarchy of Fear: A Philosopher Looks at Our Political Crisis* (New York: Simon and Schuster, 2018), chap. 6.

11. See Anne Eaton, "A Sensible Antiporn Feminism," *Ethics* 117 (2007): 674–715.

12. See Kate Manne's *Down Girl: The Logic of Misogyny* (New York: Oxford University Press, 2018).

13. See the excellent discussion in Manne's *Down Girl*, on which I elaborate in *The Monarchy of Fear*, chap. 6.

14. See also Martha C. Nussbaum, *Hiding from Humanity: Disgust, Shame, and the Law* (Princeton, NJ: Princeton University Press, 2004); and Nussbaum, *From Disgust to Humanity: Sexual Orientation and Constitutional Law* (Oxford: Oxford University Press, 2010).

15. Much of the poem is quoted in Nussbaum, *Monarchy of Fear*, chap. 4.

16. See Zoya Hasan et al., eds., *The Empire of Disgust: Prejudice, Discrimination, and Policy in India and the US* (New Delhi, India: Oxford University Press, 2018), a binational collaboration between Indian and U.S. scholars, edited by Zoya Hasan and Vidhu Verma on the Indian side, and by Aziz Huq and me on the U.S. side.

17. For a list of examples, see Nussbaum, *Monarchy of Fear*, chap. 6.

CHAPTER 3: VICES OF VICTIMHOOD

1. I analyze this play in detail in the final chapter of *The Fragility of Goodness: Luck and Ethics in Greek Tragedy and Philosophy*, updated ed. (1986; repr., Cambridge: Cambridge University Press, 2001).

2. Of course I do not share these views, either of the "bestial" in general or of dogs in particular. Indeed, these acts of betrayal could have been committed only by a human.

3. On this transformation, see especially Martha C. Nussbaum, *The Monarchy of Fear: A Philosopher Looks at Our Political Crisis* (New York: Simon and Schuster, 2018), chap. 3.

4. See Aristotle, *Nicomachean Ethics* 1100b33–1101a10. For analysis of all the relevant passages, see Nussbaum, *Fragility of Goodness*, chap. 11. In the section on aging in his *Rhetoric*, however (1389b13–1390a24), Aristotle does insist that bad experiences over time can breed a lack of trust and confidence, thus eroding the virtues: see *Fragility of Goodness*, 338–89.

5. E. L. Abramson, "Euripides' Tragedy of Hecuba," *Transactions of the American Philological Association* 83 (1952): 120–29; for discussion of attacks on the play, see Nussbaum, *Fragility of Goodness*, 505.

6. Immanuel Kant, *Grounding for the Metaphysics of Morals: On a Supposed Right to Lie Because of Philanthropic Concerns*, trans. James W. Ellington, 3rd ed. (Indianapolis, IN: Hackett, 1993), Akad. p. 394 (the standard Akademie pagination that is used in all editions of Kant).

7. Mary Wollstonecraft, *A Vindication of the Rights of Woman*, ed. Miriam Brody (1792; repr., London: Penguin, 2004).

8. Jon Elster, *Sour Grapes: Studies in the Subversion of Rationality* (Cambridge: Cambridge University Press, 1983).

9. See my discussion of Elster, Sen, and others in Martha C. Nussbaum, *Women and Human Development* (Cambridge: Cambridge University Press, 2000), chap. 2.

10. For a good discussion of this victim-blaming tradition, see Lisa Tessman, *Burdened Virtues: Virtue Ethics for Liberatory Struggles* (New York: Oxford University Press, 2005), chap. 2.

11. Tessman, *Burdened Virtues*, 45, speaking of Shelby Steele.

12. For a cogent assessment and critique, see Rosa Terlazzo, "Conceptualizing Adaptive Preferences Respectfully: An Indirectly Substantive Account," *Journal of Political Philosophy*, 23, no. 3 (2016): 206–26; she has a series of other valuable articles on this theme, which can be found on her website at the Philosophy Department, University of Rochester.

13. See Justin Wolfers, David Leonhardt, and Kevin Quealy, "1.5 Million Missing Black Men," *New York Times*, April 20, 2015, https://www.nytimes.com/interactive/2015/04/20/upshot/missing-black-men.html.

14. Laurence Thomas, "Sexism and Racism: Some Conceptual Differences," *Ethics* 90 (1980): 239–50.

15.   See Bernard Williams, "Ethical Consistency," in *Problems of the Self: Philosoph-ical Papers 1956–1972* (Cambridge: Cambridge University Press, 1973), 166–86; see also Michael Walzer, "Political Action and the Problem of Dirty Hands," *Phi-losophy and Public Affairs* 2 (1973): 160–80.

16.   Barbara Herman, "Could It Be Worth Thinking about Kant on Sex and Mar-riage?" in *A Mind of One's Own: Feminist Essays on Reason and Objectivity*, ed. Louise Antony and Charlotte Witt (Boulder, CO: Westview, 1993), 49–67.

17.   Sandra Lee Bartky, "Feminine Masochism and the Politics of Personal Transfor-mation," 1984, reprinted in Bartky, *Femininity and Domination: Studies in the Phenomenology of Oppression* (New York: Routledge, 1990), 45–62.

18.   Sandra Lee Bartky, "Foucault, Femininity, and the Modernization of Patriarchal Power," in *Feminism & Foucault: Reflections on Resistance*, ed. Irene Diamond and Lee Quinby (Boston: Northeastern University Press, 1988), 61–86.

19.   Claudia Card, "Gender and Moral Luck," in Virginia Held, ed., *Justice and Care: Essential Readings in Feminist Ethics* (Boulder, CO: Westview, 1995), 79–100; also Card's book *The Unnatural Lottery: Character and Moral Luck* (Philadel-phia: Temple University Press, 1996).

20.   Thomas Hill, "Servility and Self-Respect," *Monist* 57 (1973): 87–104.

21.   See especially Marcia L. Homiak, "Feminism and Aristotle's Rational Ideal," in *A Mind of One's Own: Feminist Essays on Reason and Objectivity*, ed. Louise M. Antony and Charlotte E. Witt (Boulder, CO: Westview, 1993), 1–18; and Homiak, "On the Malleability of Character," in *On Feminist Ethics and Politics*, ed. Clau-dia Card (Lawrence: University Press of Kansas, 1999).

22.   Tessman, *Burdened Virtues*; see also Tessman, *Moral Failure: On the Impossible Demands of Morality* (New York: Oxford University Press, 2015).

23.   See Miranda Fricker, *Epistemic Injustice: Power and the Ethics of Knowing* (New York: Oxford University Press, 2007).

24.   CNN International TV news broadcast, December 13, 2013.

25.   See my analysis of this issue in *Anger and Forgiveness* (New York: Oxford Uni-versity Press, 2016), chap. 5, with many references to the legal literature on this question.

26.   These plurals are important. The "Western tradition" contains many different voices. In India, we need to deal with Hindu, Buddhist, Islamic, and Christian traditions, and it is important to remember that the Hindu tradition is highly plu-ral and regionally specific.

27.   Quoted in James A. Washington, ed., *A Testament of Hope: The Essential Writings and Speeches of Martin Luther King, Jr.* (New York: HarperCollins, 1986), 32.

THE DOMAIN OF LEGAL ACTION

1.   Linda Hirshman's *Reckoning: The Epic Battle against Sexual Abuse and Harass-ment* (New York: Houghton Mifflin, 2019), for example, presents a (flawed) history

of sexual harassment law as if it were a history, as well, of the law of rape and sexual assault, not cluing people in to the huge differences between these two spheres.

2. Still more confusingly, Title IX of the same law, applying to universities, typically runs together sexual assault with other forms of sexual harassment. And when universities establish their own codes defining sexual harassment and sexual assault, they typically, again, run the two together and treat them as offenses by individuals. For further discussion, see Interlude: Thoughts about Sexual Assault on College Campuses.

3. Stephen J. Schulhofer, *Unwanted Sex: The Culture of Intimidation and the Failure of Law* (Cambridge, MA: Harvard University Press, 1998).

4. Susan Estrich, *Real Rape: How the Legal System Victimizes Women Who Say No* (Cambridge, MA: Harvard University Press, 1987).

5. The formative case in making "no means no" a prevalent legal standard (the case on which the movie *The Accused* was based), which I'll discuss in Chapter 4, was a Massachusetts case argued by local prosecutors.

CHAPTER 4: ACCOUNTABILITY FOR SEXUAL ASSAULT

1. See Stephen J. Schulhofer, *Unwanted Sex: The Culture of Intimidation and the Failure of Law* (Cambridge: Harvard University Press, 1998), 24. See also N.Y. Penal Law § 130.00(8) (McKinney 1965).

2. *People v. Hughes*, 41 A.D.2d 333 (N.Y. App. Div. 1973).

3. *People v. Warren*, 446 N.E.2d 591 (Ill. App. 1983). This case, and others in this section, are helpfully discussed in Schulhofer, *Unwanted Sex*, 1–10, 33–34.

4. *People v. Warren.*

5. *State v. Rusk*, 289 Md. 230, 424 A.2d 720 (1981).

6. *State v. Rusk.*

7. *State v. Thompson*, 792 P.2d 1103 (Mont. 1990).

8. *State in Interest of M.T.S.*, 609 A.2d 1266, 1267 (N.J. 1992).

9. Joseph Raz, *The Morality of Freedom* (Oxford: Clarendon, 1986), 374. Raz is actually not aiming his example at sexual assault, and the gender of the victim is chosen simply for balance; he is talking mainly about how poverty removes choice, but his argument is general.

10. James Boswell, *The Life of Samuel Johnson, L.L.D.* (London: John Murray, 1835), 3:47.

11. See the exploration of these ideas in Justin Driver, "Of Big Black Bucks and Golden-Haired Little Girls: How Fear of Interracial Sex Informed *Brown v. Board of Education* and Its Resistance," in *The Empire of Disgust: Prejudice, Discrimination, and Policy in India and the US* (New Delhi, India: Oxford University Press, 2018), 41–61.

12. See E. R. Shipp, "Tyson Gets 6-Year Prison Term for Rape Conviction in Indiana," *New York Times*, March 27, 1992, http://www.nytimes.com/1992/03/27/

sports/tyson-gets-6-year-prison-term-for-rape-conviction-in-indiana .html?pagewanted=all.

13. *Commonwealth v. Lefkowitz*, 20 Mass. App. 513, 481 N.E.2d 277, 232 (1985).

14. A vivid description of the gang rape of a young woman of lower class and bad reputation, spurred on by the mythology in question, is in Joyce Carol Oates, *We Were the Mulvaneys* (New York: Plume, 1996).

15. *People v. Libereta* 474 N.E.2d 567, 572 (N.Y. 1984).

16. *The Accused*, directed by Jonathan Kaplan (1988; Paramount Pictures).

17. *Commonwealth v. Vieira*, 401 Mass. 828, 830 (Mass. 1988).

18. *Commonwealth v. Vieira.*

19. "Witness's Testimony Implicates Two Men in Tavern Rape Case," *New York Times*, March 1, 1984, www.nytimes.com/1984/03/01/us/witness-s-testimony -implicates-two-men-in-tavern-rape-case.html.

20. The source for this quote was accessed in 2000 but can no longer be traced.

21. Jay Pateakos, "After 26 Years, Brothers Break Silence," *Wicked Local*, October 26, 2009, www.wickedlocal.com/x884487240/After-26-years-brothers-break-silence.

22. See, for example, Charlene Muehlenhard and Lisa Hollabaugh, "Do Women Sometimes Say No When They Mean Yes?" *Journal of Personality and Social Psychology* 54 (1988): 872–79, an article that does not show how frequent such confusions are.

23. See also Schulhofer, *Unwanted Sex*, 39. People still think rape is a crime of violence.

24. See Stephen J. Schulhofer, "Taking Sexual Autonomy Seriously," *Law and Philosophy* 11, no. 1/2 (1992): 35–94.

25. See Allen E. Buchanan and Dan W. Brock, *Deciding for Others: The Ethics of Surrogate Decision-Making* (Cambridge: Cambridge University Press, 1989), a landmark book.

26. These ages vary, state by state, between sixteen and eighteen. Many states used to have a higher age of consent to homosexual than to heterosexual intercourse, but this asymmetry no longer exists in the United States.

27. See Miranda Fricker, *Epistemic Injustice: Power and the Ethics of Knowing* (New York: Oxford University Press, 2007).

28. Saul Levmore and Martha C. Nussbaum, "Unreported Sexual Assault," *Nebraska Law Review* 97 (2019): 607–27.

CHAPTER 5: WOMEN IN THE PROUD MALE WORKPLACE

1. See a report by MIT professor Mary Rowe: "The Saturn's Rings Phenomenon" (1973)—though Rowe insists that the term was already in use in women's groups in the 1970s. Catharine MacKinnon is sometimes credited with coining the term, but in her book *Sexual Harassment of Working Women* (New Haven, CT: Yale University Press, 1979) she denies this, crediting earlier feminists. A Cornell Uni-

versity group is sometimes credited with the name, but their work was slightly later than Rowe's; perhaps it was an independent coinage. At any rate, Lin Farley, of the Cornell group in question, testified in 1975 before the Commission on Human Rights in New York City and used the term, saying that workplace sexual harassment is "extremely widespread . . . literally epidemic." See Kyle Swenson, "Who Came Up with the Term 'Sexual Harassment'?" *Washington Post*, November 22, 2017, https://www.washingtonpost.com/news/morning-mix/wp/2017/11/22/who-came-up-with-the-term-sexual-harassment. MacKinnon credits her own focus on the issue to a visit to the Cornell Women's Resource Center (where she was earning money by singing): she heard of a case of harassment where a female employee, harassed to the point of stress-related physical illness, was denied unemployment benefits because she left her job "for personal reasons." "When I read that," she said, "it exploded in my brain! I remember it to this day" (Sasha Arutyunova, "Catharine MacKinnon and Gretchen Carlson Have a Few Things to Say," *New York Times*, March 17, 2018), https://www.nytimes.com/2018/03/17/business/catharine-mackinnon-gretchen-carlson.html.

2. MacKinnon, *Sexual Harassment of Working Women*, 173. See also MacKinnon's "Reflections on Sex Equality under Law," *Yale Law Journal* 100 (1991): 1281–1328.

3. MacKinnon in Arutyunova, "Catherine MacKinnon," quoting Gloria Steinem.

4. Legal theorists identify several different functions of law: the retributive (which I criticize and reject), the deterrent, the educational, and the expressive (meaning making a statement about social values); see Martha C. Nussbaum, *Anger and Forgiveness* (New York: Oxford University Press, 2016), chap. 6.

5. On Murray's career, see Sabina Mayeri, *Reasoning from Race: Feminism, Law, and the Civil Rights Revolution* (Cambridge, MA: Harvard University Press, 2011); on Title VII, pp. 22–23.

6. *Bostock v. Clayton County*, Georgia, 590 U.S. ___ (2020). Decided June 15, 2020.

7. Among important lower-court cases on the sexual orientation/gender identity issue, the parallel with sexual harassment is made with particular eloquence in *Hively v. Ivy Tech Community College*, 853F 3d 339 (7th Cir. 1990), where an 8–3 majority of the Seventh Circuit ruled that discrimination on the basis of sexual orientation counts as sex discrimination; the majority opinion by Chief Judge Diane Wood makes a clear textualist argument; the dissent argues that sexual orientation was not on the mind of Congress. This case was not further appealed, so it forms no explicit part of the Supreme Court decision.

8. Diane P. Wood, "Sexual Harassment Litigation with a Dose of Reality," *University of Chicago Legal Forum* 2019, art. 23 (2019). I am grateful to Judge Wood for showing me her article in penultimate draft.

9. *Williams v. Saxbe*, 413 F. Supp. 654, 657-8 (D.D.C. 1974).

10. *Barnes v. Costle* (1977), *Tomkins v. Public Service Electric & Gas Co.* (1977), and *Miller v. Bank of America* (1979).

11. *Alexander v. Yale University*, 631 F.2d 178 (2d Cir. 1980).

12. See Anne E. Simon, "*Alexander v. Yale University*: An Informal History," in *Directions in Sexual Harassment Law*, ed. Catharine A. MacKinnon and Reva B. Siegel (New Haven, CT: Yale University Press, 2004), 51–59.

13. Personal conversations at the time with members of the Yale University Classics Department (my profession).

14. *Reed v. Reed*, 404 U.S. 71 (1971).

15. *Craig v. Boren*, 429 U.S. 190 (1976).

16. As she is portrayed in Linda Hirshman, *Reckoning: The Epic Battle against Sexual Abuse and Harassment* (New York: Houghton Mifflin, 2019).

17. MacKinnon was appointed assistant professor at the University of Minnesota in 1982 and finally was tenured at the University of Michigan in 1989. "Wandering in the desert . . . was my tenure process," she told the *New York Times*; see Philip Galanes, "Catharine MacKinnon and Gretchen Carlson Have a Few Things to Say," *New York Times*, March 17, 2018, https://www.nytimes.com/2018/03/17/business/catharine-mackinnon-gretchen-carlson.html.

18. See Mayeri, *Reasoning from Race*.

19. *Brown v. Board of Education*, 347 U.S. 483 (1954).

20. *Loving v. Virginia*, 388 U.S. 1 (1967).

21. Herbert Wechsler, "Toward Neutral Principles of Constitutional Law," *Harvard Law Review* 73 (1959): 1–35. I discuss Wechsler and subsequent reasoning in that style in Martha C. Nussbaum, "Constitutions and Capabilities: 'Perception' against Lofty Formalism," Supreme Court Foreword, *Harvard Law Review* 121 (2007): 4–97.

22. Wechsler, "Toward Neutral Principles," 34.

23. Before introducing the Houston anecdote, Wechsler says that segregation is a source of guilt for the southern white (Wechsler, "Toward Neutral Principles," 34); he was not of southern origin himself, but when the incident took place, both he and Houston were working in the South, so it's not clear whether he intends to apply this reference to himself.

24. Wechsler, "Toward Neutral Principles," 33–34.

25. From a speech at the Sundance Film Festival, quoted in Galanes, "Catherine MacKinnon and Gretchen Carlson."

26. I don't name the judge only because illness prevents him from giving permission for this ascription.

27. *Meritor Savings Bank v. Vinson*, 477 U.S. 57 (1986).

28. *Oncale v. Sundowner Offshore Services*, 523 U.S. 75 (1998).

29. Another point MacKinnon makes is that the equality theory, unlike the difference theory, can support programs of affirmative action in which differential treatment is aimed at eradicating hierarchy; see MacKinnon, "Reflections on Sex Equality," 1287.

30. Another false view about MacKinnon is that she neglects racial hierarchy and the

intersectional wrongs of women of color. This view is clearly mistaken; her book frequently discusses this intersection, and the case she brought to the Supreme Court as the first test of her theory was the case of Mechelle Vinson, a Black woman.

31. *Meritor*, 477 U.S. 57.

32. See also an excellent law review article on the case, written by Victoria Bartels: "*Meritor Savings Bank v. Vinson*: The Supreme Court's Recognition of the Hostile Environment in Sexual Harassment Claims," *Akron Law Review* 20 (1987): 575–89.

33. *Harris v. Forklift Systems*, 510 U.S. 17 (1993).

34. *Baskerville v. Culligan*, 50 F.3d 428 (1995).

35. See *King v. Board of Regents of the University of Wisconsin*, 898 F. 2d 533 (7th Cir. 1990); and my analysis in Martha C. Nussbaum, "'Carr,' Before and After: Power and Sex in '*Carr v. Allison Gas Turbine Division, General Motors*,'" *University of Chicago Law Review* 74, Special Issue (2007): 1831–44.

36. *Carr v. Allison Gas Turbine Division, General Motors*, 32 F.3d 1007 (7th Cir. 1994). I analyze this case in Nussbaum, "'Carr,' Before and After."

37. *Oncale*, 523 U.S. 75.

38. See Wood, "Sexual Harassment Litigation."

39. *Baskerville*, 50 F.3d 428. I discuss this case also in Nussbaum, "'Carr,' Before and After."

40. *Wetzel v. Glen St. Andrew Living Community, LLC, et al.*, 901 F.3d 856 (2018). See Martha C. Nussbaum, "Harassment and Capabilities: Discrimination and Liability in *Wetzel v. Glen St. Andrew Living Community*," *University of Chicago Law Review* 87 (2020), 2437–2452.

41. See Wood, "Sexual Harassment Litigation."

42. *Bostock*, 590 U.S. ____ (2020).

43. *Altitude Express, Inc. v. Zarda*, 590 U.S. ____ (2020).

44. *R. G. and G. R. Harris Funeral Homes, Inc. v. Equal Employment Opportunity Commission*, 590 U.S. ____ (2020).

45. The split was three circuits to one, not two to one, since the Seventh Circuit had ruled the same way as the Second and Sixth, but the Seventh Circuit case was not appealed: *Hively*, 853 F.3d 339.

46. *Phillips v. Martin Marietta Corp.*, 400 U.S. 542 (1971).

47. *Los Angeles Dept. of Water and Power v. Manhart*, 435 U.S. 702 (1978).

48. *Bostock*, 590 U.S. ____ (2020).

49. One dissenting opinion was written by Justice Alito, and joined by Justice Thomas. Justice Kavanaugh wrote a separate dissent, making virtually identical arguments but taking the opportunity to express personal respect for the struggles of LGBTQ people and for their dignity; he just wants them to achieve their goals through legislation.

50. Neil M. Gorsuch, *A Republic, If You Can Keep It* (New York: Crown, 2019).

51. Of course, workplaces have bathrooms, but Justice Gorsuch leaves that issue, as well as the issue of bathrooms generally, for later resolution.

52. See *Wetzel*, 901 F.3d.

53. *Bostock*, 590 U.S. ___ (2020).

54. Importantly, MacKinnon has never proposed to ban pornography; instead she has attempted to create a civil cause of action for women injured through the use of pornography, against its makers and distributors, modeling her proposal on "dangerous product" litigation against, for example, tobacco companies.

INTERLUDE: THOUGHTS ABOUT SEXUAL ASSAULT ON COLLEGE CAMPUSES

1. Nick Anderson, Susan Svrluga, and Scott Clement, "Survey: More than 1 in 5 Female Undergrads at Top Schools Suffer Sexual Attacks," *Washington Post*, September 21, 2015, https://www.washingtonpost.com/local/education/survey-more-than-1-in-5-female-undergrads-at-top-schools-suffer-sexual-attacks/2015/09/19/c6c80be2-5e29-11e5-b38e-06883aacba64_story.html.

2. Charlene L. Muehlenhard et al., "Evaluating the One-in-Five Statistic: Women's Risk of Sexual Assault While in College," *Journal of Sex Research* 54, no. 4 (May 16, 2017): 565, https://doi.org/10.1080/00224499.2017.1295014. As discussed there, evidence does not support the assumption that college students experience more sexual assault than nonstudents.

3. In this area, my two research assistants did such superb and meticulous work on this topic, which naturally interested them greatly, that their work is worthy of note in itself and is on file with me: Sarah Hough, "Legal Approaches toward On-Campus Sexual Violence in the US: A Brief Overview," unpublished paper, July 1, 2019; and Jared I. Mayer, "Memo on De Vos's Changes to Campus Title IX Proceedings," unpublished paper, May 20, 2020.

4. National Sexual Violence Resource Center, "Dear Colleague Letter: Sexual Violence" (US Department of Education, Office of Civil Rights, 2011), https://www.nsvrc.org/publications/dear-colleague-letter-sexual-violence. The NSVRC website also contains much helpful background information.

5. See "Department of Education Issues New Interim Guidance on Campus Sexual Misconduct," US Department of Education, September 22, 2017, https://www.ed.gov/news/press-releases/department-education-issues-new-interim-guidance-campus-sexual-misconduct.

6. "Rethink Harvard's Sexual Harassment Policy" (Opinion), *Boston Globe*, October 14, 2014, https://www.bostonglobe.com/opinion/2014/10/14/rethink-harvard-sexual-harassment-policy/HFDDiZN7nU2UwuUuWMnqbM/story.html.

7. For an overview of the notice-and-comment system of regulation making, see "A Guide to the Rulemaking Process," Office of the Federal Register, January 2011, https://www.federalregister.gov/uploads/2011/01/the_rulemaking_process.pdf.

8. "Nondiscrimination on the Basis of Sex in Education Programs or Activities Receiving Federal Financial Assistance," *Federal Register*, November 29, 2018, https://www.federalregister.gov/documents/2018/11/29/2018-25314/nondiscrimination-on-the-basis-of-sex-in-education-programs-or-activities-receiving-federal.

9. See 20 U.S.C. § 1681(a) (2018). A helpful memo clarifying the content of the Final Rule is Apalla U. Chopra et al., "Analysis of Key Provisions of the Department of Education's New Title IX Regulations," O'Melveny & Myers LLP, May 15, 2020, https://www.omm.com/resources/alerts-and-publications/alerts/analysis-of-key-provisions-of-doe.

10. National Sexual Violence Resource Center, "Dear Colleague Letter."

ABUSES OF POWER AND LACK OF ACCOUNTABILITY

1. See David Yaffe-Bellany, "McDonald's CEO Fired over a Relationship That's Becoming Taboo," *New York Times*, November 4, 2019, https://www.nytimes.com/2019/11/04/business/mcdonalds-ceo-fired.html.

CHAPTER 6: PRIDE AND PRIVILEGE

1. This salary arrangement is partial compensation for the financial loss typically incurred by a lawyer who becomes a judge. Judges not only make much less than most practicing lawyers; they are also forbidden from accepting speaking fees and other honoraria. An option for judges who want a smaller workload but don't want to retire also exists: they may choose "senior" status, meaning that they still sit on cases, but fewer.

2. Most other countries either do not have tenure at all or have tenure capped by a mandatory retirement age, which can be as early as sixty-five. Most other countries also have mandatory retirement for judges.

3. The Seventh Circuit has the good fortune to be geographically centralized, holding all of its oral arguments in Chicago. Other circuits typically have several different centers of activity, making it more difficult for collegiality to develop.

4. Alex Kozinski, "Confessions of a Bad Apple," *Yale Law Journal* 100 (1991): 1707–30. The "confessions" in question had nothing to do with sexual harassment or bullying; he was simply talking about hiring clerks earlier than the official deadline—a ubiquitous practice despite many reform attempts.

5. *Maintaining the Public Trust: Ethics for Federal Judicial Law Clerks*, 4th ed. (Federal Judicial Center, 2013).

6. Another code, the Model Employment Dispute Resolution Plan (2010), which provides an alternative avenue of complaint, does mention as forbidden all discrimination on grounds of race, religion, and sex, and includes pregnancy discrimination and sexual harassment as examples of sex discrimination. However,

this Model Plan, while put forward as a suggestive model by the national Judicial Conference, is not binding on any circuit; each judicial circuit must draw up its own plan.

7. His father survived internment in concentration camps during the Second World War.

8. Daphne Wysham, "Mining Whistleblower Speaks Out against Massey," Institute for Policy Studies, July 23, 2010, https://www.ips-dc.org/blog/mining_whistleblower_speaks_out_against_massey.

9. "Kozinski, Alex," Federal Judicial Center, accessed October 2014–February 2020, https://www.fjc.gov/history/judges/kozinski-alex.

10. The lecture honored Herbert Morris, one of the giants in legal theory, who was himself in attendance, but it was also about sex—about the role of disgust in homophobia in both the United States and India. Kozinski's presence might have been explained by either of these facts, or both.

11. Cited in Chris Chrystal, "Senate Panel to Reopen Kozinski Hearing," UPI, October 31, 1985, https://www.upi.com/Archives/1985/10/31/Senate-panel-to-reopen-Kozinski-hearing/3933499582800.

12. The blog was started by David Lat, who also used to edit the highly influential semi-serious legal blog *Above the Law*, of which more later.

13. Alex Kozinski to Article III Groupie, "Courthouse Forum: The Hot. Alex Kozinski," *Underneath the Robes* (blog), June 28, 2004, https://underneaththeirrobes.blogs.com/main/2004/06/courthouse_foru.html.

14. Dahlia Lithwick, "He Made Us All Victims and Accomplices," *Slate*, December 13, 2017.

15. Kathryn Rubino, "*Above the Law*'s Dangerous Love of Federal Judges: Did We Help Support Sexual Harassment?" *Above the Law*, September 10, 2018.

16. "Who's Afraid of Commercial Speech?" *Virginia Law Review* 76 (1990): 627.

17. Akela Lacy reached a similar conclusion in "What Did Brett Kavanaugh Know about His Mentor Alex Kozinski's Sexual Harassment? A Timeline Suggests an Awful Lot," *Intercept*, September 20, 2018.

18. Third Circuit, "In re: Complaint of Judicial Misconduct," JC no. 03-08-90050 (Judicial Council of the Third Circuit, 2009). The story broke in the *LA Times*: Scott Glover, "9th Circuit's Chief Judge Posted Sexually Explicit Matter on His Website," *Los Angeles Times*, June 11, 2008, https://www.latimes.com/local/la-me-kozinski12-2008jun12-story.html.

19. Third Circuit, "In re: Complaint," JC no. 03-08-90050.

20. See Third Circuit, "Proceeding in Review of the Order and Memorandum of the Judicial Council of the Ninth Circuit," JC nos. 09-12-90026, 09-12-90032 (January 2014).

21. Matt Zapotosky, "Prominent Appeals Court Judge Alex Kozinski Accused of Sexual Misconduct," *Washington Post*, December 8, 2017; and Zapotosky, "Nine

More Women Say Judge Subjected Them to Inappropriate Behavior, Including Four Who Say He Touched or Kissed Them," *Washington Post*, December 15, 2017.

22. Heidi Bond, "Me Too," "Thinking of You," "Gag List Emails Received between 2006 and 2007," all on her blog *Courtney Milan*, http://www.courtneymilan.com. Heidi Bond, "I Received Some of Kozinski's Infamous Gag List Emails. I'm Baffled by Kavanaugh's Responses to Questions about Them," *Slate*, September 14, 2018.

23. Lithwick, "He Made Us All Victims"; and Katherine Ku, "Pressuring Harassers to Quit Can End Up Protecting Them," *Washington Post*, January 7, 2018.

24. Bond, *Courtney Milan*.

25. Ninth Circuit, "In re: Complaint of Judicial Misconduct," JC no. 02-17-90118 (Judicial Council of the Ninth Circuit, 2017).

26. John F. Roberts Jr., "Letter to Chief Judge Robert Katzmann," *Supreme Court of the United States*, December 15, 2017.

27. Matt Zapotosky, "Judge Who Quit over Harassment Allegations Reemerges, Dismaying Those Who Accused Him," *Washington Post*, July 24, 2018.

28. The judges are Judge Walter Smith, US District Court for the Western District of Texas (2014 complaint, for sexually harassing a clerk); Judge Edward Nottingham, US District Court for the District of Colorado (2007–8, various complaints, including drunkenly attending a strip club and soliciting a prostitute); Judge Richard Cebull, US District Court for the District of Montana (2012 complaint, discussed earlier); Judge Richard Kent of the US District Court for the Southern District of Texas (2017 complaint, for sexually harassing a judicial employee, which evidence showed was part of a pattern); and Judge Richard Roberts, US District Court for the District of Columbia (2017 complaint, for coercing a sixteen-year-old witness into performing sex acts, while serving as a federal prosecutor prior to his judicial appointment). In the last case, despite Roberts's retirement, an inquiry into his conduct was opened, but the investigation concluded that his prejudicial actions were not justiciable under the judicial code.

29. John G. Roberts, "2017 Year-End Report on the Federal Judiciary," in *Report of the Federal Judiciary Workplace Conduct Working Group to the Judicial Conference of the United States*, June 1, 2018, https://www.uscourts.gov/sites/default/files/workplace_conduct_working_group_final_report_0.pdf, appdx. 2.

30. Roberts, "2017 Year-End Report," 6.

31. *Protecting Federal Judiciary Employees from Sexual Harassment, Discrimination, and Other Workplace Misconduct: Hearing before the Subcommittee on Courts, Intellectual Property, and the Internet*, 116th Cong. (2020) (testimony of Olivia Warren), https://judiciary.house.gov/calendar/eventsingle.aspx?EventID=2791.

32. Debra Cassens Weiss, "Over 70 Former Reinhardt Clerks Urge Judiciary to

Change Reporting Procedures and Training," *ABA Journal*, February 21, 2020, https://www.abajournal.com/news/article/former-reinhardt-clerks-urge-judiciary-to-change-reporting-procedures-and-training.

33. "To the Judicial Conference (Honorable Chief Justice John G. Roberts, Jr., Presiding)," https://ylw.yale.edu/wp-content/uploads/2020/02/Judicial-Misconduct-Letter.pdf.

34. Vivia Chen, "The Careerist: Why Haven't Women in Law Firms Called Out Kozinski?" *Connecticut Law Tribune*, December 20, 2017, https://www.law.com/ctlawtribune/sites/therecorder/2017/12/20/why-havent-women-in-law-firms-called-out-kozinski.

35. Ross Todd, "Alex Kozinski Set to Return to 9th Circuit as Oral Advocate," *Recorder*, December 5, 2019, https://www.law.com/therecorder/2019/12/05/alex-kozinski-set-to-return-to-9th-circuit-as-oral-advocate/?slreturn=20191117125149; and Todd, "Alex Kozinski Makes Post-retirement Debut at Ninth Circuit in 'Shape of Water' Case," *Am Law Litigation Daily*, December 9, 2019, https://www.law.com/litigationdaily/2019/12/09/kozinski-contends-playwrights-due-process-rights-are-at-stake-in-copyright-case-against-shape-of-water-filmmakers-407-11110.

CHAPTER 7: NARCISSISM AND IMPUNITY

1. 1. Malcolm Gay and Kay Lazar, "In the Maestro's Thrall," *Boston Globe*, March 2, 2018.

2. Associated Press, "Opera Star Plácido Domingo Receives Standing Ovation for 50th Anniversary in Milan," *USA Today*, December 16, 2019.

3. Lyric Opera of Chicago, for example, got 43 percent from donors in 2018–19, and only 31 percent from ticket sales. The Metropolitan Opera has a similar breakdown.

4. A famous case is the basso Samuel Ramey, who was training to be a music teacher at Kansas State University when a teacher recognized his talent. At that time he had never been to an opera. (Lecture by Ramey to the Wagner Society of America, about twelve years ago.) The tenor Lawrence Brownlee was discovered by a choir director in his church in Youngstown, Ohio, who told him that opera was for him and even specified the type of role (florid bel canto tenor) that he now sings as well as anyone in the world. (Lawrence Brownlee, interview in my class on opera at the University of Chicago, spring 2017.)

5. At the top end, opera chorus employment is very lucrative: at the Metropolitan Opera, the average full-time chorus member earns $200,000 plus $100,000 in benefits. Salary and benefits are similar for the average member of the Metropolitan Opera orchestra; in most leading symphony orchestras it is similar, though both salary and pension plans have been sticking points in recent negotiations.

6. *Meritor Savings Bank v. Vinson*, 477 U.S. 57 (1986).

7.   There is much dispute about the extent to which countertenors use falsetto, and which ones do and which do not. This issue needn't concern us here.

8.   Castrati were extremely tall and thick, as a result of their castration. Deller showed, however, that a male of "normal" sexual development could sing such roles—and he went to great lengths to emphasize his credentials as a straight, married man with three children, thus destigmatizing the countertenor career for cautious operagoers and younger singers. Another leading promoter and teacher of countertenor singing was the American Russell Oberlin (1928–2016), whose recordings of Bach and Handel introduced young people of my generation to this unique sound (and he is one who, everyone agrees, used no falsetto).

9.   The role of Oberon in Benjamin Britten's *Midsummer Night's Dream*, the role of Trinculo in Thomas Adès's *Tempest*, and the title role in Philip Glass's *Aknaten* are all written for a male countertenor.

10. Daniels also performed Britten's Oberon and Adès's Trinculo.

11. This opera, based on Oscar Wilde's trial and death rather than on his wit and achievements, was generally accounted a failure, denounced for its sanctimonious libretto and its musical mediocrity. One thing that was not criticized, to my knowledge, was the odd choice to cast a countertenor as Wilde, although by all accounts Wilde had a resonant, deep voice that mesmerized even the miners of Leadville, Colorado! The opera purported to attack stereotypes of the gay man, but in its vocal writing it surely affirmed one silly stereotype.

12. David Jesse, "U-M Trying to Out Former Graduate Student as Gay, Court Filing Claims," *Detroit Free Press*, July 31, 2019.

13. Gus Burns, "Report Reveals New Misconduct Claims against University of Michigan Professor David Daniels," *MLive*, August 14, 2019, https://www.mlive .com/news/2019/08/report-reveals-new-misconduct-claims-against-university-of -michigan-professor-david-daniels.html.

14. Burns, "Report Reveals New Misconduct Claims"; Anastasia Tsioulcas, "Memos Lay Out Sexual Misconduct Allegations against Opera Star David Daniels," NPR, August 8, 2019, https://www.npr.org/2019/08/08/749368222/memos-lay -out-sexual-misconduct-allegations-against-opera-star-david-daniels.

15. Isobel Grant, "Findings of David Daniels Investigation May Be Kept from the Public," *Michigan Daily*, September 19, 2019, https://www.michigandaily.com/ section/news-briefs/findings-david-daniels-investigation-may-be-kept-public.

16. For Schultz's story, see Norman Lebrecht, "A Baritone Writes: I Was Raped," *Slipped Disc*, July 15, 2018, https://slippedisc.com/2018/07/a-baritone-writes-i -was-raped; and D. L. Groover, "#MeToo at the Opera, the Samuel Schultz Story," *Houston Press*, August 27, 2018, https://www.houstonpress.com/arts/samuel -schultz-says-he-was-drugged-and-raped-after-an-hgo-performance-10798013.

17. Groover, "#MeToo at the Opera."

18. Michael Levenson, "Opera Star, Charged with Sexual Assault, Is Fired by Uni-

versity of Michigan," *New York Times*, March 26, 2020, https://www.nytimes
.com/2020/03/26/us/david-daniels-michigan-opera-singer-fired.html.

19. Joshua Kosman, "SF Opera Removes David Daniels from Production amid
    Sexual Assault Allegations," *San Francisco Chronicle*, November 8, 2018,
    https://datebook.sfchronicle.com/music/sf-opera-removes-david-daniels-from
    -production-amid-sexual-assault-allegations.

20. Jocelyn Gecker, "Famed Conductor Charles Dutoit Accused of Sexual Miscon-
    duct," *AP News*, December 21, 2017, https://apnews.com/278275ccc09442d98a7
    94487a78a67d4/AP-Exclusive:-Famed-conductor-accused-of-sexual-misconduct;
    and Jocelyn Gecker and Janie Har, "Famed Conductor Dutoit Faces New Sex
    Claims, Including Alleged Rape," *Boston Globe*, January 11, 2018, https://
    www.bostonglobe.com/arts/2018/01/11/famed-conductor-faces-new-sex-claims
    -including-rape/I6e3hq3rDlqaCBdYXGCoAO/story.html.

21. Jocelyn Gecker, "Famed Conductor Accused of Sexual Misconduct," *AP News*,
    December 22, 2017, https://apnews.com/278275ccc09442d98a794487a78a67d4/
    AP-Exclusive:-Famed-conductor-accused-of-sexual-misconduct.

22. Jocelyn Gecker and Janie Har, "Philly Orchestra Latest to Break Ties with Dutoit
    amid Scandal," *Philadelphia Tribune*, December 23, 2017, https://www.phillytrib
    .com/entertainment/music/philly-orchestra-latest-to-break-ties-with-dutoit-amid
    -scandal/article_887237a8-635f-5994-82c4-477cd273bb98.html.

23. Gecker and Har, "Philly Orchestra Latest to Break Ties"; and "BSO: Sexual Mis-
    conduct Claims against Dutoit Credible," WAMC, accessed January 2020, https://
    www.wamc.org/post/bso-sexual-misconduct-claims-against-dutoit-credible.

24. I last saw him in the summer of 2016, and at this point it seems best to use the
    past tense.

25. Gay and Lazar, "In the Maestro's Thrall."

26. The question is poorly thought out: Is the point that the Ninth itself is in danger
    of disappearing altogether? Or only that a precious manuscript in Beethoven's
    hand is endangered? Obviously, many editions and copies, and countless recorded
    performances, preserve the work.

27. Michael Cooper, "Met Opera Suspends James Levine after New Sexual Abuse
    Allegations," *New York Times*, December 3, 2017.

28. Jeremy Eichler, "Levine Allegations Prompt BSO Review of Sex Harassment
    Policies," *Boston Globe*, December 5, 2017, https://www.bostonglobe.com/
    arts/music/2017/12/05/levine-allegations-prompt-bso-review-sex-harassment
    -policies/hLqts5V0h9pxqK19v8okRN/story.html.

29. Anastasia Tsioulcas, "James Levine Accused of Sexual Misconduct by 5 More Men,"
    NPR, May 19, 2018, https://www.npr.org/sections/therecord/2018/05/19/612621436/
    james-levine-accused-of-sexual-misconduct-by-5-more-men.

30. Ronald Blum, "Levine Fired by Met After It Finds Evidence of Sexual Abuse,"
    AP News, March 12, 2018, https://apnews.com/1f1d30df52ca447db82a0fd1db6
    91a5f/Levine-fired-by-Met-after-it-finds-evidence-of-sexual-abuse; and Michael

Cooper, "James Levine's Final Act at the Met Ends in Disgrace," *New York Times*, March 12, 2018, https://www.nytimes.com/2018/03/12/arts/music/james -levine-metropolitan-opera.html.

31. Anastasia Tsioulcas, "Majority of James Levine's Defamation Claims against Met Opera Dismissed," NPR, March 27, 2019, https://www.npr.org/2019/03/27/7071 47886/majority-of-james-levines-defamation-claims-against-met-opera-dismissed.

32. Cooper, "Met Opera Suspends James Levine." See also Pai's statements in ibid. "It has really messed me up."

33. Cooper, "James Levine's Final Act."

34. Cooper, "Met Opera Suspends James Levine."

35. James B. Stewart and Michael Cooper, "The Met Opera Fired James Levine, Citing Sexual Misconduct. He Was Paid $3.5 Million," *New York Times*, September 20, 2020, https://www.nytimes.com/2020/09/20/arts/music/met-opera-james -levine.html

36. Jocelyn Gecker and Jocelyn Noveck, "Singer Says Opera's Domingo Harassed Her, Grabbed Her Breast," *AP News*, September 7, 2019, https://apnews.com/3b af2ccc59144284b227f29eb7d44797; Jocelyn Gecker, "Women Accuse Opera Legend Domingo of Sexual Harassment," *AP News*, August 13, 2019, https://apnews .com/c2d51d690d004992b8cfba3bad827ae9.

37. Gecker, "Women Accuse Opera Legend Domingo."

38. Gecker and Noveck, "Singer Says Opera's Domingo Harassed Her."

39. Associated Press, "Plácido Domingo's Accusers: Nothing 'Chivalrous' about Groping Women," *Hollywood Reporter*, December 3, 2019, https://www .hollywoodreporter.com/news/placido-domingo-s-accusers-nothing-chivalrous -groping-women-1259453.

40. Adriana Gomez Licon, "Andrea Bocelli Questions Shunning of Accused Opera Star Plácido Domingo: 'This Is Absurd,'" *USA Today*, November 12, 2019, https://www.usatoday.com/story/entertainment/celebrities/2019/11/12/andrea -bocelli-appalled-absurd-treatment-placido-domingo/2578364001.

41. Jessica Gelt, "Plácido Domingo Apologizes for 'Hurt That I Caused' as Investigation Finds Misconduct," *Los Angeles Times*, February 24, 2020, https://www .latimes.com/entertainment-arts/story/2020-02-24/placido-domingo-allegations -apologizes-opera-guild-investigation.

42. There was a dispute over the public release of the AGMA report, which apparently was at first intended to be confidential. Some parties claim that a deal had been worked out whereby Domingo would pay $500,000 as a fine in exchange for confidentiality; others deny that there was ever such a deal. I shall not pursue that issue further here.

43. "LA Opera Independent Investigation: Summary of Findings and Recommendations," LA Opera, March 10, 2020, https://www.laopera.org/about-us/press -room/press-releases-and-statements/statement-summary-of-findings.

44. Gelt, "Plácido Domingo Apologizes."

45. Anastasia Tsioulcas, "Plácido Domingo Backpedals on Public Apology; Meanwhile, Union Seeks Leakers," NPR, February 27, 2020, https://www.npr.org/2020/02/27/809995613/pl-cido-domingo-backpedals-on-public-apology-meanwhile-union-seeks-leakers.

46. Alex Marshall, "Plácido Domingo Walks Back Apology on Harassment Claims," *New York Times*, February 27, 2020, https://www.nytimes.com/2020/02/27/arts/music/placido-domingo-apology.html.

47. Philip Kennicott, "Plácido Domingo's Reputation as a Performer Enabled the Opera World to Ignore His Predatory Behavior," February 26, 2020, https://www.washingtonpost.com/entertainment/music/placido-domingo-apologizes-after-union-finds-he-engaged-in-inappropriate-activity/2020/02/25/19ac42ac-57e9-11ea-ab68-101ecfec2532_story.html. It is unlikely that Kennicott is the source of the headline, since in the article he credits Domingo with being not just a reputation but a bold and revolutionary performer, though his moral judgment is severe. The only behavior that possibly justifies the label "predatory" would appear to be the behavior described by one complainant as like "stalking." As I've said, Domingo's persistence in making unwelcome overtures seems to qualify as an element in a "hostile environment," but whether it is really stalking is harder to determine without a fuller adjudication of the facts.

48. "AFL-CIO Anti-Discrimination and Anti-Harassment Policy," accessed January 2020, AFL-CIO, https://aflcio.org/about-us/afl-cio-anti-discrimination-and-anti-harassment-policy.

49. The general policy of pro bono representation was described in detail by Anthony Freud, general director and CEO of Lyric Opera of Chicago, in his lecture "Careers for Lawyers in the Performing Arts" (Law Students for the Creative Arts, University of Chicago Law School, April 2019).

50. Peter Dobrin, "Philadelphia Orchestra Has Played 650 Concerts with Charles Dutoit, the Conductor Accused of Sexual Misconduct," *Philadelphia Inquirer*, December 21, 2017, http://www.philly.com/philly/entertainment/charles-dutoit-sexual-misconduct-philadelphia-orchestra-20171221.html.

51. Michael Cooper, "Charles Dutoit, Conductor Accused of Sexual Assault, Leaves Royal Philharmonic," *New York Times*, January 11, 2018.

52. Gecker and Noveck, "Singer Says Opera's Domingo Harassed Her."

CHAPTER 8: MASCULINITY AND CORRUPTION

1. 1. Joseph Zucker, "Jameis Winston After 30 INT Season: 'You Look at My Numbers, I'm Ballin'," Bleacher Report, December 29, 2019, https://bleacherreport.com/articles/2868964-jameis-winston-after-30-int-season-you-look-at-my-numbers-im-ballin

2. Some might argue that we should worry, nonetheless, about rappers and hip-hop

artists who glorify violence. I think this worry is overblown, but this is not the place to investigate it.

3. Soccer is becoming much more popular, yet it lags very far behind in terms of spectators. See Marketing Charts, "How Many Americans Are Sports Fans?" October 23, 2017, https://www.marketingcharts.com/industries/sports-industries-80768. More than 50 percent of Americans say they are baseball fans, and between 60 and 70 percent say they are professional football fans, while 40 percent are fans of professional basketball; but only 28 percent are professional soccer fans. Young women do find heroes in women's soccer, but the same seems far less true of males and men's soccer, at least in the United States.

4. Quoted in Willie Mays and John Shea, *24: Life Stories and Lessons from the Say Hey Kid* (New York: St. Martin's, 2020). Mays is surely one of my heroes, along with Nelson Mandela, Martin Luther King Jr., and Jawaharlal Nehru.

5. Alanna Vagianos, "NFL Player to Elementary School Class: Girls Are 'Supposed to Be Silent,'" *Huffington Post*, February 23, 2017, www.huffingtonpost.com/entry/jameis-winston-accused-of-rape-to-elementary-class-girls-are-supposed-to-be-silent_us_58af20a2e4b0a8a9b78012e6.

6. Vagianos, "NFL Player to Elementary School Class."

7. Jim Bouton, *Ball Four: My Life and Hard Times Throwing the Knuckleball in the Big Leagues*, ed. Leonard Schecter (New York: World, 1970).

8. John Feinstein, "Jim Bouton Opened the Lid on the Closed Ol' Boy Network of Baseball," *Washington Post*, July 12, 2019, https://www.washingtonpost.com/sports/jim-bouton-opened-the-lid-on-the-closed-ol-boy-network-of-baseball/2019/07/12/4580a4c8-a442-11e9-bd56-eac6bb02d01d_story.html

9. Adam Silver, email to author, January 14, 2019.

10. Steve Almasy and Homero De la Fuente, "San Francisco Giants' Alyssa Nakken Becomes First Female Full-Time Coach in MLB History," CNN, January 17, 2020, https://www.cnn.com/2020/01/16/us/san-francisco-giants-female-coach-spt-trnd/index.html.

11. Jill Martin, "NBA Commissioner Adam Silver Wants More Women as Referees and Coaches," CNN, May 10, 2019, https://www.cnn.com/2019/05/10/sport/adam-silver-wants-more-women-as-referees-and-coaches-in-nba-trnd/index.html.

12. Louis Bien, "A Complete Timeline of the Ray Rice Assault Case," SB Nation, updated November 28, 2014, https://www.sbnation.com/nfl/2014/5/23/5744964/ray-rice-arrest-assault-statement-apology-ravens.

13. Paul Hagen, "MLB, MLBPA Reveal Domestic Violence Policy," MLB Advanced Media, August 21, 2015, https://www.mlb.com/news/mlb-mlbpa-agree-on-domestic-violence-policy/c-144508842.

14. Mark Gonzales, "Cubs' Addison Russell Addresses Domestic Violence Suspension: 'I Am Not Proud of the Person I Once Was,'" *Chicago Tribune*, February 15,

2019, https://www.chicagotribune.com/sports/cubs/ct-spt-cubs-addison-russell
-speaks-20190215-story.html.

15. Tyler Kepner, "Yankees' Domingo German Suspended 81 Games for Domestic Violence," *New York Times*, January 2, 2020, https://www.nytimes.com
/2020/01/02/sports/baseball/domingo-german-suspension.html.

16. Silver email, January 14, 2019.

17. Al Neal, "Which of the Big 4 Has the Best Domestic Violence Policy?" Grand-
stand Central, August 24, 2018, https://grandstandcentral.com/2018/society/best
-domestic-violence-policy-sports.

18. Neal, "Which of the Big 4."

19. An instance of the uneasy relationship between teams and league is the case of
Tyreek Hill of the Kansas City Chiefs. In 2014, Hill pled guilty to misdemeanor
domestic violence (a grisly case involving strangulation); his college team, Okla-
homa State, cut him, and he went to a lower-level team, West Alabama. Then, in
2019, playing with the Chiefs (who drafted him in the fifth round), he was accused
by the same girlfriend of child abuse. The Chiefs suspended him, but some months
later the NFL cleared him of the child abuse charge, allegedly after reviewing the
medical evidence, and he is now back with the Chiefs.

20. Neal, "Which of the Big 4."

21. Sexual corruption in professional soccer in Europe has been under-investigated;
FIFA (the international governing body of soccer) is clearly corrupt in many
respects, but whether the corruption includes covering up wrongdoing by players
needs further study. At any rate, we can say this: the system *could* adopt clear
public rules on sexual assault and enforce them, because the overall structure is
similar to that of American professional leagues.

22. For two good stories about European soccer academies, see David Conn, " 'Football's Biggest Issue': The Struggle Facing Boys Rejected by Academies," *Guardian*,
October 6, 2017, https://www.theguardian.com/football/2017/oct/06/football
-biggest-issue-boys-rejected-academies; and Michael Sokolove, "How a Soccer
Star Is Made," *New York Times Magazine*, June 2, 2010, https://www.nytimes
.com/2010/06/06/magazine/06Soccer-t.html.

23. In reality, the system is somewhat more complicated than that, but the details are
not relevant to my argument.

24. Ben Maller, "College Graduation Rates of MLB Players," The PostGame, May 18,
2012, http://www.thepostgame.com/blog/dish/201205/grandy-man-only-educated
-bronx-bomber.

25. Roger Kahn, *The Boys of Summer* (New York: Harper, 1972).

26. See the comprehensive study in Richard T. Karcher, "The Chances of a Drafted
Baseball Player Making the Major Leagues: A Quantitative Study," *Baseball
Research Journal* 46, no. 1 (Spring 2017), https://sabr.org/research/chances
-drafted-baseball-player-making-major-leagues-quantitative-study.

27. One famous case is that of Brock Turner, a white swimming star at Stanford who

raped a woman who had passed out, and was convicted of three counts of sexual assault but then treated leniently by a judge, who referred to his athletic talent and his bright future in sentencing him to only six months in prison (he served just three). The case generated widespread outrage, and in 2019 the victim, Chanel Miller, published a memoir discussing her experience: *Know My Name: A Memoir* (New York: Viking).

28. Richard Johnson, "Northwestern's New Football Practice Facility Is Literally on a Beach," SB Nation, April 10, 2018, https://www.sbnation.com/college-football/2018/4/10/17219292/northwestern-new-practice-facility.

29. A few states have a basketball coach at the top, and a few others have university medical professionals in that position: see "Who's the Highest-Paid Person in Your State?" ESPN, March 20, 2018, http://www.espn.com/espn/feature/story/_/id/22454170/highest-paid-state-employees-include-ncaa-coaches-nick-saban-john-calipari-dabo-swinney-bill-self-bob-huggins.

30. "NCAA Salaries," *USA Today*, accessed November 2019–February 2020, https://sports.usatoday.com/ncaa/salaries.

31. Dan Bauman, Tyler Davis, and Brian O'Leary, "Executive Compensation at Public and Private Colleges," *Chronicle of Higher Education*, July 17, 2020, https://www.chronicle.com/interactives/executive-compensation#id=table_public_2018.

32. This figure is supported by William Bowen's analyses; see William G. Bowen and Sarah A. Levin, *Reclaiming the Game: College Sports and Educational Values* (Princeton, NJ: Princeton University Press, 2005); and the earlier James L. Shulman and William G. Bowen, *The Game of Life: College Sports and Educational Values* (Princeton, NJ: Princeton University Press, 2002). See also Mike McIntire, *Champions Way: Football, Florida, and the Lost Soul of College Sports* (New York: W. W. Norton, 2017), 90.

33. Bowen and Levin, *Reclaiming the Game*; Shulman and Bowen, *Game of Life*.

34. Myles Brand, "Academics First: Reforming College Athletics" (speech, National Press Club, Washington, DC, January 23, 2001).

35. See Joshua Hunt, *University of Nike: How Corporate Cash Bought American Higher Education* (Brooklyn, NY: Melville House, 2018).

36. Hunt, *University of Nike*.

37. Paula Lavigne and Mark Schlabach, *Violated: Exposing Rape at Baylor University amid College Football's Sexual Assault Crisis* (New York: Center Street, 2017).

38. In general, I will cite specific pages of McIntire's book in parentheses in the text, but all his claims are buttressed by extensive citations: to news stories, interviews with the participants, court documents, and so on. The interested reader can track the sources there.

39. A complete summary of relevant data, compiled by my research assistant Jared Mayer, can be accessed on my faculty webpage; the data were compiled and the analytical summary written by Jared I. Mayer, JD expected 2021, University of Chicago Law School.

40. Jeremy Bauer-Wolf, "NCAA: No Academic Violations at UNC," *Inside Higher Ed*, October 16, 2017, https://www.insidehighered.com/news/2017/10/16/ breaking-ncaa-finds-no-academic-fraud-unc. Despite the damning facts, the toothless NCAA gave the school a free pass.

41. Winston refused McIntire's attempts to interview him, but all material ascribed to him in his own words comes either from his own social media accounts or from press interviews; narrative material comes from multiple sources, some confidential.

42. Walt Bogdanich, "A Star Player Accused, and a Flawed Rape Investigation," *New York Times*, April 16, 2014, https://www.nytimes.com/interactive/2014/04/16/ sports/errors-in-inquiry-on-rape-allegations-against-fsu-jameis-winston.html.

43. Bogdanich, "Star Player Accused."

44. Kristopher Knox, "The Best Potential Landing Spots for Jameis Winston Next Season," *Bleacher Report*, January 7, 2020, https://bleacherreport.com/articles/2870001 -the-best-potential-landing-spots-for-jameis-winston-next-season.

45. Jenna Laine, "Uber Driver Sues Jameis Winston over Alleged Groping Incident," ESPN, September 18, 2018, https://www.espn.com/nfl/story/_/id/24726850/ jameis-winston-tampa-bay-buccaneers-sued-uber-driver-alleged-2016-incident.

46. Tom Schad, "Jameis Winston Suspended for Three Games, Apologizes for Uber Incident," *USA Today*, June 28, 2018, https://www.usatoday.com/story/sports/ nfl/buccaneers/2018/06/28/jameis-winston-suspended-tampa-bay-buccaneers -uber/742691002.

47. For the latest evidence, see Dennis Thompson, "Nearly All NFL Players in Study Show Evidence of Brain Disorder CTE," UPI, July 25, 2017, https://www.upi.com/ Health_News/2017/07/25/Nearly-all-NFL-players-in-study-show-evidence-of -brain-disorder-CTE/7201500998697. Accountability for the likely concealment of this evidence belongs to many, and yet, for the financial reasons I've discussed, those who participated are unlikely to face any penalty. Ninety-nine percent of former NFL players show evidence of CTE! This issue of accountability is huge, but it lies beyond the scope of this article.

48. See Lavigne and Schlabach, *Violated*; and Associated Press, "Ken Starr Leaves Baylor after Complaints It Mishandled Sex Assault Inquiry," *New York Times*, August 19, 2016, https://www.nytimes.com/2016/08/20/us/ken-starr-resigns-as -professor-cutting-last-tie-to-baylor-university.html.

49. John Wagner, Josh Dawsey, and Michael Brice-Saddler, "Trump Expands Legal Team to Include Alan Dershowitz, Kenneth Starr as Democrats Release New Documents," *Washington Post*, January 17, 2020, https://www.washingtonpost .com/politics/impeachment-trial-live-updates/2020/01/17/df59d410-3917 -11ea-bb7b-265f4554af6d_story.html?utm_campaign=post_most&utm_ medium=Email&utm_source=Newsletter&wpisrc=nl_most&wpmm=1.

50. NCAA, "Louisville Men's Basketball Must Vacate Wins and Pay Fine" ("Decision of the National College Athletic Association Division I Infractions Appeals

Committee"), Louisville Cardinals, February 20, 2018, https://gocards.com/ documents/2018/2/20/NCAA_Appeals_Decision.PDF. See also Jeff Greer, "A Timeline of the Louisville Basketball Investigation: From 2015 to 2018," *Courier-Journal* (Louisville, KY), February 20, 2018, https://www.courier-journal .com/story/sports/college/louisville/2018/02/20/louisville-basketball-ncaa -investigation-timeline/1035815001.

51. Marc Tracy, "N.C.A.A. Coaches, Adidas Executive Face Charges; Pitino's Pro-gram Implicated," *New York Times*, September 26, 2017, https://www.nytimes .com/2017/09/26/sports/ncaa-adidas-bribery.html?hp=&action=click&pgt ype=Homepage&clickSource=story-heading&module=inline&region=top -news&WT.nav=top-news.

52. In addition to known public facts, I base my claims about Notre Dame on a writ-ten statement and a lengthy interview with Notre Dame professor of political sci-ence Eileen Hunt Botting, August 24, 2019, for years a member of the faculty athletics committee.

53. Botting interview, August 24, 2019, recording her own experience and impressions.

54. Randy Gurzi, "2017 NFL Draft: Each Team's Biggest Draft Bust in Past 5 Years," Fansided, accessed August and September 2019, https://nflspinzone .com/2017/01/26/nfl-draft-2017-biggest-bust-each-team-last-5-years/27.

55. Texts quoted by Botting in her statement.

56. Melinda Henneberger, "Why I Won't Be Cheering for Old Notre Dame," *Wash-ington Post*, December 4, 2012, https://www.washingtonpost.com/blogs/she -the-people/wp/2012/12/04/why-i-wont-be-cheering-for-old-notre-dame; Todd Lighty and Rich Campbell, "Ex-Notre Dame Player's Remarks Reopen Wound," *Chicago Tribune*, February 26, 2014, https://www.chicagotribune.com/news/ct -xpm-2014-02-26-ct-seeberg-interview-met-20140226-story.html.

57. Ryan Glasspiegel, "Atlanta Falcons LB Prince Shembo Allegedly Kicked and Killed Girlfriend's Dog," The Big Lead, May 29, 2015, https://www.thebiglead .com/2015/05/29/prince-shembo-animal-cruelty.

58. Darin Gantt, "Felony Charges against Former Falcons Dog-Killer Prince Shembo Dropped," NBC Sports, *Pro Football Talk* (blog), August 12, 2015, https:// profootballtalk.nbcsports.com/2015/08/12/felony-charges-against-former -falcons-dog-killer-prince-shembo-dropped.

59. Derek Wittner, "The Risks When Colleges Reopen" (Opinion), *New York Times*, June 13, 2020, https://www.nytimes.com/2020/06/13/opinion/letters/coronavirus -college-reopening.html?smid=em-share. My source, Eileen Botting, has an elo-quent letter in this exchange, daring Notre Dame's president, Father Jenkins, to show true moral courage by delaying or deferring the reopening, in order to protect safety. She says that her letter has been taken very seriously by the president and provost.

60. "Penn State Scandal Fast Facts," CNN, July 1, 2020, https://www.cnn .com/2013/10/28/us/penn-state-scandal-fast-facts/index.html.

61. "Penn State Scandal Fast Facts."

62. The abuse of very young athletes is also a feature of the notorious case of sports physician Larry Nassar at Michigan State, but since that case was under the aegis of USA Gymnastics in the Olympic Movement, it is not part of my topic here, although MSU clearly behaved very badly, and its football program had a major sex scandal around the same time. The Nassar incident led Congress to pass, in 2017, the Protecting Young Victims from Abuse and Safe Sport Authorization Act, which sets clear reporting requirements for college administrators. Another sports powerhouse, the University of Southern California (USC), participated in a cover-up by another team gynecologist in 2016.

63. This influence is described in great detail in Hunt, *University of Nike*.

64. Peg Brand Weiser, Brand's widow and a philosopher, kindly sent me a collection of his speeches, and it is to this collection that I refer; if I have missed something, it is not in the major writings she selected.

65. At least, not in the collection of his speeches that Peg Brand Weiser gave me.

66. Although the events involving Jameis Winston postdated Brand's death, Mike McIntire's book *Champions Way* shows that corruption at FSU long predated it, and the same can be said of much of the sexual and academic corruption at other schools.

67. "Commission on College Basketball: Report and Recommendations to NCAA Board of Governors, Division I Board of Directors and NCAA President Emmert," accessed April 2018, https://wbca.org/sites/default/files/rice-commission-report.pdf.

68. The University of North Carolina academic scandal, however, involved female players and their academic advisor as well.

69. From Rice's prepared remarks introducing the report.

70. Silver email, January 14, 2019.

71. A comprehensive account of the history of the G League and its teams can be found at Wikipedia, s.v. "NBA G League," accessed January 2020, https://en.wikipedia.org/wiki/NBA_G_League.

72. Ben Golliver, "NBA's G League to Add Mexico City Franchise in 2020: 'A Historic Milestone,'" *Washington Post*, December 12, 2019, https://www.washingtonpost.com/sports/2019/12/12/nbas-g-league-add-mexico-city-franchise-historic-milestone.

73. Joe Nocera, "If NCAA Won't Pay High School Players, the NBA Will," Bloomberg, April 17, 2020, https://www.bloomberg.com/opinion/articles/2020-04-17/if-ncaa-won-t-pay-top-high-school-players-the-nba-will.

74. Chris Haynes, "Why the Nation's Top Prep Player Is Opting for the G League," Yahoo! Sports, April 16, 2020, https://sports.yahoo.com/why-the-nations-top-prep-player-is-opting-for-the-g-league-170038681.html.

75. Alan Blinder, "N.C.A.A. Athletes Could Be Paid under New California Law," *New York Times*, September 30, 2019, https://www.nytimes.com/2019/09/30/sports/college-athletes-paid-california.html.

76. "NCAA Board of Governors Federal and State Legislation Working Group Final Report and Recommendations," April 17, 2020, https://ncaaorg.s3.amazonaws .com/committees/ncaa/wrkgrps/fslwg/Apr2020FSLWG_Report.pdf, 13.

77. Earlier the NCAA issued a theoretical discussion: Deborah Wilson et al., *Addressing Sexual Assault and Interpersonal Violence: Athletics' Role in Support of Healthy and Safe Campuses* (NCAA, September 2014), https://www .ncaa.org/sites/default/files/Sexual-Violence-Prevention.pdf; recently it was followed by a set of practical rules: *Sexual Violence Prevention: An Athletics Tool Kit for a Healthy and Safe Culture*, 2nd ed. (NCAA and Sports Science Institute, August 2019), https://ncaaorg.s3.amazonaws.com/ssi/violence/SSI_ SexualViolencePreventionToolkit.pdf.

78. Liptak, Adam, "Supreme Court to Rule on N.C.A.A. Limits on Paying College Athletes," *New York Times*, December 16, 2020, https://www.nytimes.com /2020/12/16/us/supreme-court-ncaa-athletes-pay.html.

79. Tony Manfred, "LeBron James Explains Why He Won't Let His Kids Play Football," *Business Insider*, November 13, 2014, https://www.businessinsider.com/ lebron-james-explains-kids-football-2014-11.

80. Rick Stroud, "Jameis Winston Says Goodbye to the Bucs," *Tampa Bay Times*, March 21, 2020, https://www.tampabay.com/sports/bucs/2020/03/21/jameis -winston-says-goodbye-to-the-bucs.

81. Samantha Previte, "Jameis Winston Pushes SUV Uphill in NFL Free-Agency Desperation," March 23, 2020, https://nypost.com/2020/03/23/jameis-winston -pushes-suv-uphill-in-nfl-free-agency-desperation.

82. The other unsigned star during this time was Cam Newton, also Black. On June 28, Newton was signed by the Patriots. The two most successful Black quarterbacks in the NFL today, Seattle's Russell Wilson and Kansas City's Patrick Mahomes, are both from reasonably affluent middle-class backgrounds and have lighter skin. Mahomes has a white mother. As for Wilson, Wikipedia reports a calculation that his DNA is 36 percent European (Wikipedia, s.v., "Russell Wilson," accessed March 2020, https://en.wikipedia.org/wiki/Russell_Wilson), and the fact that this is prominently mentioned speaks volumes. Both of these stars have escaped the stereotyping that afflicts so many others, but it's no credit to the NFL that this is so.

83. John DeShazler, "Jameis Winston Finds Fit, Looking to 'Serve' with New Orleans Saints," New Orleans Saints, April 29, 2020, https://www.neworleanssaints.com/ news/jameis-winston-finds-fit-looking-to-serve-with-new-orleans-saints.

84. Andrew Beaton, "Drew Brees Apologizes after Backlash to Anthem Remarks," *Wall Street Journal*, June 4, 2020, https://www.wsj.com/articles/drew-brees -apologizes-after-backlash-to-anthem-remarks-11591281201; Nancy Armour, "As Protests Rage over Racial Inequality, Drew Brees' Tone-Deaf Comments Show Saints QB Is Willfully Ignorant" (Opinion), *USA Today*, June 3, 2020, https://

www.usatoday.com/story/sports/columnist/nancy-armour/2020/06/03/drew
-brees-saints-willfully-ignorant-flag-national-anthem-george-floyd/3137613001.

CONCLUSION: THE WAY FORWARD

1. See Martha C. Nussbaum, *Hiding from Humanity: Disgust, Shame, and the Law* (Princeton, NJ: Princeton University Press, 2004).
2. In chapter 5 of *Hiding from Humanity*, I investigate all five at some length, setting the objections against the arguments of Dan Kahan, the main legal proponent of shame-based punishments.

INDEX